THE

LINCOLN MEMORIAL

ALBUM-IMMORTELLES.

ORIGINAL LIFE PICTURES, WITH AUTOGRAPHS,

FROM THE HANDS AND HEARTS OF EMINENT

AMERICANS AND EUROPEANS,

CONTEMPORARIES OF THE GREAT MARTYR TO LIBERTY,

Abraham Lincoln.

*TOGETHER WITH EXTRACTS FROM HIS SPEECHES,
LETTERS AND SAYINGS.*

COLLECTED AND EDITED

BY

OSBORN H. OLDROYD.

WITH AN INTRODUCTON BY

MATTHEW SIMPSON, D.D., LL.D.,

AND A SKETCH OF THE PATRIOT'S LIFE BY

HON. ISAAC N. ARNOLD.

D. L. GUERNSEY, PUBLISHER,
61 CORNHILL, BOSTON. MASS.

Printing Statement:

Due to the very old age and scarcity of this book,
many of the pages may be hard to read due to the
blurring of the original text, possible missing pages,
missing text, dark backgrounds and other issues
beyond our control.

Because this is such an important and rare work, we
believe it is best to reproduce this book regardless of
its original condition.

Thank you for your understanding.

TO

THE AMERICAN PEOPLE,

THESE

LITERARY IMMORTELLES TO ABRAHAM LINCOLN,

THE PRESIDENT

WHO ROSE FROM THE RANKS OF THE PLAIN PEOPLE;

THE PATRIOT

WHO GAVE HIS LIFE FOR HIS COUNTRY;

AND

THE LIBERATOR

WHO BOUND UP THE UNION, AND UNBOUND THE SLAVES,

ARE

Dedicated.

PREFACE.

IN offering this volume to the public a few words from the editor may not seem out of place.

On the fifteenth day of April, 1880, I was standing near the monument of Abraham Lincoln, waiting for the Lincoln Guard of Honor to begin their first memorial service on the fifteenth anniversary of the death of Abraham Lincoln. The gathering was a small one, it being only about twenty-two minutes after seven o'clock in the morning. As I gazed on the pinnacle of the towering shaft, that marks the resting-place of him whom I had learned to love in my boyhood's years, when, in the spirited campaign of 1860, "Old Abe" was the watchword of every Republican, I fell to wondering whether it might not be possible for me to contribute my mite toward adding luster to the fame of this great product of American institutions. I had begun as early as 1860 to collect trophies from his campaign, and had ever since then carefully preserved every article I could secure that related in any way to his memory. The first thought that came into my mind, as I stood looking at that noble monument, was that of building a Memorial Hall in which to preserve the memorials I then possessed and those which I might subsequently secure, and I then and there adopted this plan. I have continued up to this time to gather Lincoln mementos, and have now in my possession nearly two thousand books, sermons, eulogies, poems, songs, portraits, badges, autograph letters, pins, medals, envelopes, statuettes, etc., etc. The fact is, I have collected everything I could find sacred to Lincoln's memory, from a newspaper scrap to his large cook-stove and other household articles. I desire here to thank the many friends to whom I am under obligations for valuable contributions. I have the promise of several more, that will be sent me in due time, and I shall always be thankful for any Lincoln relic sent me, no matter how trifling it may seem to the owner. The accumulation of Lincoln relics induced me to collect the opinions of the great men of the world in regard to the noble martyr, in order to demonstrate how universally Mr. Lincoln was beloved and respected. Letters were sent to distinguished persons East and West, North and South in our country, as well as to persons in England, requesting them to express their estimate of Lincoln's public and private character and of his services ; and the more than two hundred responses to be found in this volume, over the *fac-similes* of the writer's names, shows the unexpected success I met with in this effort. Their publication in book form, together with the other reminiscences of Lincoln found in this volume, will, I have no doubt, be approved by the public. It has been my purpose to produce a work the contents of which might in some degree shed luster on the name of the immortal emancipator, and the external appearance of which might be an ornament in any house or library. How far I have succeeded in attaining the goal of my ambition, of this a generous public will have to judge. Surely the gathering of the material for this volume has been the greatest pleasure of my life. It has been a source of profound gratification to me, not only to receive the many tributes of great men's thoughts upon the life and character of Lincoln, but also to visit the old friends of his boyhood and listen to their simple and unvarnished stories illustrating the goodness of his heart. What a noble example was his whole life ! I have often thought what a beautiful book for boys might be made out of the boyhood of Lincoln if the past were collected and properly presented. All the friends of his youth whom I have seen give testimony of the purity and nobleness of his character; they say he always wanted to see fair play and that he was honest and upright in all things. He found great delight in helping any one in need. An old friend of Mr. Lincoln's, now living in Petersburg, Ill., told me how he at one time was building a house and was unable to make a brace fit. Mr. Lincoln happened to come that way, and the former said to him that if he would cut him a brace he would vote for him the first time he ran for President. Lincoln took a slate and pencil, and after getting the distance between the joists, he estimated its dimensions, made a pattern and the brace slipped in, a perfect fit. " I did not vote for Lincoln," added the man who related the story, "as I promised to do, but I have regretted it ever since." Few better examples of industry could be furnished to young men than the life of Lincoln. He was always as busy as a bee. He always carried some good book in his pocket, and when not otherwise engaged he would read, and was usually seen reading when going to and from his work. It is hoped that the sketch of Lincoln given in this work, the many extracts from his speeches, and the numerous thoughts and utterances in reference to his life and character by the foremost men of our time may be made accessible to the youth of our land, in order that thus many a young heart may be stimulated to industry, honesty, goodness and patriotism, and may find encouragement for higher aspirations and good deeds. The names of some persons will be missed in this work by many of the readers. In reference to this I have only to say that the fault is not mine. For some reason or other they did not respond to my *urgent* solicitations. It now remains to me to express my most hearty thanks to all those persons who have so kindly aided me in the preparation of this volume. I am particularly indebted for their special interest to Rev. Matthew Simpson, Hon. I. N. Arnold, Prof. Rasmus B.

Anderson, Benson J. Lossing. LL.D., Rev. Theo. L. Cuyler, T. W. S. Kidd, Joshua F. Speed, Joseph Gillespie and Jesse W. Fell. Their generous assistance has been a great comfort and help to me.

All I ask is that with the sale of this book I may realize some funds with which to build a Memorial Hall, where I may display to the public, free of charge, my life work in the collection of memorials and souvenirs of Abraham Lincoln, which will in due time be bequeathed to the public.

I am aware that there are many imperfections in all human enterprises, and am not blind to the faults of this work, but I can truly say that it has not been undertaken for the purpose of making money, but solely as an outcome of my enthusiasm and reverence for its great hero. I have spared neither pains nor expense, and, in view of this fact, it may not seem immodest if I bespeak for my effort the generosity of the critic and the liberality of the public.

Osborn Hamiline Oldroyd.

SPRINGFIELD, ILLINOIS, JULY, 1882.

GENERAL CONTENTS.

INDEX

TO THE

WRITINGS, SPEECHES AND SAYINGS

BY

Abraham Lincoln.

ALPHABETICAL

LIST OF CONTRIBUTORS.

————◆◆————

THE angels of your thoughts are climbing still
  The shining ladder of his fame,
And have not reached the top, nor ever will,
  While this low life pronounces his high name.

But yonder, where they dream, or dare, or do,
  The "good" or "great" beyond our reach,
To talk of him must make old language new
  In heavenly, as it did in human, speech.

Elizabeth Stuart Phelps.

ANDOVER, MASS., NOVEMBER, 1881.

[xxi]

INTRODUCTION.

THE name of *Abraham Lincoln* is imperishable. His fame is world-wide. Born in comparative poverty, trained in obscurity, mingling with the sons of toil in early manhood, he yet rose to one of earth's proudest positions, and at his death the world was in tears. He was not born great, as the heir of a great name, or of an estate; yet he was born great in having a strong intellect and a noble heart. Without the surrounding of friends, without the influence of wealth, he rose slowly but surely. Step by step he ascended the great pyramid until he stood upon its lofty summit. As we read history, how few names survive. Multiplied millions pass away in every generation; a few hundreds only are honored by coming ages. In early history the names which live are chiefly those of warriors or founders of nations; but Lincoln was no warrior; he drew no sword; he fought no bloody battles; he had no stars upon his breast. Others, as the founders of schools of philosophy, have left a name; as Plato, and Socrates, and

Aristotle. You hear of Crœsus through his untold wealth; but Lincoln was neither teacher nor millionaire. First, his name lives through his honesty and unselfishness, in his business, in his profession of the law, and in all his transactions among men, he gained the grand title of *honest.* His word was not doubted. No man believed that he ever betrayed any trust.

When in after life he had millions under his control, not even an enemy whispered a suspicion of his illegally or selfishly controlling a dollar of public money. If an honest man is the noblest work of God, then Mr. Lincoln's title to high nobility is clear and unquestioned.

In his busiest moment, in his most anxious hours during the war, he was ever ready to listen to the story of distress; many a widow's heart was cheered by his words and acts of kindness.

Secondly, he adhered firmly to what he believed to be right. Endowed with strong intellectual powers, which he had carefully exercised, he loved to study great principles. Deeply interested in the welfare of the nation, he inquired how it might become strong and be perpetuated. He followed not the crowd; he sought not personal popularity; he had faith in the ultimate triumph of truth and right. Perceiving the antagonism between slave labor and free labor, espousing the cause of equal rights and of human freedom, he early became the opponent of the encroachments of the slave power. He stood firmly with a small minority while others quailed before an imperious and threatening majority. He risked his position as a leader, his reputation as a statesman, as he disputed the right of slavery to the territories, and championed the cause of freedom. In his speeches which he made through his State are embodied most noble sentiments and trenchant thoughts; and though unpopular for a time, his sentiments became the sentiments of the great West.

Thirdly, when, in a season of great national excitement, he was unexpectedly called to the Presidency of the nation, he left his Western home with a presentiment that he would probably never return. The dangers of rebellion and civil war were before him. Threats of treachery and assassination were heard. But he determined, if needful, to lay down his life for the nation. He was not a warrior, but he was a hero. Through the weary years of that fearful war he bore anxieties and labors, and passed through perils that were exhausting and fearful. He lived to see the cause of the nation triumph, to behold the nation victorious, and coming peace smiled upon the land. Just at that moment the hand of the assassin sped the fatal ball. He died a martyr for his country.

Fourthly, in that terrible contest he had the distinguished honor and power of showing that "the pen is mightier than the sword." Fearful had been the contest. Disaster had sometimes attended our armies; despondency brooded over the minds of the people until he issued the famous Proclamation of Emancipation. That act became the turning-point of the war. Four millions of men were changed by it from slaves to citizens. Manacles were melted by its electric thrill. Success began to crown the movements of the army, and soon triumph rested on our banners.

Nor was it only from the millions of slaves that chains had been removed; the whole nation had been in bondage; free speech had been suppressed. Men dared not utter their convictions. An inquisition had been made in the postal service; the pulpit had frequently been over-awed by excited assemblies and utterances. Our great nation was reproached by the nations of the earth as violating the principles of freedom by holding men in slavery. The Proclamation of Emancipation not only freed the slave, but freed the nation. Free speech was restored. The pulpit and the press were unshackled. The dark blot that had rested upon our national honor was removed, and the nation stood proudly a united and free people among the nations of the earth. This act linked the name of Lincoln with the rights and progress of humanity, and while human freedom and true progress continue shall that name be held in reverence. We look not only to the past, but his life is a living power for the present and the future. It is a glowing commentary on the principles of the American Government and on the possibilities of human elevation. In older nations the rulers are found in hereditary families, among names that have been noble for generations; where wealth has been accumulated, and centuries of honored memories have clustered around the name. Mr. Lincoln's elevation shows that in America every station in life may be honorable; that there is no barrier against the humblest; but that merit, wherever it exists, has the opportunity to be known. His life also is an inspiration for the young. There are few, indeed, more humble in their birth, more obscure in their early associations, more pressed with life's surroundings and cares, with fewer apparent prospects of success; to all these his example and his elevation becomes a living power. What he became they may aspire to be; and the humblest youth looking through the coming years beholds the possibility of occupying any position to which his talents and his efforts may fit him.

Nor is it uninstructive to see how a name unknown but a few years before may become world-wide. As a President of the United States his position was equal, at least, to that of the monarchs of Europe; and yet those monarchs had been unwilling to recognize as an equal the President of a youthful nation, whose term of office was limited to a few years. But when suddenly smitten, the national sympathy of the masses and of the monarchs was strongly touched; words of sympathy and condolence were sent from nearly every throne, and the masses of the people in all their associations joined in the general mourning, recognizing that a friend of humanity had fallen. It is very fitting that proper mementos should be prepared and widely diffused. The volume now offered to the public embraces some of these mementos, and is a collection of some of the best thoughts and utterances in reference to his distinguished career. It is hoped that it may have a wide circulation, and may stimulate many a youthful heart to noble aspirations and to noble deeds.

M. Simpson

PHILADELPHIA, 1882.

ABRAHAM LINCOLN.

BY.HON. ISAAC N. ARNOLD.

THE noblest inheritance we, Americans, derive from our British ancestors is the memory and example of the great and good men who adorn your history. They are as much appreciated and honored on our side of the Atlantic as on this. In giving to the English-speaking world Washington and Lincoln we think we repay, in large part, our obligation. Their pre-eminence in American history is recognized, and the republic, which the one *founded* and the other *preserved*, has, already, crowned them as models for her children.

In the annals of almost every great nation some names appear standing out clear and prominent, names of those who have influenced or controlled the great events which make up history. Such were Wallace and Bruce in Scotland, Alfred and the Edwards, William the Conqueror, Cromwell, Pitt, Nelson and Wellington, in England, and such, in a still greater degree, were Washington and Lincoln.

I am here, from near his home, with the hope that

I may, to some extent, aid you in forming a just and true estimate of Abraham Lincoln. I knew him, somewhat intimately, in private and public life for more than twenty years. We practiced law at the same bar, and during his administration, I was a member of Congress, seeing him and conferring with him often, and therefore, I may hope without vanity, I trust, that I shall be able to contribute something of value in enabling you to judge of him. We in America, as well as you in the old world, believe that "blood will tell;" that it is a great blessing to have had an honorable and worthy ancestry. We believe that moral principle, physical and intellectual vigor, in the forefathers are qualities likely to be manifested in the descendants. Fools are not the fathers or mothers of great men. I claim for Lincoln, humble as was the station to which he was born and rude and rough as were his early surroundings, that he had such ancestors. I mean that his father and mother, his grandfather and grandmother, and still further back, however humble and rugged their condition, were physically and mentally strong, vigorous men and women ; hardy and successful pioneers on the frontier of American civilization. They were among the early settlers in Virginia, Kentucky, and Illinois, and knew how to take care of themselves in the midst of difficulties and perils ; how to live and succeed when the weak would perish. These ancestors of Lincoln, for several generations, kept on the very crest of the wave of Western settlements— on the frontier, where the struggle for life was hard and the strong alone survived.

His grandfather, Abraham Lincoln, and his father, Thomas, were born in Rockingham County, Virginia.

About 1781, while his father was still a lad, his grandfather's family emigrated to Kentucky, and was a contemporary with Daniel Boone, the celebrated Indian fighter and early hero of that State. This, a then wild and wooded territory, was the scene of those fierce and desperate conflicts between the settlers and the Indians which gave it the name of "The dark and bloody ground."

When Thomas Lincoln, the father of the President, was six years old, his father (Abraham, the grandfather of the President) was shot and instantly killed by an Indian. The boy and his father were at work in the corn-field, near their log-cabin home. Mordecai, the elder brother of the lad, at work not far away, witnessed the attack. He saw his father fall, and ran to the cabin, seized his ready-loaded rifle and springing to the loop-hole cut through the logs, he saw the Indian, who had seized the boy, carrying him away. Raising his rifle and aiming at a silver medal, conspicuous on the breast of the Indian, he instantly fired. The Indian fell, and the lad, springing to his feet, ran to the open arms of his mother, at the cabin door. Amidst such scenes, the Lincoln family naturally produced rude, rough, hardy, and fearless men, familiar with wood-craft; men who could meet the extremes of exposure and fatigue, who knew how to find food and shelter in the forest; men of great powers of endurance—brave and self-reliant, true and faithful to their friends and dangerous to their enemies. Men with

minds to conceive and hands to execute bold enterprises.

It is a curious fact that the grandfather, Abraham
Lincoln, is noted on the surveys of Daniel Boone as having purchased of the Government five hundred acres of
land. Thomas Lincoln, the father, was also the purchaser
of government land, and President Lincoln left, as a part
of his estate, a quarter-section (one hundred and sixty
acres), which he had received from the United States for
services rendered in early life as a volunteer soldier, in the
Black-Hawk Indian war. Thus for three generations the
Lincoln family were land-owners directly from the Government.

Such was the lineage and family from which President
Lincoln sprung. Such was the environment in which his
character was developed.

He was born in a log-cabin, in Kentucky, on the 12th
of February, 1809.

It will aid you in picturing to yourself this young man
and his surroundings, to know that, from boyhood to the
age of twenty-one, in winter his head was protected from
the cold by a cap made of the skin of the coon, fox, or
prairie-wolf, and that he often wore the buckskin breeches
and hunting-shirt of the pioneer.

He grew up to be a man of majestic stature and Herculean strength. Had he appeared in England or Nor-
mandy, some centuries ago, he would have been the
founder of some great baronial family, possibly of a
royal dynasty. He could have wielded, with ease, the
two-handed sword of Guy, the great Earl of Warwick, or
the battle-axe of Richard of the Lion-heart.

HIS EDUCATION AND TRAINING.

The world is naturally interested in knowing what was the education and training which fitted Lincoln for the great work which he accomplished. On the extreme frontier, the means of book-learning was very limited. The common free schools, which now closely follow the heels of the pioneer and organized civil government, and prevail all over the United States, had not then reached the Far West. An itinerant school-teacher wandered occasionally into a settlement, opened a private school for a few months, and, at such, Lincoln attended at different times, in all about twelve months. His mother, who was a woman of practical good sense, of strong physical organization, of deep religious feeling, gentle and self-reliant, taught him to read and write.

Although she died when he was only nine years old, she had already laid deep the foundations of his excellence. Perfect truthfulness and integrity, love of justice, self-control, reverence for God, these constituted the solid basis of his character. These were all implanted and carefully cultivated by his mother, and he always spoke of her with the deepest respect and the most tender affection. "All that I am, or hope to be," said he, when President, "I owe to my sainted mother."

He early manifested the most eager desire to learn, but there were no libraries, and few books in the back settlements in which he lived. Among the stray volumes which he found in the possession of the illiterate families by which he was surrounded, were Æsop's Fables, Bunyan's Pilgrim's Progress, a life of Washington, the poems

3

of Burns, and the Bible. To these his reading was confined, and he read them over and over again, until they became as familiar almost as the alphabet. His memory was marvelous, and I never yet met the man more familiar with the Bible than Abraham Lincoln. This was apparent in after life, both from his conversation and writings, scarcely a speech or state paper of his in which illustrations and illusions from the Bible cannot be found.

While a young man, he made for himself, of coarse paper, a scrap-book, into which he copied everything which particularly pleased him. He found an old English grammar, which he studied by himself; and he formed, from his constant study of the Bible, that simple, plain, clear Anglo-Saxon style, so effective with the people. He illustrated the maxim that it is better to know thoroughly a few good books than to skim over many. When fifteen years old, he began (with a view of improving himself) to write on various subjects and to practice in making political and other speeches. These he made so amusing and attractive that his father had to forbid his making them in working-hours, for, said he, "when Abe begins to speak, all the hands flock to hear him." His memory was so retentive that he could repeat, *verbatim*, the sermons and political speeches which he heard.

While his days were spent in hard manual labor, and his evenings in study, he grew up strong in body, healthful in mind, with no bad habits; no stain of intemperance, profanity or vice of any kind. He used neither tobacco nor intoxicating drinks, and, thus living, he grew to be six feet four inches high, and a giant in strength. In all athletic sports he had no equal. I have heard an old comrade say, "he could strike the hardest blow with the woodman's axe, and the maul of the rail-splitter, jump higher, run faster than any of his fellows, and there were none, far or near, who could lay him on his back." Kind and cordial, he early developed so much wit and humor, such a capacity for narrative and story-telling, that he was everywhere a most welcome guest.

A LAND SURVEYOR.

Like Washington, he became, in early life, a good practical surveyor, and I have in my library the identical book from which, at eighteen years of age, he studied the art of surveying. By his skill and accuracy, and by the neatness of his work, he was sought after by the settlers, to survey and fix the boundaries of their farms, and in this way, in part, he earned a support while he studied law. In 1837, self-taught, he was admitted and licensed, by the Supreme Court of Illinois, to practice law.

A LAWYER.

It is difficult for me to describe, and, perhaps, more difficult for you to conceive the contrast when Lincoln began to practice law, between the forms of the administration of justice in Westminster Hall, and in the rude log court-houses of Illinois. I recall to-day what was said a few years ago by an Illinois friend, when we visited, for the first time, Westminster Abbey, and as we passed into Westminster Hall. "This," he exclaimed, "this is the grandest forum in the world.   Here Fox, Burke, and Sheridan hurled their denunciations against Warren Hastings.   Here Brougham defended Queen Caroline.   And this," he went on to repeat, in the words of Macaulay, (words as familiar in America as here), "This is the great hall of William Rufus, the hall which has resounded with acclamations at the inauguration of thirty kings, and which has witnessed the trials of Bacon and Somers and Strafford and Charles the First."   "And yet," I replied, "I have seen justice administered on the prairies of Illinois without pomp or ceremony, everything simple to rudeness, and yet when Lincoln and Douglass led at that bar, I have seen justice administered by judges as pure, aided by advocates as eloquent, if not as learned, as any who ever presided, or plead, in Westminster Hall."

The common law of England (said to be the perfection of human wisdom) was administered in both forums, and the decisions of each tribunal were cited as authority in the other; both illustrating that reverence for, and obedience to, law, which is the glory of the English-speaking race.

Lincoln was a great lawyer.   He sought to convince rather by the application of principle than by the citation of authorities.   On the whole, he was stronger with the jury than with the court.   I do not know that there has ever been, in America, a greater or more successful advocate before a jury, on the right side, than Abraham Lincoln.   He had a marvelous power of conciliating and impressing every one in his favor.   A stranger entering the court, ignorant of the case, and listening a few moments to Lincoln, would find himself involuntarily on his side and wishing him success. He was a quick and accurate reader of character, and seemed to comprehend, almost intuitively, the peculiarities of those with whom he came in contact. His manner was so candid, his methods so direct, so fair, he seemed so anxious that truth and justice should prevail, that every one wished him success. He excelled in the statement of his case. However complicated, he would disentangle it, and present the important and turning-point in a way so clear that all could understand. Indeed, his statement often alone won his cause, rendering argument unnecessary. The judges would often stop him by saying, "If that is the case, brother Lincoln, we will hear the other side."

His ability in examining a witness, in bringing out clearly the important facts, was only surpassed by his skillful cross-examinations, He could often compel a witness to tell the truth, where he meant to lie. He could make a jury laugh, and generally weep, at his pleasure. On the right side, and when fraud or injustice were to be exposed, or innocence vindicated, he rose to the highest range of eloquence, and was irresistible. But he must have faith in his cause to bring out his full strength. His wit and humor, his quaint and homely illustrations, his inexhaustible stores of anecdote, always to the point, added greatly to his power as a jury-advocate.

He never misstated evidence or misrepresented his opponent's case, but met it fairly and squarely.

He remained in active practice until his nomination, in May, 1860, for the presidency. He was employed in the leading cases in both the federal and state courts, and had a large clientelage not only in Illinois, but was frequently called, on special retainers, to other States.

AN ILLINOIS POLITICIAN.

By his eloquence and popularity he became, early in life, the leader of the old Whig party, in Illinois. He served as member of the State Legislature, was the candidate of his party for speaker, presidential elector, and United States senator, and was a member of the lower house of Congress.

SLAVERY.

When the independence of the American republic was established, African slavery was tolerated as a local and temporary institution. It was in conflict with the moral sense, the religious convictions of the people, and the political principles on which the government was founded.

But having been tolerated, it soon became an organized aggressive power, and, later, it became the master of the government. Conscious of its inherent weakness, it demanded and obtained additional territory for its expansion. First, the great Louisiana territory was purchased, then Florida, and then Texas.

By the repeal, in 1854, of the prohibition of slavery north of the line of 36°, 30′ of latitude (known in America as the "Missouri Compromise"), the slavery question became the leading one in American politics, and the absorbing and exciting topic of discussion. It shattered into fragments the old conservative Whig party, with which Mr. Lincoln had, theretofore, acted. It divided the Democratic party, and new parties were organized upon issues growing directly out of the question of slavery.

The leader of that portion of the Democratic party which continued, for a time, to act with the slavery party, was Stephen Arnold Douglas, then representing Illinois in the United States Senate. He was a bold, ambitious, able man, and had, thus far, been uniformly successful. He had introduced and carried through Congress, against the most vehement opposition, the repeal of the law prohibiting slavery, called the Missouri Compromise.

THE CONTEST BETWEEN FREEDOM AND SLAVERY IN THE TERRITORIES.

The issue having been now distinctly made between freedom and the extension of slavery into the territories, Lincoln and Douglas, the leaders of the Free-soil and Democratic parties, became more than ever antagonized. The conflict between freedom and slavery now became earnest, fierce, and violent, beyond all previous political controversies, and from this time on, Lincoln plead the cause of liberty with an energy, ability, and eloquence, which rapidly gained for him a national reputation. From this time on, through the tremendous struggle, it was he who grasped the helm and led his party to victory. Conscious of a great cause, inspired by a generous love of liberty, and animated by the moral sublimity of his great theme, he proclaimed his determination, ever thereafter, "to speak for freedom, and against slavery, until every·

where the sun shall shine, the rain shall fall, and the wind blow upon no man who goes forth to unrequited toil."

THE LINCOLN AND DOUGLAS DEBATE.

The great debate between Lincoln and Douglas, in 1858, was, unquestionably, both with reference to the ability of the speakers and its influence upon opinion and events, the most important in American history. I do not think I do injustice to others, nor over-estimate their importance, when I say that the speeches of Lincoln published, circulated, and read throughout the Free States, did more than any other agency in creating the public opinion, which prepared the way for the overthrow of slavery. The speeches of John Quincy Adams, and those of Senator Sumner, were more learned and scholarly, and those of Lovejoy and Wendell Phillips were more vehement and impassioned; Senators Seward, Chase, and Hale spoke from a more conspicuous forum, but Lincoln's speeches were as philosophic, as able, as earnest as any, and his manner had a simplicity and directness, a clearness of illustration, and his language a plainness, a vigor, an Anglo-Saxon strength, better adapted than any other, to reach and influence the understanding and sentiment of the common people.

At the time of this memorable discussion, both Lincoln and Douglas were in the full maturity of their powers, Douglas being forty-five and Lincoln forty-nine years old. Douglas had had a long training and experience as a popular speaker. On the hustings (stump, as we say in America) and in Congress, and, especially in the United

States Senate, he had been accustomed to meet the ablest debaters of his State and of the Nation.

His friends insisted that never, either in conflict with a single opponent, or when repelling the assaults of a whole party, had he been discomfited. His manner was bold, vigorous, and aggressive. He was ready, fertile in resources, familiar with political history, strong and severe in denunciation, and he handled, with skill, all the weapons of the dialectician. His iron will, tireless energy, united with physical and moral courage, and great personal magnetism, made him a natural leader, and gave him personal popularity.

Lincoln was also now a thoroughly trained speaker. He had contended successfully at the bar, in the legislature, and before the people, with the ablest men of the West, including Douglas, with whom he always rather sought than avoided a discussion. But he was a courteous and generous opponent, as is illustrated by the following beautiful allusion to his rival, made in 1856, in one of their joint debates. "Twenty years ago, Judge Douglas and I first became acquainted; we were both young then; he a trifle younger than I. Even then, we were both ambitious, I, perhaps, quite as much as he. With me, the race of ambition has been a flat failure. With him, it has been a splendid success. His name fills the nation, and it is not unknown in foreign lands. I affect no contempt for the high eminence he has reached; so reached, that the oppressed of my species might have shared with me in the elevation, I would rather stand on that eminence than wear the richest crown that ever pressed a monarch's brow."

We know, and the world knows, that Lincoln did reach that high, nay, far higher eminence, and that he did reach it in such a way that the "oppressed" did share with him in the elevation.

Such were the champions who, in 1858, were to dis- cuss, before the voters of Illinois, and with the whole nation as spectators, the political questions then pending, and especially the vital questions relating to slavery. It was not a single combat, but extended through a whole campaign.

On the return of Douglas from Washington, to Illinois, in July, 1858, Lincoln and Douglas being candi- dates for the Senate, the former challenged his rival to a series of joint debates, to be held at the principal towns in the State. The challenge was accepted, and it was agreed that each discussion should occupy three hours, that the speakers should alternate in the opening and the close—the opening speech to occupy one hour, the reply one hour and a-half, and the close half an hour. The meetings were held in the open air, for no hall could hold the vast crowds which attended.

In addition to the immense mass of hearers, reporters, from all the principal newspapers in the country, attended, so that the morning after each debate, the speeches were published, and eagerly read by a large part, perhaps a majority, of all the voters of the United States.

The attention of the American people was thus arrested, and they watched with intense interest, and devoured every argument of the champions.

Each of these great men, I doubt not, at that time, sincerely believed he was right. Douglas's ardor, while in such a conflict, would make him think, for the time being, he was right, and I *know* that Lincoln argued for freedom against the extension of slavery with the most profound conviction that on the result hung the fate of his country. Lincoln had two advantages over Douglas; he had the best side of the question, and the best temper. He was always good-humored, always had an apt story for illustration, while Douglas sometimes, when hard pressed, was irritable.

Douglas carried away the most popular applause, but Lincoln made the deeper and more lasting impression. Douglas did not disdain an immediate *ad captandum* triumph, while Lincoln aimed at permanent conviction. Sometimes, when Lincoln's friends urged him to raise a storm of applause (which he could always do by his happy illustrations and amusing stories), he refused, saying the occasion was too serious, the issue too grave. "I do not seek applause," said he, "nor to amuse the people; I want to convince them."

It was often observed, during this canvass, that while Douglas was sometimes greeted with the loudest cheers, when Lincoln closed, the people seemed solemn and serious, and could be heard, all through the crowd, gravely and anxiously discussing the topics on which he had been speaking.

Douglas secured the immediate object of the struggle, but the manly bearing, the vigorous logic, the honesty and sincerity, the great intellectual powers, exhibited by Mr. Lincoln, prepared the way, and, two years later, secured his nomination and election to the presidency. It is a touching incident, illustrating the patriotism of both these statesmen, that, widely as they differed, and keen as had been their rivalry, just as soon as the life of the republic was menaced by treason, they joined hands, to shield and save the country they loved.

The echo and the prophecy of this great debate was heard, and inspired hope in the far-off cotton and rice-fields of the South. The toiling blacks, to use the words of Whittier, began hopefully to pray:

> "We pray de Lord He gib us signs
> Dat some day we be free.
> De Norf wind tell it to de pines,
> De wild duck to de sea.

> "We tink it when de church-bell ring,
> We dream it in de dream,
> De rice-bird mean it when he sing,
> De eagle when he scream."

THE COOPER INSTITUTE SPEECH.

In February, 1860, Mr. Lincoln was called to address the people of New York, and, speaking to a vast audience, at the Cooper Institute (the Exeter Hall of the United States), the poet Bryant presiding, he made, perhaps, the most learned, logical, and exhaustive speech to be found in American anti-slavery literature. The question was, the power of the National Government to exclude slavery from the territories. The orator from the prairies, the morning after this speech, awoke to find himself famous.

He closed with these words, " Let us have faith that *right* makes *might*, and in that faith let us, to the end, do our duty as we understand it."

This address was the carefully finished product of, not an orator and statesman only, but also of an accurate student of American history. It confirmed and elevated the reputation he had already acquired in the Douglas debates, and caused his nomination and election to the presidency.

If time permitted, I would like to follow Mr. Lincoln, step by step, to enumerate his measures one after another, until, by prudence and courage, and matchless statesmanship, he led the loyal people of the republic to the final and complete overthrow of slavery and the restoration of the Union.

From the time he left his humble home, in Illinois, to assume the responsibilities of power, the political horizon black with treason and rebellion, the terrific thunder-clouds,—the tempest which had been gathering and growing more black and threatening for years, now ready to explode,—on and on, through long years of bloody war, down to his final triumph and death — what a drama! His eventful life terminated by his tragic death, has it not the dramatic unities and the awful ending of the Old Greek tragedy?

HIS FAREWELL TO HIS NEIGHBORS.

I know of nothing, in history, more pathetic than the scene when he bade good-bye to his old friends and neighbors. Conscious of the difficulties and dangers before him, difficulties which seemed almost insurmountable, with a sadness as though a presentiment that he should return no more was pressing upon him, but with a deep religious trust which was characteristic, on the platform of the rail-carriage, which was to bear him away to the capital, he paused and said, " No one can realize the sadness I feel at this parting. Here I have lived more than a quarter of a century. Here my children were born, and here one of them lies buried. I know not how soon I shall see you again. I go to assume a task more difficult than that which has devolved upon any other man since the days of Washington. He never would have succeeded but for the aid of Divine Providence, upon which, at all times, he relied. * * * I hope you, my dear friends, will all pray that I may receive that Divine assistance, without which I cannot succeed, but with which, success is certain."

And as he waved his hand in farewell to the old home, to which he was never to return, he heard the response from many old friends, " God bless and keep you." "God protect you from all traitors." His neighbors "sorrowing most of all," for the fear "that they should see his face no more."

HIS INAUGURAL AND APPEAL FOR PEACE.

In his inaugural address, spoken in the open air, and from the eastern portico of the Capitol, and heard by thrice ten thousand people, on the very verge of civil war, he made a most earnest appeal for peace. He gave the most solemn assurance, that "the property, peace, and security of no portion of the republic should be endangered by his administration." But he declared, with firmness, that the union of the States must be "per-

petual," and that he should "execute the laws faithfully
in every State." "In doing this," said he, "there need be
no bloodshed nor violence, nor shall there be, unless
forced upon the national authority." In regard to the
difficulties which thus divided the people, he appealed to
all to abstain from precipitate action, assuring them that
intelligence, patriotism, and a firm reliance on Him, who
has never yet forsaken the republic, "were competent
to adjust, in the best way, all existing troubles."

His closing appeal, against civil war, was most touching, "In your hands," said he, and his voice for the first
time faltered, "In your hands, and not in mine, are the
momentous issues of civil war."   *   *   "You can
have no conflict without being yourselves the aggressors."
*   *   "I am," continued he, "loath to close; we are
not enemies, but friends. We must not be enemies.
Though passion may strain, it must not break. the bonds
of affection."

The answer to these appeals was the attack upon
Fort Sumter, and immediately broke loose all the mad-
dening passions which riot in blood and carnage and
civil war.

I know not how I can better picture and illustrate
the condition of affairs, and of public feeling, at that
time, than by narrating two or three incidents.

DOUGLAS'S PROPHECY, JANUARY 1, 1861.

In January, 1861, Senator Douglas, then lately a candidate for the presidency, with Mrs. Douglas, one of the
beautiful and fascinating women in America, a relative

of Mrs. Madison, occupied, at Washington, one of the most magnificent blocks of dwellings, called the "Minnesota Block." On New Year's day, 1861, General Charles Stewart, of New York, from whose lips I write an account of the incident, says,

"I was making a New Year's call on Senator Douglas; after some conversation, I asked him,

"'What will be the result, Senator, of the efforts of Jefferson Davis, and his associates, to divide the Union?' We were," said Stewart, "sitting on the sofa together, when I asked the question. Douglas rose, walked rapidly up and down the room for a moment, and then pausing, he exclaimed, with deep feeling and excitement:

"'The Cotton States are making an effort to draw in the Border States, to their schemes of secession, and I am but too fearful they will succeed. If they do, there will be the most fearful civil war the world has ever seen, lasting for years.'

"Pausing a moment, he looked like one inspired, while he proceeded: 'Virginia, over yonder, across the Potomac,' pointing toward Arlington, 'will become a charnel-house—but in the end the Union will triumph. They will try,' he continued, 'to get possession of this capital, to give them *prestige* abroad, but in that effort they will never succeed; the North will rise *en masse* to defend it. But Washington will become a city of hospitals, the churches will be used for the sick and wounded. This house,' he continued, 'the *Minnesota Block*, will be devoted to that purpose before the end of the war.'

"Every word he said was literally fulfilled—all the churches nearly were used for the wounded, and the

Minnesota Block, and the very room in which this declaration was made, became the ' Douglas Hospital.'

"What justification for all this?' said Stewart.

"'There is no justification,' replied Douglas.

"'I will go as far as the Constitution will permit to
maintain their just rights. But,' said he, rising upon his
feet and raising his arm, 'if the Southern States attempt
to secede, I am in favor of their having just so many
slaves, and just so much slave territory, as they can hold
at the point of the bayonet, and no more.'"

WILL THE NORTH FIGHT?

Many Southern leaders believed there would be no
serious war, and labored industriously to impress this
idea on the Southern people.

Benjamin F. Butler, who, as a delegate from Massachusetts, to the Charlestown Convention, had voted
many times for Breckenridge, the extreme Southern
candidate for president, came to Washington, in the winter of 1860–1, to inquire of his old associates what they
meant by their threats.

"We mean," replied they, "we mean separation — a
Southern Confederacy. We will have our independence,
a Southern government—with no discordant elements."

"Are you prepared for war?" said Butler, coolly.

"Oh, there will be no war; the North won't fight."

"The North *will* fight," said Butler; "the North will
send the *last man* and expend the *last dollar* to maintain
the Government."

"But," replied Butler's Southern friends, "the North
can't fight, we have too many allies there."

4

"You have friends," responded Butler, "in the North, who will stand by you so long as you fight your battles in the Union, but the moment you fire on the flag, the North will be a unit against you. And," Butler continued, "you may be assured that if war comes, *slavery ends.*"

THE SPECIAL SESSION OF CONGRESS, JULY, 1861

On the brink of this civil war, the President summoned Congress to meet on the 4th of July, 1861, the anniversary of our independence. Seven States had already seceded, were in open revolt, and the chairs of their representatives, in both houses of Congress, were vacant. It needed but a glance at these so numerous vacant seats to realize the extent of the defection, the gravity of the situation, and the magnitude of the impending struggle. The old pro-slavery leaders were absent, some in the rebel government, set up at Richmond, and others marshalling troops in the field. Hostile armies were gathering, and from the dome of the Capitol, across the Potomac and on toward Fairfax, in Virginia, could be seen the Confederate flag.

Breckenridge, late the Southern candidate for President, now Senator from Kentucky, and soon to lead a rebel army, still lingered in the Senate. Like Catiline among the Roman Senators, he was regarded with aversion and distrust. Gloomy and, perhaps, sorrowful he said, "I can only look with sadness on the melancholy drama that is being enacted."

Pardon the digression, while I relate an incident which occurred in the Senate, at this special session.

Senator Baker, of Oregon, was making a brilliant and impassioned reply to a speech of Breckenridge, in which he denounced the Kentucky Senator, for giving aid and encouragement to the enemy, by his speeches. At length he paused, and, turning toward Breckenridge, and fixing his eye upon him, asked, "What would have been thought if, after the battle of Cannæ, a Roman Senator had risen, amidst the Conscript Fathers, and denounced the war, and opposed all measures for its success."

Baker paused, and every eye in the Senate, and in the crowded galleries, was fixed upon the almost solitary senator from Kentucky. Fessenden broke the painful silence, by exclaiming, in low deep tones, which gave expression to the thrill of indignation which ran through the hall, "He would have been hurled from the Tarpeian Rock."

Congress manifested its sense of the gravity of the situation by authorizing a loan of two hundred and fifty millions of dollars, and enpowering the President to call into the field five hundred thousand men, and as many more as he might deem necessary.

SURRENDER OF MASON AND SLIDELL.

No act of the British Government, since the "stamp act" of the Revolution, has ever excited such intense feeling of hostility toward Great Britain, as her haughty demand for the surrender of Mason and Slidell. It required *nerve*, in the President, to stem the storm of popular feeling and yield to that demand, and it was, for a time, the most unpopular act of his administration. But when the excitement of the day had passed, it was approved by the sober judgment of the nation.

Prince Albert is kindly and gratefully remembered in America, where it is believed that his action, in modifying the terms of that demand, probably saved the United States and Great Britain from the horrors of war.

LINCOLN AND THE ABOLITION OF SLAVERY.

When in June, 1858, at his home in Springfield, Mr. Lincoln startled the people with the declaration, "This government cannot endure, permanently, half slave and half free," and when, at the close of his speech, to those who were laboring for the ultimate extinction of slavery, he exclaimed, with the voice of a prophet, "We shall not fail, if we stand firm, we shall *not* fail. Wise councils may accelerate, or mistakes delay, but sooner or later, the victory is sure to come;" he anticipated success, through years of discussion, and final triumph through peaceful and constitutional means by the ballot. He did not foresee, nor even dream (unless in those dim mysterious shadows, which sometimes startle by half revealing the future), his own elevation to the presidency. He did not then suspect that he had been appointed by God, and should be chosen by the people, to proclaim the emancipation of a race, and to save his country. He did not foresee that slavery was so soon to be destroyed, amidst the flames of war which itself kindled.

HIS MODERATION.

He entered upon his administration with the single

purpose of maintaining national unity, and many reproached and denounced him for the slowness of his anti-slavery measures. The first of the series was the abolition of slavery at the National Capitol. This act gave freedom to three thousand slaves, with compensation to their loyal masters. Contemporaneous with this was an act conferring freedom upon all colored soldiers who should serve in the Union armies and upon their families. The next was an act which I had the honor to introduce, prohibiting slavery in all the territories, and wherever the National Government had jurisdiction. But the great, the decisive act of his administration, was the "Emancipation Proclamation."

EMANCIPATION PROCLAMATION.

The President had urged, with the utmost earnestness, on the loyal slave-holders of the Border States, gradual and compensated emancipation, but in vain. He clearly saw, all saw, that the slaves, as used by the Confederates, were a vast power, contributing immensely to their ability to carry on the war, and that, by declaring their freedom, he would convert millions of freedmen into active friends and allies of the Union. The people knew that he was deliberating upon the question of issu- Union men of the Border States made an appeal to him to withhold the edict, and suffer slavery to survive.

They selected John J. Crittenden, a venerable and eloquent man, and their ablest statesman, to make, on the floor of Congress, a public appeal to the President, to withhold the proclamation. Mr. Crittenden had been governor of Kentucky, her senator in Congress, attorney-general of the United States, and now, in his old age, covered with honors, he accepted, like John Quincy Adams, a seat in Congress, that in this crisis he might help to save his country.

He was a sincere Union man, but believed it unwise to disturb slavery. In his speech he made a most eloquent and touching appeal, from a Kentuckian to a Kentuckian. He said, among other things, "There is a niche, near to that of Washington, to him who shall save his country. If Mr. Lincoln will step into that niche, the *founder* and the *preserver* of the Republic shall stand side by side." * * Owen Lovejoy, the brother of Elijah P. Lovejoy, who had been mobbed and murdered because he would not surrender the liberty of the press, replied to Crittenden. After his brother's murder, kneeling upon the green sod which covered that brother's grave, he had taken a solemn vow, of eternal war upon slavery. Ever after, like Peter the Hermit, with a heart of fire and a tongue of lightning, he had gone forth, preaching his crusade against slavery. At length, in his reply, turning to Crittenden, he said, "The gentleman from Kentucky says he has a niche for Abraham Lincoln, where is it?"

Crittenden pointed toward heaven.

Lovejoy continuing said, "He points upward, but, sir! if the President follows the counsel of that gentleman, and becomes the perpetuator of slavery, he should point *downward*, to some dungeon in the temple of Moloch, who feeds on human blood, and where are forged chains for human limbs; in the recesses of whose temple woman is scourged and man tortured, and outside the walls are lying dogs, gorged with human flesh, as Byron describes them, lying around the walls of Stamboul." " That," said Lovejoy, " is a suitable place for the statue of him who would perpetuate slavery."

" I, too," said he, " have a temple for Abraham Lincoln, but it is in Freedom's holy fane,   *   *   * not surrounded by slave fetters and chains, but with the symbols of freedom—not dark with bondage, but radiant with the light of Liberty. In that niche he shall stand proudly, nobly, gloriously, with broken chains and slave's whips beneath his feet.   *   *   That is a fame worth living for, aye, more, it is a fame worth dying for, though that death led through Gethsemane and the agony of the accursed tree."   *   *   *

" It is said," continued he, " that Wilberforce went up to the judgment-seat with the broken chains of eight hundred thousand slaves ! Let Lincoln make himself the Liberator, and his name shall be enrolled, not only in this earthly temple, but it shall be traced on the living stones of that temple which is reared amid the thrones of Heaven."

Lovejoy's prophecy has been fulfilled—in this world— you see the statues to Lincoln, with broken chains at his feet, rising all over the world, and—in that other world— few will doubt that the prophecy has been realized.

In September, 1862, after the Confederates, by their defeat at the great battle of Antietam, had been driven back from Maryland and Pennsylvania, Lincoln issued the Proclamation. It is a fact, illustrating his character, and showing that there was in him what many would call a tinge of superstition, that he declared, to Secretary Chase, that he had made a solemn vow to God, saying, "if General Lee is driven back from Pennsylvania, I will crown the result with the declaration of FREEDOM TO THE SLAVE." The final Proclamation was issued on the first of January, 1863. In obedience to American custom, he had been receiving calls on that New Year's day, and, for hours, shaking hands. As the paper was brought to him by the Secretary of State, to be signed, he said, "Mr. Seward, I have been shaking hands all day, and my right hand is almost paralyzed. If my name ever gets into history, it will be for this act, and my whole soul is in it. If my hand trembles when I sign the proclamation, those who examine the document hereafter, will say, 'he hesitated.'"

Then, resting his arm a moment, he turned to the table, took up the pen, and slowly and firmly wrote *Abraham Lincoln.* He smiled as, handing the paper to Mr. Seward, he said, "that will do."

From this day, to its final triumph, the tide of victory seemed to set more and more in favor of the Union cause. The capture of Vicksburg, the victory of Gettysburg, Chattanooga, Chickamauga, Lookout-Mountain, Missionary Ridge, Sheridan's brilliant campaign in the Valley of the Shenandoah; Thomas's decisive victory at Nashville; Sherman's march, through the Confederacy, to the sea; the capture of Fort McAllister; the *sinking of the Alabama;* the taking of Mobile by Farragut; the occupation of Columbus, Charlestown, Savannah; the evacuation of Petersburg and Richmond; the surrender of Lee to Grant; the taking of Jefferson Davis a prisoner; the triumph everywhere of the national arms; such were the events which followed (though with delays and bloodshed) the "Proclamation of Emancipation."

THE AMENDMENT TO THE CONSTITUTION.

Meanwhile Lincoln had been triumphantly re-elected; Congress had, as before stated, abolished slavery at the Capital, prohibited it in all the territories, declared all negro soldiers in the Union armies, and their families, free, and had repealed all laws which sanctioned or recognized slavery, and the President had crowned and consummated all, by the Proclamation of Emancipation. One thing alone remained to perfect, confirm, and make everlastingly permanent these measures, and this was to embody in the Constitution itself, the prohibition of slavery everywhere within the republic.

To change the organic law required the adoption by a two-thirds vote of a joint resolution, by Congress, and that this should be submitted to, and ratified by, two-thirds of the States.

The President, in his annual message and in personal interviews with members of Congress, urged the passage of such resolution. To test the strength of the measure, in the House of Representatives, I had the honor, in February, 1864, to introduce the following resolution :

"*Resolved*, That the Constitution should be so amended as to abolish slavery in the United States wherever it now exists, and to prohibit its existence in every part thereof forever" (Cong. Globe, vol. 50, p. 659). This was adopted by a decided vote, and was the first

resolution ever passed by Congress in favor of the entire
abolition of slavery.   But, although it received a majority,
it did not receive a majority of two-thirds.

The debates on the Constitutional Amendment
(perhaps the greatest in our congressional history, certainly the most important since the adoption of the Constitution) ran through two sessions of Congress.   Charles
Sumner, the learned Senator from Massachusetts, brought
to the discussion, in the Senate, his ample stores of historical illustration, quoting largely in its favor from the
historians, poets, and statesmen of the past.

The resolution was adopted in the Senate by the
large vote of ayes, 38, noes, 6.

In the lower house, at the first session, it failed to
obtain a two-thirds' vote, and, on a motion to reconsider,
went over to the next session.

Mr. Lincoln again earnestly urged its adoption, and,
in a letter to Illinois friends, he said, "The signs look
better.   *   *   Peace does not look so distant as
it did.   I hope it will come soon, and come to stay, and
so come as to be worth keeping in all future time."

I recall, very vividly, my New Year's call upon the
President, January, 1864.   I said :

"I hope, Mr. President, one year from to-day I may
have the pleasure of congratulating you on the occurrence
of three events which now seem probable."

"What are they?" inquired he.

"1. That the rebellion may be entirely crushed.

"2. That the Constitutional Amendment, abolishing
and prohibiting slavery, may have been adopted.

"3. And that Abraham Lincoln may have been re-elected President."

"I think," replied he, with a smile, "I would be glad to accept the first two as a compromise."

General Grant, in a letter, remarkable for that clear good-sense and practical judgment for which he is distinguished, condensed into a single sentence the political argument in favor of the Constitutional Amendment. "The North and South," said he, "can *never* live at peace with each other except as *one nation* and *that without slavery.*"

GARFIELD'S SPEECH.

I would be glad to quote from this great debate, but must confine myself to a brief extract from the speech of the present President, then a member of the House. He began by saying, "Mr. Speaker, we shall never know why slavery dies so hard in this republic, and in this hall, until we know why sin outlives disaster and Satan is immortal." * * "How well do I remember," he continued, "the history of that distinguished predecessor of mine, *Joshua R. Giddings*, lately gone to his rest, who, with his forlorn hope of faithful men, took his life in his hands, and, in the name of justice, protested against the great crime, and who stood bravely in his place until his white locks, like the plume of Henry of Navarre, marked where the battle of freedom raged fiercest." * * "In its mad arrogance, slavery lifted its hand against the Union, and since that fatal day it has been a fugitive and a vagabond upon the earth."

Up to the last roll-call, on the question of the passage

of the resolution, we were uncertain and anxious about the result. We needed Democratic votes. We knew we should get some, but whether enough to carry the measure none could surely tell.

As the Clerk called the names of members, so perfect was the silence, that the sound of a hundred pencils keeping tally could be heard through the Hall.

Finally, when the call was completed, and the Speaker announced that the resolution was adopted, the result was received by an uncontrollable burst of enthusiasm. Members and spectators (especially the galleries, which were crowded with convalescent soldiers) shouted and cheered, and, before the Speaker could obtain quiet, the roar of artillery on Capitol Hill proclaimed to the city of Washington, the passage of the resolution. Congress adjourned, and we hastened to the White House to congratulate the President on the event.

He made one of his happiest speeches. In his own peculiar words, he said, "*The great job is finished.*" "I can not but congratulate," said he, "all present, myself, the country, and the whole world, on this great moral victory."

PERSONAL CHARACTERISTICS.

And now, with an attempt to sketch very briefly some of his peculiar personal characteristics, I must close.

This great Hercules of a man had a heart as kind and tender as a woman. Sterner men thought it a weakness. It saddened him to see others suffer, and he shrunk from inflicting pain. Let me illustrate his kindness and tenderness by one or two incidents. One summer's day, walking along the shaded path leading from the Executive mansion to the War-office, I saw the tall, awkward form of the President seated on the grass under a tree. A wounded soldier, seeking back-pay and a pension, had met the President, and, having recognized him, asked his counsel. Lincoln sat down, examined the papers of the soldier, and told him what to do, sent him to the proper bureau with a note, which secured prompt attention.

After the terribly destructive battles between Grant and Lee, in the Wilderness of Virginia, after days of dreadful slaughter, the lines of ambulances, conveying the wounded from the steamers on the Potomac to the great field hospitals on the heights around Washington, would be continuous,—one unbroken line from the wharf to the hospital. At such a time, I have seen the President in his carriage, driving slowly along the line, and he looked like one who had lost the dearest members of his own family. On one such occasion, meeting me, he stopped and said, "I cannot bear this; this suffering, this loss of life—is dreadful."

I recalled to him a line from a letter he had years before written to a friend, whose great sorrow he had sought to console. Reminding him of the incident, I asked him, "So you remember writing to your suffering friend these words :

> "*And this too shall pass away,*
> *Never fear. Victory will come.*"

In all his State papers and speeches during these years of strife and passion, there can be found no words of bitterness, no denunciation. When others railed, he railed not again. He was always dignified, magnanimous, patient, considerate, manly, and true. His duty was ever performed "with malice toward none, with charity for all," and with "firmness in the right as God gives us to see the right."

NEVER A DEMAGOGUE.

Lincoln was never a demagogue. He respected and loved the people, but never flattered them. No man ever heard him allude to his humble life and manual labor, in a way to obtain votes. None knew better than he, that splitting rails did not qualify a man for public duties. He realized painfully the defects of his education, and labored diligently and successfully to supply his deficiencies.

HIS CONVERSATION.

He had no equal as a talker in social life. His conversation was fascinating and attractive. He was full of wit, humor, and anecdote, and at the same time, original, suggestive, and instructive. There was in his character a singular mingling of mirthfulness and melancholy. While his sense of the ludicrous was keen, and his fun and mirth were exuberant, and sometimes almost irrepressible, his conversation sparkling with jest, story, and anecdote, and in droll description, he would pass suddenly to another mood, and become sad and pathetic; a melancholy expression of his homely face would show that he was "a man of sorrows and acquainted with grief."

HIS STORIES.

The newspapers in America have always been full of Lincoln's stories and anecdotes, some true and many fabulous.

He always had a story ready, and, if not, he could improvise one, just fitted for the occasion. The following may, I think, be said to have been *adapted:*

An Atlantic port, in one of the British provinces, was, during the war, a great resort and refuge for blockade-runners, and a large contraband trade was said to have been carried on from that port with the Confederates. Late in the summer of 1864, while the election of President was pending, Lincoln being a candidate, the Governor-General of that province, with some of the principal officers, visited Washington, and called to pay their respects to the Executive. Mr. Lincoln had been very much annoyed by the failure of these officials to enforce very strictly the rules of neutrality, but he treated his guests with great courtesy. After a pleasant interview, the Governor, alluding to the approaching presidential election, said, jokingly, but with a grain of sarcasm, "I understand, Mr. President, everybody votes in this country. If we remain until November, can we vote?"

"You remind me," replied the President, "of a countryman of yours, a green emigrant from Ireland. Pat arrived in New York on election day, and was, perhaps, as eager as Your Excellency, to vote, and to vote early and late and often. So, upon his landing at Castle Garden, he hastened to the nearest voting place, and, as he approached, the judge who received the ballots inquired, 'Who do you want to vote for? on which side are you?' Poor Pat was embarrassed; he did not know who were the candidates. He stopped, scratched his head, then, with the readiness of his countrymen, he said:

"'I am fornent the Government, anyhow. Tell me, if your honor plases, which is the rebellion side, and I'll tell you how I want to vote. In Ould Ireland, I was always on the rebellion side, and, by Saint Patrick, I'll stick to that same in America.'

"Your Excellency," said Mr. Lincoln, "would, I should think, not be at all at a loss on which side to vote."

THE BOOKS HE READ.

The two books he read most were the Bible and Shakespeare. With them he was familiar, reading and quoting from them constantly. Next to Shakespeare, among the poets, was Burns, with whom he had a hearty sympathy, and upon whose poetry he wrote a lecture. He was extremely fond of ballads, and of simple, sad and plaintive music.

I called one day at the White House, to introduce two officers of the Union army, both Swedes. Immediately he began and repeated from memory, to the delight of his visitors, a long ballad, descriptive of Norwegian scenery, a Norse legend, and the adventures of an old Viking among the fiords of the North.

He said he had read the poem in a newspaper, and the visit of these Swedes recalled it to his memory.

On the last Sunday of his life, as he was sailing up

the Potomac, returning to Washington from his visit to Richmond, he read aloud many extracts from Macbeth, and, among others, the following, and with a tone and accent so impressive that, after his death, it was vividly recalled by those who heard him:

> "Duncan is in his grave;
> After life's fitful fever, he sleeps well;
> Treason has done his worst: nor steel, nor poison,
> Malice domestic, foreign levy, nothing,
> Can touch him further!"

After his assassination, those friends could not fail to recall this passage from the same play:

> "This Duncan
> Hath borne his faculties so meek, hath been
> So clear in his great office, that his virtues
> Will plead like angels, trumpet-tongued, against
> The deep damnation of his taking-off."

HIS RELIGION.

It is strange that any reader of Lincoln's speeches and writings should have had the hardihood to charge him with infidelity, but the charge, having been repeatedly made, I reply, in the light of facts accessible to all, that no more reverent Christian (not excepting Washington) ever filled the chair of President. Declarations of his trust in God, his faith in the efficacy of prayer, pervade his speeches and writings. From the time he left Springfield, to his death, he not only himself continuedly prayed for Divine assistance, but never failed to ask the prayers of others for himself and his country.

His reply to the negroes of Baltimore, who, in 1864,

5

presented him with a beautiful Bible, as an expression of their love and gratitude, ought to have silenced all who have made such charges. After thanking them, he said, " This great book is the best gift God has given to man. All the good from the Saviour of the world is communicated through this book."

When a member of Congress, knowing his religious character, asked him " Why he did not join some church ?" Mr. Lincoln replied, " Because I found difficulty, without mental reservation, in giving my assent to their long and complicated confessions of faith. When any church will inscribe over its altar the Saviour's condensed statement of law and gospel, ' Thou shalt love the Lord thy God with all thy heart, with all thy soul, and with all thy mind, and thy neighbor as thyself,' that church will I join with all my heart."

WHAT HE ACCOMPLISHED.

Let us try to sum up in part what he accomplished.

When he assumed the duties of the Executive, he found an empty treasury, the National credit gone, the little nucleus of an army and navy scattered and disarmed, the officers, who had not deserted to the rebels, strangers ; the party which elected him in a minority (he having been elected only because his opponents were divided between Douglas, Breckenridge, and Everett), the old Democratic party, which had ruled most of the time for half a century, hostile, and even that part of it in the North, from long association, in sympathy with the insurgents ; his own party made up of discordant elements, and neither he nor his party had acquired prestige and the confidence of the people.

It is the exact truth to say that when he entered the *White House* he was the object of personal prejudice to a majority of the American people, and of contempt to a powerful minority. He entered upon his task of restoring the integrity of a broken Union, without sympathy from any of the great powers of Western Europe. Those which were not hostile manifested a cold neutrality, exhibiting toward him and his government no cordial good-will, nor extending any moral aid. Yet, in spite of all, he crushed the most stupendous rebellion, supported by armies more vast, by resources greater, and an organization more perfect, than ever before undertook the dismemberment of a nation. He united and held together, against contending factions, his own party, and strengthened it by securing the confidence and winning the support of the best part of all parties. He composed the quarrels of rival generals ; and, at length, won the respect and confidence and sympathy of all nations and peoples. He was re-elected, almost by acclamation, and, after a series of brilliant victories, he annihilated all armed opposition. He led the people, step by step, to Emancipation, and saw his work crowned by an amendment of the Constitution, eradicating and prohibiting slavery forever, throughout the republic.

Such is a brief and imperfect summary of his achievements during the last five years of his life. And this good man, when the hour of victory came, made it not the hour of vengeance, but of forgiveness and reconciliation. These five years of incessant labor and fearful responsi-

bility told even upon his strength and vigor. He left
Illinois, for the Capital, with a frame of iron and nerves
of steel. His old friends, who had known him as a man
who did not know what illness was ; who had seen him
on the prairies before the Illinois courts, full of life, genial, and sparkling with fun ; now saw the wrinkles on his
forehead deepened into furrows—the laugh of the old days
lost its heartiness ; anxiety, responsibility, care, and hard
work wore upon him, and his nerves of steel at times
became irritable. He had had no respite, had taken no
holidays. When others fled away from the dust and heat
of the Capital, he stayed. He would not leave the helm
until all danger was past, and the good ship of state had
made her port.

I will not dwell upon the unutterable sorrow of the
American people, at his shocking death. But I desire to
express here, in this great city of this grand empire, the
sensibility with which the people of the United States
received, at his death, the sympathy of the English-speaking race.

That sympathy was most eloquently expressed by all.
It came from Windsor Castle to the White House ; from
England's widowed queen to the stricken and distracted
widow at Washington. From Parliament to Congress,
from the people of all this magnificent empire, as it
stretches round the world, from England to India, from
Canada to Australia, came words of deep feeling, and
they were received by the American people, in their sore
bereavement, as the expression of a kindred race.

I cannot forbear referring in particular to the words
spoken in Parliament on that occasion, by Lords Russell

and Derby, and, especially, by that great and picturesque leader, so lately passed away, Lord Beaconsfield. After a discriminating eulogy upon the late President, and the expression of profound sympathy, he said :

" Nor is it possible for the people of England, at such a moment, to forget that he sprang from the same father-land and spake the same mother-tongue."

God grant that, in all the unknown future, nothing may ever disturb the friendly feeling and respect which each nation entertains for the other. May there never be another quarrel in the family.

Isaac N. Arnold

CHICAGO, 1882.

LETTER FROM MRS. ANNE C. BOTTA.

Buckingham Palace Hotel,
June 22d, 1881.

My DEAR MR. ARNOLD :

An hour ago I opened the pamphlet you gave me yesterday, intending to glance at the contents and lay it aside to read when I reached home, but I found myself unable to lay it down until I had carefully read every word from first to last. It is certainly the most clear, exhaustive, and eloquent tribute to Mr. Lincoln that I have ever seen. But the pleasure it has given me is quite equaled by the pride I feel in knowing that it was listened to by the London Historical Society, to whom it must have been as novel as interesting. As a good American, I thank you cordially for thus giving to the English people so noble a picture of our great President, while, at the same time, you presented to them in person his able friend and coadjutor.

Very truly yours,

ANNE C. BOTTA.

ADDRESS OF TITO PAGLIARDIRRI, ESQ.,

COUNCIL OF THE ROYAL HISTORICAL SOCIETY, LONDON, ENGLAND.

MR. CHAIRMAN, LADIES, and GENTLEMEN :—Seldom have I listened to a paper that has so deeply interested me. It has given us a living portrait of one of the most remarkable individualities of recent times—a portrait, too, traced by the hand of one who, having himself taken a prominent part in the great national struggle which put an end to slavery, had constant opportunities of seeing and studying in every phase of his life the eminent man he has so graphically portrayed. And though it has been said that familiarity breeds contempt, and that there is no hero for his valet, yet men of the Garibaldi and Lincoln type, whose influence on their country and mankind at large is chiefly due to *moral* force, can only gain by a closer view of them in their prosaic every-day life. When we see the gentler feelings of the human heart combined in a prominent man with a rigid sense of duty and the intellectual power and perseverance necessary to fulfill that duty, we not only admire that man but revere and love him. Hence Abraham Lincoln, the preserver, as Washington was the founder of the great Union, always, I must confess, stood higher in my estimation and love than all the Alexanders, Cæsars, and Napoleons

who have reddened the pages of history with their brilliant exploits.

Before his time, I was often taunted by my French
republican friends for showing but scant enthusiasm for
" La grande République Américaine." In answer, I
pointed to the huge *black* spot which, though it only
covered half, yet extended its moral taint to the whole of
the otherwise glorious Union. That could not be the
model land of Liberty where millions of our fellow-creatures were born to slavery, to be bought and sold like
swine.

But when the great deliverer arose, humble though
his origin, as is that of most deliverers, my sentiments
towards America changed. I hailed him with enthusiasm
and stood almost alone in my circle, composed chiefly of
readers of the conservative and semi-conservative press ;
for, to their shame and ultimate discomfiture, the leading
papers almost all took the wrong side, prophesying continuous disasters to the anti-slavery party and a consequent
disruption of the Union. Their grand but specious argument, which misled many honest minds, ignorant of
the history of the several States, was that the South had
as much right to fight for their liberty as the United
States themselves had to fight for their independence
against England. Liberty, indeed! The liberty to perpetuate the curse of slavery!

But Americans must not judge of British sentiments
by the conservative press, which only represents a portion
of the public, but which, unfortunately, was that which
most easily found its way across the Atlantic. The real
heart of Great Britain was from the beginning with the

'North.   Indeed, Lincoln's warmest sympathizers were those who suffered most from the direful American civil contest—the cotton-spinners and the whole body of the working classes.   And as nothing succeeds like success, I am bound to add that in the process of time the undaunted determination of the Northern States, under a series of alarming defeats, with their best-trained generals and officers, and their chief arsenals, on the side of the slaveholders, gradually gained for them and for their great inspirer, Abraham Lincoln, the respect and admiration of all parties—and this admiration and this respect were vastly increased when, in the hour of victory, all cries for vengeance were hushed, and the hand of brotherhood was held out to the defeated party by the noble-hearted President, with the full consent of his victorious countrymen.

And now that what was deemed impossible is an accomplished fact, *viz.:* the abomination of slavery eradicated forever from the great American Republic, and peace and prosperity restored throughout the land, I trust that, in Mr. Arnold's own words, "nothing may ever disturb the friendly feeling and respect which each of the great Anglo-Saxon nations entertains for the other."

Already have they given a striking proof of their advanced civilization and friendly feelings, and a noble example to all other civilized nations, in the peaceful settlement of the burning Alabama question, which, but one generation ago would most certainly have led to an obstinate war, ruinous to both countries.   That the decision of the neutral body of arbitrators was impartial and toler-

ably just was proved by its giving at the time entire satisfaction to neither party, the whole question being, however, soon after completely dropped, leaving no angry feel-
ings behind, as would have done a war, however successful in the end. May God grant that any future differences between these two great nations having a common
origin, a common language, a common literature, and so
many institutions in common, be settled in the same just
friendly, and rational manner. No fratricidal war must
or can ever arise between them. All their future battles
must be fought on the peaceful fields of science, literature,
and the industrial arts. Victories on these fields will
benefit both, and the whole human race into the bargain.

I will now conclude these hasty remarks by proposing
a hearty vote of thanks to the Hon. Isaac N. Arnold for
his very valuable and interesting paper.

Which was unanimously adopted.

FAC SIMILE OF THE GOLD MEDAL PRESENTED TO MRS. ABRAHAM LINCOLN BY 40,000 FRENCH PEOPLE, RAISED BY A SUBSCRIPTION FUND OF TWO SOUS EACH.

Napoleon III, adverse to this movement, would not allow it to be struck in France, so it was produced in Switzerland, but presented from Paris, October 13, 1866.

On one side of the medal is a correct likeness of Mr. Lincoln, with inscription. On the reverse, Victory stands with anchor and wreath. Two freedmen, one pointing to the American Eagle, the other is placing a palm branch on the altar.

THE ripest and fairest fruit that has yet 'fallen from our American tree of civilization is Abraham Lincoln. His private character was stainless, his public life pure, wise, courageous, statesmanlike. In both, he will shine the brighter as years and centuries roll on. Among the many orbs that illuminate the pages of our history, he is the sun himself, whose light was not darkened by the most cloudy and stormy days of our civil war. When he had saved our country, and wiped out the black stain that marred the beauty of so many of our fair states, envy could find no more shining mark for its poisoned shafts, and like the good Balder in our ancient mythology, and like Christ and Socrates of old, he was made to *die*, that truth and righteousness might *live*. I can name no name of any age or country that in private and public life outshines that of the great ABRAHAM LINCOLN. His memory will be cherished by the latest generations of this earth.

MADISON, 1880.

EXTRACT FROM A SPEECH DELIVERED
DECEMBER, 1839.

Of the slave power he said, Broken by it? I, too, may be asked to bow to it, I never will! The probability that we may fail in the struggle ought not to deter us from the support of a cause which I deem to be just. It shall not deter me. If I ever feel the soul within me elevate and expand to dimensions not wholly unworthy of its almighty Architect, it is when I contemplate the cause of my country, deserted by all the world beside, and I standing up boldly and alone, and hurling defiance at her victorious oppressors. Here, without contemplating consequences, before high Heaven, and in the face of the world, I swear eternal fidelity to the just cause, as I deem it, of the land of my life, my liberty, and my love!

And who that thinks with me, will not adopt the oath that I take? Let none falter who thinks he is right, and we may succeed. But if, after all, we shall fall, be it so. We shall have the proud consolation of saying to our conscience, and to the departed shade of our country's freedom, that the course approved by our judgments and adored by our hearts, in disaster, in chains, in torture, and in death, We never faltered in defending.

ABRAHAM LINCOLN was a man of noble character,—of lofty aims. He brought to the duties of
the presidential office the highest qualities of manhood,
a wide knowledge of humanity, and a superb courage to
carry out his convictions. It was a most fortunate circumstance that he was our President during those momentous years in our country's history.

U. S ARMY,
1882.

RESOLUTIONS UPON DOMESTIC SLAVERY IN THE ILLINOIS LEGISLATURE.

March 3, 1837.

The following protest was presented to the House, which was read and ordered to be spread on the journals, to wit:

"Resolutions upon the subject of domestic slavery having passed both branches of the General Assembly, at its present session, the undersigned hereby protest against the passage of the same.

"They believe that the institution of slavery is founded on both injustice and bad policy; but that the promulgation of abolition doctrines tends rather to increase than abate its evils.

"They believe that the Congress of the United States has no power, under the Constitution, to interfere with the institution of slavery in the different States.

"They believe that the Congress of the United States has the power, under the Constitution, to abolish slavery in the District of Columbia; but that the power ought not to be exercised unless at the request of the people of said District. The difference between these opinions and those contained in the said resolutions, is their reason for entering this protest.

(Signed)

"DAN. STONE,
"A. LINCOLN,
"Representatives from the County of Sangamon."

TO comprehend the current of history sympathetically, to appreciate the spirit of the age, prophetically, to know what God, by his providence, is working out in the epoch and the community, and so to work with him as to guide the current and embody in noble deeds the spirit of the age in working out the divine problem,—this is true greatness. The man who sets his powers, however gigantic, to stemming the current and thwarting the divine purposes, is not truly great.

Abraham Lincoln was made the Chief Executive of a nation whose Constitution was unlike that of any other nation on the face of the globe. We assume that, ordinarily, public sentiment will change so gradually that the nation can always secure a true representative of its purpose in the presidential chair by an election every four years. Mr. Lincoln held the presidential office at a time when public sentiment was revolutionized in less than four years. When he was called to the presidency, only a very insignificant minority in the nation was willing that slavery should be interfered with, and only a bare majority of the loyal North were prepared even to enforce the laws in rebellious States. Before his term of office had expired, a great body of the North were ready, not only to put down rebellion by force of arms, but in doing this to enfranchise the negro and to put arms into his hands. It was the peculiar genius of Abraham Lincoln, that he was able, by his sympathetic insight, to perceive the change in public sentiment without waiting for it to be formulated in any legislative action; to keep pace with it, to lead and direct it, to quicken laggard spirits, to hold in the too ardent, too impetuous, and too hasty ones, and thus, when he signed the emancipation proclamation, to make his signature, not the act of an individual man, the edict of a military imperator, but the representative act of a great nation. He was the greatest President in American History, because in a time of revolution he comprehended the spirit of American institutions, grasped the purposes of the American people, and embodied them in an act of justice and humanity which was in the highest sense the act of the American Republic.

Lyman Abbott,

CORNWALL-ON-HUDSON,
    1881.

PERSONALLY I never saw President Lincoln more than twice in my life, and then for a very few minutes. He then frankly told me that my mission to Great Britain had not been altogether his selection, but I believe he became well satisfied afterwards. So, on the other hand, I became from a very lukewarm admirer of his, one of the most appreciative of his high qualities, and mourners of his great loss. I shall never forget the moment when, in London, the tidings of this loss were brought to me. It seemed as if we were all afloat in the midst of a boundless ocean.

Charles Francis Adams.

BOSTON, 1880.

AN ADDRESS

DELIVERED BEFORE THE SPRINGFIELD WASHINGTONIAN
TEMPERANCE SOCIETY, AT THE SECOND PRESBYTER-
IAN CHURCH, ON THE 22D DAY OF FEBRUARY,
1842, BY ABRAHAM LINCOLN, ESQ.

Although the Temperance Cause has been in progress
for nearly twenty years, it is apparent to all that it is just
now being crowned with a degree of success, hitherto
unparalleled.

The list of its friends is daily swelled by the additions
of fifties, of hundreds, and of thousands. The cause
itself seems suddenly transformed from a cold abstract
theory, to a living, breathing, active and powerful chief-
tain, going forth "conquering and to conquer." The
citadels of his great adversary are daily being stormed
and dismantled; his temples and his altars, where the
rites of his idolatrous worship have long been performed,
and where human sacrifices have long been wont to be
made, are daily desecrated and deserted. The trump of
the conqueror's fame is sounding from hill to hill, from
sea to sea, and from land to land, and calling millions to
his standard at a blast.

For this new and splendid success we heartily rejoice.
That that success is so much greater now, than heretofore, is doubtless owing to rational causes; and if we
would have it continue, we shall do well to inquire what
those causes are.

The warfare heretofore waged against the demon Intemperance, has, somehow or other, been erroneous. Either the champions engaged, or the tactics they adopted, have not been the most proper. These champions, for the most part, have been preachers, lawyers and hired agents; between these and the mass of mankind, there is a want of *approachability*, if the term be admissible, partial at least, fatal to their success. They are supposed to have no sympathy of feeling or interest with those very persons whom it is their object to convince and persuade.

And again, it is so easy and so common to ascribe motives to men of these classes, other than those they profess to act upon. The preacher, it is said, advocates temperance because he is a fanatic, and desires a union of the church and state; the lawyer from his pride, and vanity of hearing himself speak; and the hired agent for his salary.

But when one who has long been known as a victim of intemperance bursts the fetters that have bound him, and appears before his neighbors "clothed and in his right mind," a redeemed specimen of long-lost humanity, and stands up with tears of joy trembling in his eyes, to tell of the miseries once endured, now to be endured no more forever, of his once naked and starving children, now clad and fed comfortably, of a wife, long weighed down with woe, weeping, and a broken heart, now restored to health, happiness and a renewed affection, and how easily it is all done, once it is resolved to be done; how simple his language; there is a logic and an eloquence in it that few with human feelings can resist. They cannot say that he desires a union of church and state, for he is not a church-member; they cannot say he is vain of hearing himself speak, for his whole demeanor shows he would gladly avoid speaking at all; they cannot say he speaks for pay, for he receives none, and asks for none. Nor can his sincerity in any way be doubted, or his sympathy for those he would persuade to imitate his example be denied.

In my judgment it is to the battles of this new class of champions that our late success is greatly, perhaps chiefly, owing. But had the old-school champions themselves been of the most wise selecting? Was their system of tactics the most judicious? It seems to me it was not. Too much denunciation against dram-sellers and dram-drinkers was indulged in. This, I think, was both impolitic and unjust. It was impolitic, because it is not much in the nature of man to be driven to anything; still less to be driven about that which is exclusively his own business; and least of all, where such driving is to be submitted to at the expense of pecuniary interest, or burning appetite. When the dram-seller and drinker were incessantly told, not in the accents of entreaty and persuasion, diffidently addressed by erring man to an erring brother, but in the thundering tones of anathema and denunciation, with which the lordly judge often groups together all the crimes of the felon's life, and thrusts them in his face just ere he passes sentence of death upon him, that they were the authors of all the vice and misery and crime in the land; that they were the manufacturers and material of all the thieves and robbers and murderers that infest the earth; that their houses were the work-shops of the devil, and that their persons should be shunned by all the good and virtuous, as moral pestilences,—I say, when they were told all this, and in this way, it is not wonderful that they were slow, very slow, to acknowledge the truth of such denunciations, and to join the ranks of their denouncers, in a hue and cry against themselves.

To have expected them to do otherwise than they did —to have expected them not to meet denunciation with denunciation, crimination with crimination, and anathema with anathema,—was to expect a reversal of human nature, which is God's decree, and can never be reversed.

When the conduct of men is designed to be influenced, persuasion, kind, unassuming persuasion, should ever be adopted. It is an old and a true maxim, "that a drop of honey catches more flies than a gallon of gall." So with men. If you would win a man to your cause, first convince him that you are his sincere friend. Therein is a drop of honey that catches his heart; which, say what he will, is the great high road to his reason, and which, when once gained, you will find but little trouble in convincing his judgment of the justice of your cause, if, indeed, that cause really be a just one. . On the contrary, assume to dictate to his judgment, or to command his action, or to mark him as one to be shunned and despised, and he will retreat within himself, close all the avenues to his head and his heart, and though your cause be naked truth itself, transformed to the heaviest lance, harder than steel, and sharper than steel can be made, and though you throw it with more than herculean force and precision, you shall be no more able to pierce him, than to penetrate the hard shell of a tortoise with a rye-straw. Such is man, and so must he be understood by those who would lead him, even to his own best interests.

On this point, the Washingtonians greatly excel the temperance advocates of former times. Those whom they desire to convince and persuade are their old friends and companions. They know they are not demons, nor even the worst of men; they know that generally they are kind, generous and charitable, even beyond the example of their more staid and sober neighbors. They are practical philanthropists; and they glow with a generous and brotherly zeal, that mere theorizers are incapable of feeling. Benevolence and charity possess their hearts entirely; and out of the abundance of their hearts their tongues give utterance, " Love through all their actions run, and all their words are mild :" in this spirit they speak and act, and in the same they are heard and regarded. And when such is the temper of the advocate, and such of the audience, no good cause can be unsuccessful. But I have said that denunciations against dram-sellers and dram-drinkers are unjust, as well as impolitic. Let us see.

I have not inquired at what period of time the use of intoxicating liquors commenced; nor is it important to know. It is sufficient that to all of us who now inhabit the world, the practice of drinking them is just as old as the world itself—that is, we have seen the one, just as long as we have seen the other. When all such of us as have now reached the years of maturity, first opened our eyes upon the stage of existence, we found intoxicating liquors recognized by everybody, used by everybody, repudiated by nobody. It commonly entered into the first draught of the infant, and the last draught of the dying man. From the sideboard of the parson, down to the ragged pocket of the houseless loafer, it was constantly found. Physicians prescribed it, in this, that and the other disease; Government provided it for soldiers and sailors; and to have a rolling or raising, a husking or "hoe-down" anywhere about without it, was *positively unsufferable.* So too, it was everywhere a respectable article of manufacture and of merchandise. The making of it was regarded as an honorable livelihood, and he could make most, was the most enterprising and respectable. Large and small manufactories of it were everywhere erected, in which all the earthly goods of their owners were invested. Wagons drew it from town to town; boats bore it from clime to clime, and the winds wafted it from nation to nation; and merchants bought and sold it, by wholesale and retail, with precisely the same feelings on the part of the seller, buyer and by-stander as are felt at the selling and buying of plows, beef, bacon, or any other of the real necessaries of life. Universal public opinion not only tolerated, but recognized and adopted its use.

It is true, that even then it was known and acknowledged that many were greatly injured by it; but none seemed to think the injury arose from the use of a bad thing, but from the abuse of a very good thing. The victims of it were to be pitied and compassionated, just as are the heirs of consumption, and other hereditary diseases. Their failing was treated as a misfortune, and not as a crime, or even as a disgrace.

If then, what I have been saying is true, is it wonderful, that some should think and act now, as all thought and acted twenty years ago, and is it just to assail, condemn, or despise them for doing so? The universal sense of mankind, on any subject, is an argument, or at least an influence, not easily overcome. The success of the argument in favor of the existence of an over-ruling Providence, mainly depends upon that sense; and men ought not, in justice, to be denounced for yielding to it in any case, or giving it up slowly, especially when they are backed by interest, fixed habits, or burning appetites.

Another error, as it seems to me, into which the old reformers fell, was the position that all habitual drunkards were utterly incorrigible, and therefore, must be turned adrift, and damned without remedy, in order that the grace of temperance might abound, to the temperate then, and to all mankind some hundreds of years thereafter. There is in this something so repugnant to humanity, so uncharitable, so cold-blooded and feelingless, that it never did, nor never can enlist the enthusiasm of a popular cause. We could not love the man who taught it—we could not hear him with patience. The heart could not throw open its portals to it, the generous man could not adopt it, it could not mix with his blood. It looked so fiendishly selfish, so like throwing fathers and brothers overboard, to lighten the boat for our security—that the noble-minded shrank from the manifest meanness of the thing. And besides this, the benefits of a reformation to be effected by such a system, were too remote in point of time, to warmly engage many in its behalf. Few can be induced to labor exclusively for posterity; and none will do it enthusiastically. Posterity has done nothing for us ; and theorize on it as we may, practically we shall do very little for it unless we are made to think, we are, at the same time, doing something for ourselves.

What an ignorance of human nature does it exhibit, to ask or expect a whole community to rise up and labor for the temporal happiness of others, after themselves shall be consigned to the dust, a majority of which community take no pains whatever to secure their own eternal welfare at no greater distant day. Great distance in either time or space has wonderful power to lull and render quiescent the human mind. Pleasures to be enjoyed, or pains to be endured, after we shall be dead and gone, are but little regarded, even in our own cases, and much less in the cases of others.

Still, in addition to this, there is something so ludicrous, in promises of good, or threats of evil, a great way off, as to render the whole subject with which they are connected, easily turned into ridicule. " Better lay down that spade you're stealing, Paddy—if you don't, you'll pay for it at the day of judgment." " Be the powers, if ye'll credit me so long I'll take another jist."

By the Washingtonians this system of consigning the habitual drunkard to hopeless ruin is repudiated. They adopt a more enlarged philanthropy, they go for present as well as future good. They labor for all now living, as well as hereafter to live. They teach hope to all—despair to none. As applying to their cause, they deny the doctrine of unpardonable sin ; as in Christianity it is taught, so in this they teach—

> "While the lamp holds out to burn,
> The vilest sinner may return."

And, what is a matter of the most profound congratulation, they, by experiment upon experiment, and example upon example, prove the maxim to be no less true in the one case than in the other. On every hand we behold those, who but yesterday were the chief of sinners, now the chief apostles of the cause. Drunken devils are çast out by ones, by sevens, by legions; and their unfortunate victims, like the poor possessed, who was redeemed from his long and lonely wanderings in the tombs, are publishing to the ends of the earth how great things have been done for them.

To these new champions, and this new system of tactics, our late success is mainly owing; and to them we must mainly look for the final consummation. The ball is now rolling gloriously on, and none are so able as they to increase its speed, and its bulk—to add to its momentum and its magnitude—even though unlearned in letters, for this task none are so well educated. To fit them for this work they have been taught in the true school. They have been in that gulf, from which they would teach others the means of escape. They have passed that prison wall, which others have long declared impassable; and who that has not, shall dare to weigh opinions with them as to the mode of passing?

But if it be true, as I have insisted, that those who have suffered by intemperance personally, and have reformed, are the most powerful and efficient instruments to push the reformation to ultimate success, it does not follow that those who have not suffered have no part left them to perform. Whether or not the world would be vastly benefitted by a total and final banishment from it of all intoxicating drinks, seems to me not now an open question. Three-fourths of mankind confess the affirmative with their tongues; and, I believe, all ·the rest acknowledge it in their hearts.

Ought any, then, to refuse their aid in doing what the good of the whole demands? Shall he who cannot do much, be, for that reason, excused if he do nothing? "But," says one, "what good can I do by signing the pledge? I never drink, even without signing." This question has already been asked and answered more than a million of times. Let it be answered once more. For the man to suddenly, or in any other way, to break off from the use of drams, who has indulged in them for a long course of years, and until his appetite for them has grown ten or a hundred fold stronger and more craving than any natural·appetite can be, requires a most powerful moral effort. In such an undertaking he needs every moral support and influence that can possibly be brought to his aid, and thrown around him. And not only so, but every moral prop should be taken from whatever argument might rise in his mind, to lure him to his backsliding. When he casts his eyes around him, he should be able to see all that he respects, all that he admires, all that he loves, kindly and anxiously pointing him onward, and none beckoning him back to his former misesable "wallowing in the mire."

But it is said by some, that men will think and act for themselves; that none will disuse spirits or anything else because his neighbors do; and that moral influence is not that powerful engine contended for. Let us examine this. Let me ask the man who could maintain this position most stiffly, what compensation he will accept to go to church some Sunday and sit during the sermon with his wife's bonnet upon his head? Not a trifle, I'll venture. And why not? There would be nothing irreligious in it, nothing immoral, nothing uncomfortable—then why not? Is it not because there would be something egregiously unfashionable in it? Then it is the influence of fashion; and what is the influence of fashion but the influence that other people's actions have on our own actions—the strong inclination each of us feels to do as we see all our neighbors do? Nor is the influence of fashion confined to any particular thing or class of things. It is just as strong on one subject as another. Let us make it as unfashionable to withhold our names from the temperance pledge, as for husbands to wear their wives' bonnets to church, and instances will be just as rare in the one case as the other.

"But," say some, "we are no drunkards, and we shall not acknowledge ourselves such, by joining a reformed drunkards' society, whatever our influence might be." Surely, no Christian will adhere to this objection.

If they believe as they profess, that Omnipotence condescended to take on himself the form of sinful man, and, as such, to die an ignominious death for their sakes, surely, they will not refuse submission to the infinitely lesser condescension, for the temporal, and perhaps eternal salvation, of a large, erring, and unfortunate class of their fellow-creatures. Nor is the condescension very great. In my judgment such of us as have never fallen

victims, have been spared more from the absence of appe
tite, than from any mental or moral superiority over those
who have. Indeed, I believe, if we take habitual drunkards as a class, their heads and their hearts will bear an
advantageous comparison with those of any other class.
There seems ever to have been a proneness in the brilliant and warm-blooded to fall into this vice—the demon
of intemperance ever seems to have delighted in sucking
the blood of genius and generosity. What one of us
but can call to mind some relative, more promising in
youth than all his fellows, who has fallen a sacrifice to
his rapacity? He ever seems to have gone forth like
the Egyptian angel of death, commissioned to slay, if not
the first, the fairest born of every family. Shall he now
be arrested in his desolating career? In that arrest, all
can give aid that will; and who shall be excused that can,
and will not? Far around as human breath has ever
blown, he keeps our fathers, our brothers, our sons, and our
friends prostrate in the chains of moral death. To all
the living, everywhere, we cry, "Come, sound the moral
trump, that these may rise and stand up an exceeding
great army."—"Come from the four winds, O breath! and
breathe upon these slain, that they may live." If the
relative grandeur of revolutions shall be estimated by the
great amount of human misery they alleviate, and the
small amount they inflict, then, indeed, will this be the
grandest the world shall ever have seen,

Of our political revolution of '76 we are all justly
proud. It has given us a degree of political freedom far
exceeding that of any other nations of the earth. In it the
world has found a solution of the long mooted problem,

as to the capability of man to govern himself. In it was
the germ which has vegetated, and still is to grow and
expand into the universal liberty of mankind,

But, with all these glorious results, past, present, and
to come, it had its evils too. It breathed forth famine,
swam in blood, and rode in fire; and long, long after, the
orphans' cry and the widows' wail continued to break the
sad silence that ensued. These were the price, the inevitable price, paid for the blessings it bought.

Turn now to the temperance revolution. In it we
shall find a stronger bondage broken, a viler slavery man-
umitted, a greater tyrant deposed—in it, more of want
supplied, more disease healed, more sorrow assuaged.
By it, no orphans starving, no widows weeping. By it,
none wounded in feeling, none injured in interest; even
the dram-maker and dram-seller will have glided into
other occupations so gradually as never to have felt the
change, and will stand ready to join all others in the universal song of gladness. And what a noble ally this, to
the cause of political freedom, with such an aid, its
march cannot fail to be on and on, till every son of earth
shall drink in rich fruition the sorrow-quenching draughts
of perfect liberty. Happy day, when, all appetites controlled, all poisons subdued, all matter subjected, mind,
all-conquering mind, shall live and move, the monarch of
the world! Glorious consummation! Hail, fall of fury!
Reign of reason, all hail!

And when the victory shall be complete—when there
shall be neither a slave nor a drunkard on the earth—
how proud the title of that *Land*, which may truly claim
to be the birth-place and the cradle of both those revo-

lutions that shall have ended in that victory. How
nobly distinguished that people, who shall have planted,
and nurtured to maturity, both the political and moral
freedom of their species.

This is the one hundred and tenth anniversary of the
birthday of Washington—we are met to celebrate this
day. Washington is the mightiest name of earth—long
since mightiest in the cause of civil liberty, still mightiest
in moral reformation. On that name a eulogy is expected. It cannot be. To add brightness to the sun, or
glory to the name of Washington is alike impossible.
Let none attempt it. In solemn awe pronounce the
name, and in its naked, deathless splendor leave it
shining on.

7

SPEECH DELIVERED AT PEORIA, ILLINOIS,
OCT. 16, 1854.

Finally I insist that if there is any *thing* which it is the duty of the *whole people* to never intrust to any hands but their own, that thing is the preservation and perpetuity of their own liberties and institutions. And if they shall think, as I do, that the extension of slavery endangers them, more than any or all other causes, how recreant to themselves if they submit the question, and with it the fate of their country, to a mere handful of men, bent only on temporary self-interest. If this question of slavery extension were an insignificant one—one having no power to do harm—it might be shuffled aside in this way; but being as it is, the great Behemoth of danger, shall the strong gripe of the nation be loosened upon him, to intrust him to the hands of such feeble keepers? I have done with this mighty argument of self-government. Go sacred thing; Go in peace! Much as I hate slavery, I would consent to the extension of it rather than see the Union dissolved, just as I would consent to any *great* evil to avoid a *greater* one. But when I go to Union-saving I must believe, at least, that the means I employ have some adaptation to the end.

A S the years pass, and we look back upon the life and work of Abraham Lincoln, during the time he was President of the United States, our admiration and reverence for the man increases. For unselfish devotion to the public welfare, purity of character, freedom from partisanship and personal ambition, and ability to comprehend and deal with the momentous questions at issue in our great struggle for national existence, he was first among the ablest statesmen and most loyal men of his time.

T. S. Arthur.

NEW YORK, 1880.

EXTRACT.FROM MR. LINCOLN'S SPEECH,

DELIVERED IN REPRESENTATIVE'S HALL, SPRINGFIELD, ILLINOIS, JUNE 26, 1857.

In those days, our Declaration of Independence was held sacred by all, and thought to include all; but now, to aid in making the bondage of the negro universal and eternal, it is assailed and sneered at, and construed, and hawked at, and torn, till, if its framers could rise from their graves, they could not at all recognize it. All the powers of earth seem rapidly combining against him. Mammon is after him, ambition follows, philosophy follows, and the theology of the day is fast joining the cry. They have him in his prison-house; they have searched his person, and left no prying instrument with him. One after another, they have closed the heavy iron doors upon him; and now they have him, as it were, bolted in with a lock of a hundred keys, which can never be unlocked without the concurrence of every key; the keys in the hands of a hundred different men, and they scattered to a hundred different and distant places; and they stand musing as to what invention, in all the dominions of mind and matter, can be produced to make the impossibility of his escape more complete than it is.

THE weary form, that rested **not,**
　　Save in a martyr's grave;
The care-worn face that none forgot,
　　Turned to the kneeling slave.

We rest in peace, where his sad eyes
　　Saw peril, strife and pain;
His was the awful sacrifice,
　　And ours, the priceless gain.

John G. Whittier

DANVERS, 1880.

EXTRACT FROM MY SERMON.

HE lived to see the rebellion in its last agonies; he lived to enter Richmond amid the acclamations of the liberated slave; he lived until Sumter's flag rose again, like a star of Bethlehem, in the southern sky; and then, with the martyr's crown upon his brow, and with four million broken fetters in his hand, he went up to meet his God. In a moment his life crystallizes into the pure, white fame that belongs only to the martyr for truth and liberty! Terrible as seems the method of his death to us, it was, after all, the most fitting and glorious. In God's sight, Lincoln was no more precious than the humblest drummer-boy, who has bled away his young life on the sod of Gettysburgh or Chattanooga. He had called on two hundred thousand heroes to lay down their lives for their country; and now he, too, has gone to make his grave beside them.

> "So sleep the brave, who sink to rest,
>   By all their country's wishes blest."

When that grave, on yonder western prairie, shall finally yield up its dead, glorious will be his resurrection! Methinks that I behold the spirit of the great *Liberator*, in that judgment scene, before the assembled hosts of heaven. Around him are the tens of thousands from whom he struck the oppressor's chain. Methinks I hear their grateful voices exclaim, "We were an hungered, and

I HAVE been working for thirteen years in Fisk University, an institution which is devoted to the elevation of the colored race in the United States. And I am more and more convinced, from year to year, that no one can fully comprehend the magnitude and grandeur of the work achieved by Abraham Lincoln, until he has learned to look upon him as the colored people regard him. To the white Northerner he is preserver of the Union and the martyred President, to the colored people he is their deliverer, their savior. The name of Abraham Lincoln is enshrined forever as sacred in the hearts of a grateful people, whom he has redeemed.

H. S. Bennett.

FISK UNIVERSITY,
1880.

EXTRACT FROM MR. LINCOLN'S SPEECH,

AT SPRINGFIELD, ILLINOIS, JUNE 17, 1858.

"A house divided against itself cannot stand." I believe this government cannot endure permanently, half slave, and half free. I do not expect the Union to be dissolved—I do not expect the house to fall—but I do expect it will cease to be divided. It will become all one thing, or all the other. Either the opponents of slavery will arrest the further spread of it, and place it where the public mind shall rest in the belief that it is in the course of ultimate extinction, or its advocates will push it forward till it shall become alike lawful in all the states, old as well as new, North as well as South.

I have always hated slavery, I think, as much as any abolitionist.

Our cause, then, must be intrusted to, and conducted by, its own doubted friends—those whose hands are free, whose hearts are in the work,—who *do care* for the result. Two years ago, the Republicans of the nation mustered over thirteen hundred thousand strong. We did this under the single impulse of resistance to a common danger, with every external circumstance against us. Of strange, discordant, and even hostile elements, we gathered from the four winds, and formed and fought the battle through, under the constant hot fire of a disciplined, proud, and pampered enemy. Did we brave all, then, to falter now,—now, when that same enemy is wavering, dissevered, and belligerent? The result is not doubtful. We shall not fail,—if we stand firm, we *shall not fail.* Wise counsels may accelerate, or mistakes delay it, but sooner or later, the victory is sure to come.

EXTRACT FROM MR. LINCOLN'S SPEECH

AT CHICAGO, ILLINOIS, JULY 10, 1858.

Now, it happens that we meet together once every year, sometimes about the 4th of July, for some reason or other. These 4th of July gatherings I suppose have their uses. If you will indulge me, I will state what I suppose to be some of them. We are now a mighty nation; we are thirty, or about one-fifteenth part of the dry land of the whole earth. We run our memory back over the pages of history for about eighty-two years, and we consider that we were then a very small people in point of numbers, vastly inferior to what we are now, with a vastly less extent of country, with vastly less of everything we deem desirable among men. We look upon the change as exceedingly advantageous to us and to our posterity, and we fix upon something that happened away back, as in some way or other being connected with this rise of prosperity. We find a race of men living in that day, whom we claim as our fathers and grandfathers; they were iron men; they fought for the principle that they were contending for; and we understood that by what they then did it has followed that the degree of prosperity which we now enjoy has come to us. We hold this annual celebration to remind ourselves of all the good done in this process of time, of how it was done and who did it, and how we are historically connected with it ; and we go from these meetings in better humor with ourselves ; we feel more attached the one to the other ; and more firmly bound to the country we inhabit. In every way we are better men in the age and race and country in which we live, for these celebrations. But after we have done all this we have not yet reached the world. There is something else connected with it.

We have, besides these men descended by blood from our ancestors, among us, perhaps half our people, who are not descendants at all of these men ; they are men who have come from Europe—German, Irish, French, and Scandinavian—men that have come from Europe themselves, or whose ancestors have come hither and settled here, finding themselves our equals in all things. If they look back through this history to trace their connection with those days by blood, they find they have none, they cannot carry themselves back into that glorious epoch and make themselves feel that they are part of us ; and when they look through that old Declaration of Independence, they find that those men say that, "we hold these truths to be self-evident, that all men are created equal," and then they feel that that moral sentiment taught in that day evidences their relation to those men ; that it is the father of all moral principle in them, and they have a right to claim it as though they were blood of the blood, and flesh of the flesh, of the men who wrote that declaration, and so they are. That is the electric cord in that declaration that links the hearts of patriotic and liberty-loving men together, that will link those patriotic hearts as long as the love of freedom exists in the minds of men through-out the world.

I am a poor hand to quote Scripture. I will try it again, however. It is said in one of the admonitions of our Lord, "As your Father in Heaven is perfect, be ye also perfect." The Savior, I suppose, did not expect that any human creature could be perfect as the Father in Heaven; but He said, "As your Father in Heaven is perfect, be ye also perfect." He set that up as a stand-ard, and he who did most toward reaching that standard, attained the highest degree of moral perfection. So I say, in relation to the principle that all men are created equal, let it be as nearly reached as we can. If we can-not give freedom to every creature, let us do nothing that will impose slavery upon any other creature. Let us then turn this government back into the channel in which the framers of the Constitution originally placed it. Let us stand firmly by each other. Let us discard all this quibbling about this man and the other man, this race and that race and the other race, being inferior, and therefore they must be placed in an inferior position— discarding our standing that we have left us. Let us discard all these things, and unite as one people through-out this land, until we shall once more stand up declaring that all men are created equal.

M R. LINCOLN, to those who knew him most intimately, was greatest.

They saw and noted the gentleness, charity, love, and tenderness of his daily life in all his harassing occupations, *while the pages of the history* of his times record the proofs of his courage and wisdom, and of his fidelity to his country, and to human liberty. He was as eminent for his patience, as for his patriotism and wisdom.

M C Meigs

EXTRACT FROM MR. LINCOLN'S SPEECH

DELIVERED AT SPRINGFIELD, ILLINOIS, JULY 17, 1858.

Senator Douglas is of world-wide renown. All the anxious politicians of his party, or who have been of his party for years past, have been looking upon him as certainly, at no distant day, to be the President of the United States. They have seen in his round, jolly, fruitful face, post-offices, land offices, marshalships, and cabinet appointments, chargeships, foreign missions, and sprouting out in wonderful exuberance, ready to be laid hold of by their greedy hands. And as they have been gazing upon this attractive picture so long, they cannot, in the little distraction that has taken place in the party, bring themselves to give up the charming hope, but with greedier anxiety they rush about him, sustain him, and give him marches, triumphal entries, and receptions beyond what, even in the days of his highest prosperity, they could have brought about in his favor.

On the contrary, nobody has ever expected me to be President. In my poor, lean, lank face, nobody has ever seen that any cabbages were sprouting out. These are disadvantages, all taken together, that the republicans labor under: *We* have to fight this battle upon principle alone. I am, in a certain sense, made the standard-bearer in behalf of the republicans. So I hope those with whom I am surrounded have principle enough to nerve themselves for the task, and leave nothing undone that can be fairly done, to bring about the right result.

My declarations upon this subject of negro slavery may be misrepresented, but cannot be misunderstood. I have said that I do not understand the Declaration to mean that all men were created equal in all respects. They are not our equal in color; but I suppose that it does mean to declare that all men are created equal in some respects; they are equal in their right to " life, liberty, and the pursuit of happiness." Certainly the negro is not our equal in color, perhaps not in many other respects; still, in the right to put into his mouth the bread that his own hands have earned, he is the equal of every other man, white or black. In pointing out that more has been given you, you cannot be justified in taking away the little which has been given him. All I ask for the negro is that if you do not like him, let him alone. If God gave him but little that little let him enjoy.

8

THE life and character of Abraham Lincoln, and his great services to this country during the war of the rebellion, will stand as a monument long after the granite monuments erected to his memory have crumbled in the dust.

Thomas A Edison

MENLO PARK, 1880.

EXTRACT FROM MR. LINCOLN'S SPEECH

AT FREEPORT, ILLINOIS, AUGUST 27, 1858.

I have supposed myself, since the organization of the Republican party at Bloomington, in May, 1856, bound as a party man, by the platforms of the party, then, and since. If, in any interrogatories which I shall answer, I go beyond the scope of what is within these platforms, it will be perceived that no one is responsible but myself.

1st. I do not now, nor ever did, stand in favor of the unconditional repeal of the Fugitive Slave Law.

2d. I do not now, or ever did, stand pledged against the admission of any more slave States into the Union.

3d. I do not stand pledged against the admission of a new State into the Union, with such a Constitution as the people of that State may see fit to make.

4th. I do not stand to-day, pledged to the abolition of slavery in the District of Columbia.

5th. I do not stand pledged to the prohibition of the slave-trade between the different States.

6th. I am implied, if not expressly, pledged to a belief in the *right* and *duty* of Congress to prohibit slavery in all the United States Territories.,

7th. I am not generally opposed to honest acquisition of territory; and, in any given case, I would or would not oppose such acquisition, accordingly as I might think such acquisition would, or would not, aggravate the slavery question among ourselves

J UST a. the moment when the people were rejoicing
over the fall of Richmond and the surrender of the
Confederate armies, the Chief Magistrate of the Nation, the most beloved and most trusted of men, fell by the
hand of an assassin. For a moment the nation was struck
dumb by the atrocity of the act, and the magnitude of the
loss that had been sustained. As the report flashed over
the wires that the beloved Chief Magistrate of the Nation,
in the midst of rejoicing over our victories and the prospect of returning peace, had been slain, what heart was
there throughout this broad land which was not filled
with anguish and apprehension ?—what thinking man did
not put to himself the questions, Can the Republic
stand this unexpected calamity? Can our popular institutions bear this new trial? The anguish remained and
still remains, but the apprehension existed but for a
moment. Scarcely had the announcement been made that
Lincoln had fallen, before it was followed by the report
that the Vice-President had taken the oath of President,
and that the functions of government were being performed as regularly and quietly as though nothing had
happened. And what followed? The body of the beloved
President was taken from Washington to Illinois through
crowded cities, among a grief-stricken and deeply excited
people, mourning as no people ever mourned, and moved
as no people were ever moved; and yet there was no
popular violence, no outbreak of popular passion; borne
a thousand miles to its last resting-place, hundreds of
thousands doing such honor to the remains as were never

paid to those of king or conqueror, and the public peace
notwithstanding intense indignation was mixed with
intense sorrow, was in no instance disturbed. Hereafter
there will be no skepticism among us in regard to the
wisdom, the excellence and the power of republican institutions. There is no country upon earth that could have
passed through the trials to which the United States have
been subjected during the four years of civil war with
out being broken into fragments.

The more I saw of Mr. Lincoln the higher became my
admiration of his ability and his character. Before I went
to Washington, and for a short period after, I doubted both
his nerve and his statesmanship ; but a closer observation
relieved me of these doubts, and before his death I had
come to the conclusion that he was a man of will, of
energy, of well-balanced mind, and wonderful sagacity.
His practice of story-telling when the government seemed
to be in imminent peril, and the sublimest events were
transpiring, surprised, if it did not sometimes disgust, those
who did not know him well; but it indicated on his part
no want of a proper appreciation of the terrible responsibility which rested upon him as the Chief Magistrate of a
great nation engaged in the suppression of a desperate
rebellion which threatened its overthrow. Story-telling
with him was something more than a habit. He was so
accustomed to it in social life and in the practice of his
profession, that it became a part of his nature, and so
accurate was his recollection, and so great a fund had he
at command, that he had always anecdotes and stories to
illustrate his arguments and delight those whose tastes
were similar to his own; but those who judged from this

trait that he lacked deep feeling or sound judgment, or a proper sense of the responsibility of his position, had no just appreciation of his character. He possessed all these qualities in an eminent degree. It was true of him, as is true of all really noble and good men, that those who knew him best had the highest admiration of him. He was not a man of genius, but he possessed, in a large degree, what is far more valuable in a public man, excellent common sense. He did not undertake to direct public opinion, but no man understood better the leadings of the popular will or the beatings of the popular heart. He did not seem to gain this knowledge from reading or from observation, for he read very few of our public journals. and was little inclined to call out the opinions of others. He was a representative of the people, and he understood what the people desired rather by a study of himself than of them. Granting that, although constitutionally honest himself, he did not put a very high valuation upon honesty in others, and that he sometimes permitted his partiality for his friends to influence his action in a manner that was hardly consistent with an upright administration of his great office, few men have held high position whose conduct would so well bear the severest criticism as Mr. Lincoln's. The people have already passed judgment in favor of the nobleness and uprightness of his character and the wisdom of his administration, and the pen of impartial history will confirm the judgment.

Hugh McCulloch

New York, 1882.

EXTRACT FROM MR. LINCOLN'S SPEECH

AT GALESBURG, ILLINOIS, OCTOBER 7, 1858.

I have all the while maintained, that in so far as it should be insisted that there was an equality between the white and black races that should produce a perfect social and political equality, it was an impossibility. This, you have seen in my printed speeches; and with it, I have said, that in their right to "life, liberty and the pursuit of happiness," as proclaimed in that old Declaration, the inferior races are our equals. And these declarations I have constantly made in reference to the abstract moral question, to contemplate and consider when we are legislating about any new country, which is not already cursed with the actual presence of the evil— slavery. I have never manifested any impatience with the necessities that spring from the actual presence of black people among us, and the actual existence of slavery among us, where it does already exist; but I have isisted that, in legislating for new countries, where it does not exist, there is no just rule, other than that of moral and abstract right! With reference to those new countries, those maxims as to the right of a people to "life, liberty and the pursuit of happiness," were the just rules to be constantly referred to. There is no misunderstanding this, except by men interested to misunderstand it. I take it that I have to address an intelligent and reading community, who will pursue what I say, weigh it, and then judge whether I advance improper or unsound views, or whether I advance hypocritical, and deceptive, and contrary views in different portions of the country. I believe myself to be guilty of no such thing as the latter, though, of course, I cannot claim that I am entirely free from all error in the opinions I advance.

I have said once before, and I will repeat it now, that Mr. Clay, when he was once answering an objection to the Colonization Society, that it had a tendency to the ultimate emancipation of the slaves, said that "those who would repress all tendencies to liberty and ultimate emancipation, must do more than put down the benevolent efforts of the Colonization Society—they must go back to the era of our liberty and independence, and muzzle the cannon that thunders its annual joyous return—they must blot out the moral lights around us—they must penetrate the human soul, and eradicate the light of reason, and the love of liberty," and I do think—I repeat, though I said it on a former occasion,—that Judge Douglas, and whoever, like him, teaches that the negro has no share, humble though it may be, in the Declaration of Independence, is going back to the era of our liberty and independence, and so far as in him lies, muzzling the cannon that thunders its annual joyous return; that he is blowing out the moral lights around us, when he contends that whoever wants slaves has a right to hold them: that he is penetrating, so far as lies in his power, the human soul, and eradicating the light of reason and the love of liberty, when he is in every possible way preparing the public mind, by his vast influence, for making the institution of slavery perpetual and national.

And now, it only remains for me to say that it is a very grave question for the people of this Union to consider—whether, in view of the fact that this slavery question has been the only one that has ever endangered our Republican institutions—the only one that has ever threatened or menaced a dissolution of the Union—that has ever disturbed us in such a way as to make us fear for the perpetuity of our liberty—in view of these facts, I think it is an exceedingly interesting, and important question for this people to consider whether we shall engage in the policy of acquiring additional territory, discarding altogether from our consideration, while obtaining new territory, the question how it may affect us in regard to this, the only endangering element to our liberties and national greatness. The Judge's view has been expressed. I, in my answers to his question, have expressed mine. I think it will become an important and practical question. Our views are before the public. I am willing and anxious that they should consider them fully—that they should turn it about, and consider the importance of the question, and arrive at a just conclusion as to whether it is, or is not, wise in the people of this Union, in the acquisition of new territory, to consider whether it will add to the disturbance that is existing among us—whether it will add to the one only danger that has ever threatened the perpetuity of the Union, or of our own liberties.

I think it is extremely important that they shall decide, and rightly decide, that question before entering upon that policy.

I LOVE Abraham Lincoln so ardently, that I scarcely dare write my opinion of him. His obscure parentage, his humble birth, his lack of childhood's joys, his exalted attainments, his peculiar talents, his natural gifts, his sympathy for the oppressed, his patriotism for his country, his loyalty to truth, his pure life, and his having had all these excellencies crowned with a martyr's death, renders him beyond doubt, one of the most illustrious men that ever labored to make goodness triumphant, and brotherly charity universal.

W. B. Affleck

Springfield, 1881.

EXTRACT FROM MR. LINCOLN'S SPEECH,

AT QUINCY, ILLINOIS, OCTOBER 13, 1858.

I was aware, when it was first agreed that Judge Douglas and I were to have these seven joint discussions, that they were the successive acts of a drama—perhaps I should say, to be enacted not mearly in the face of audiences like this, but in the face of the nation, and to some extent, by my relation to him, and not from anything in myself, in the face of the world—and I am anxious that they should be conducted with dignity and in good temper, which would be befitting the vast audiences before which it was conducted.

I was not entirely sure that I should be able to hold my own with him, but I at least had the purpose made to do as well as I could upon him; and now I say that I will not be the first to cry "hold." I think it originated with the Judge, and when he quits, I probably will. But I shall not ask any favors at all. He asks me, or he asks the audiences, if I wish to push this matter to the point of personal difficulty? I tell him, No. He did not make a mistake, in one of his early speeches, when he called me an amiable man, though perhaps he did when he called me an "intelligent" man. It really hurts me very much to suppose that I have wronged anybody on earth. I again tell him No! I very much prefer, when this canvass shall be over, however it may result, that we at least part without any bitter recollections of personal difficulties.

We have in this nation this element of domestic slavery It is a matter of absolute certainty that it is a disturbing element. It is the opinion of all the great men who have expressed an opinion upon it, that it is a dangerous element. We keep up a controversy in regard to it. That controversy necessarily springs from difference of opinion, and if we can learn exactly—can reduce to the lowest elements—what that difference of opinion is, we perhaps shall be better prepared for discussing the different system of policy that we would propose in regard to that disturbing element. I suggest that the difference of opinion, reduced to its lowest terms, is no other than the difference between the men who think slavery a wrong and those who do not think it wrong. We think it is a wrong not confining itself merely to the persons or the States where it exists, but that it is a wrong in its tendency, to say the least, that extends itself to the existence of the whole nation. Because we think it wrong we propose a course of policy that shall deal with it as a wrong. We deal with it as with any other wrong, in so far as we can prevent its growing any larger, and so deal with it that in the run of time there may be some promise of an end to it. We have a due regard to the actual presence of it among us and the difficulties of getting rid of it in any satisfactory way, and all the constitutional obligations thrown about it. I suppose that in reference both to its actual existence in the nation, and to our constitutional obligations, we have no right at all to disturb it in the States where it exists, and we profess that we have no more inclination to disturb it than we have the right to do it. We go farther than that; we don't propose to disturb it where, in one instance, we think the Constitution would permit us. We think the constitution would permit us to disturb it in the District of Columbia. Still, we do not propose to do that, unless it should be in terms which I don't suppose the nations is very likely soon to agree to—the terms of making the emancipation gradual and compensating the unwilling owners. Where we suppose we have the constitutional right, we restrain ourselves in reference to the actual existence of the institution and the difficulties thrown about it. We also oppose it as an evil so far as it seeks to spread itself. We insist on the policy that shall restrict it to its present limits. We don't suppose that in doing this we violate anything due to the actual presence of the institution, or anything due to the constitutional guaranties thrown around it.

THERE is not, to my mind, outside of Divine Writ, so convincing an evidence of the immortality of the soul, as is furnished by the growth and development of the mind and character of this greatest of American Presidents to meet the exigencies of the direction and control of a great revolution, on the successful issue of which depended the happiness of one-fifth of the world. From a poor country boy, uneducated and untrained, we find him advancing through the grades of a commonplace law practice, to the government of a great nation in one of the most perplexing political epochs that history records, controlling and directing events to a successful issue—to the most successful issue possible, as retrospection after a lapse of years proves. History furnishes scarcely a parallel to the character of this greatest of reformers. The love of power has produced wise despots, who have endured a life of earnest labor, full of privations, for the sake of innovation and improvement; Icabots have lived miserable lives, or suffered infamous deaths for an idea involving improvement, but the motive in both cases is rather personal than general. The rule with mankind as practical in politics or religion, is conservation. In the face of opposition and struggle, we shrink from responsibilities, and content ourselves with contracting the sphere of intended reforms, to our immediate surroundings.

ABRAHAM LINCOLN was the genius of common sense. In his daily life he was a representative of the American people, and probably the best leader we could have had in the crisis of our national life. He was a great leader, because to his common sense was added the gift of imagination.

Chas. Dudley Warner

HARTFORD, 1880.
9

SPEECH AT ALTON, ILLINOIS, OCTOBER 15, 1858.

On this subject of treating slavery as a wrong, and limiting its spread, let me say a word. Has anything ever threatened the existence of this Union save and except this very institution of slavery? What is it that we hold most dear among us? Our own liberty and prosperity. What has ever threatened our liberty and prosperity, save and except this institution of slavery? If this is true, how do you propose to improve the condition of things by enlarging slavery?—by spreading it out, and making it bigger? You may have a wen or cancer upon your person, and not be able to cut it out lest you bleed to death: but surely, it is no way to cure it, to ingraft it and spread it over your whole body—that is no proper way of treating what you regard a wrong. You see, this peaceful way of dealing with it as a wrong —restricting the spread of it, and not allowing it to go into new countries where it has not already existed— that is the peaceful way, the old-fashioned way, the way in which the fathers themselves set us the example.

" Is slavery wrong ?"

That is the real issue. That is the issue that will continue in this country, when these poor tongues of Judge Douglas and myself shall be silent. It is the eternal struggle between these two principles—right and wrong—throughout the world. They are two principles that have stood face to face from the beginning of time; and will ever continue to struggle. The one is the common right of humanity, and the other, the divine right of kings. It is the same principle in whatever shape it develops itself. It is the same spirit that says, "You work, and toil, and earn bread, and I'll eat it." No matter in what shapes it comes, whether from the mouth of a king, who seeks to bestride the people of his own nation, and live by the fruit of their labor, or from one race of men as an apology for enslaving another race, it is the same tyrannical principle.

I do not claim, gentlemen, to be unselfish; I do not pretend that I would not like to go to the United States Senate; I make no such hypocritical pretense; but I do say to you, that in this mighty issue it is nothing to the mass of the people of the nation, whether or not Judge Douglas or myself shall ever be heard of after this night; it may be a trifle to either of us, but in connection with this mighty question, upon which hangs the destinies of the nation, perhaps, it is absolutely nothing.

EXTRACT FROM MR. LINCOLN'S SPEECH

AT COLUMBUS, OHIO, SEPTEMBER, 1859.

Public opinion in this country is everything. In a nation like ours this popular sovereignty and squatter Sovereignty have already wrought a change in the public mind to the extent I have stated. There is no man in this crowd who can contradict it. Now, if you are opposed to slavery honestly, as much as anybody, I ask you to note that fact, and the like of which is to follow, to be plastered on, layer after layer, until very soon you are prepared to deal with the negro everywhere as with the brute. If public sentiment has not been debauched already to this point, a new turn of the screw in that direction is all that is wanting; and this is constantly being done by the teachers of this insidious popular sovereignty. You need but one or two turns further until your minds, now ripening under these teachings, will be ready for all these things, and you will receive and support or submit to, the slave trade, revived with all its horrors, a slave code enforced in our territories, and a new Dred Scott decision to bring slavery up into the very heart of the free North. This, I must say, is but carrying out those words prophetically spoken by Mr. Clay, many, many years ago—I believe more than thirty years—when he told his audience that if they would repress all tendencies to liberty and ultimate emancipation, they must go

back to the era of our independence and muzzle the cannon
which thundered its annual joyous return on the Fourth
of July; they must blow out the moral lights around us;
they must penetrate the human soul and eradicate the
love of liberty; but until they did these things, and others
eloquently enumerated by him, they could not repress all
tendencies to ultimate emancipation. I ask attention to
the fact that in a pre-eminent degree these popular sov-
ereigns are at this work; blowing out the moral lights
around us; teaching that the negro is no longer a man,
but a brute; that the Declaration has nothing to do with
him; that he ranks with the crocodile and the reptile;
that man with body and soul, is a matter of dollars and
cents.

EXTRACT FROM MR. LINCOLN'S SPEECH

AT CINCINNATI, OHIO, SEPTEMBER, 1859.

It has occurred to me here, to-night, that if I ever do shoot over the line, at the people on the other side of the line, into a slave State, and purpose to do so, keeping my skin safe, that I have now about the best chance I shall ever have. I should not wonder that there are some Kentuckians about this audience; we are close to Kentucky; and whether that be so or not, we are on elevated ground, and by speaking distinctly, I should not wonder if some of the Kentuckians would hear me on the other side of the river. For that reason, I propose to address a portion of what I have to say, to the Kentuckians.

I say, then, in the first place, to the Kentuckians, that I am what they call, as I understand it, a "Black Republican." I think slavery is wrong, morally and politically. I desire that it should be no further spread in these United States, and I should not object, if it should gradually terminate in the whole Union. While I say this for myself, I say to you, Kentuckians, that I understand you differ radically with me upon this proposition; that you believe slavery is a good thing; that slavery is right; that it ought to be extended and perpetuated in this Union. Now, there being this broad difference between us, I do not pretend, in addressing myself to you, Kentuckians, to attempt proselyting you; that would be a vain effort. I do not enter upon it. I will tell you, so far as I am authorized to speak for the opposition, what we mean to do with you. We mean to treat you, as near as we possibly can, as Washington, Jefferson, and Madison treated you. We mean to leave you alone, and in no way to interfere with your institution; to abide by all and every compromise of the Constitution, and, in a word, coming back to the original proposition, to treat you, so far as degenerated men (if we have degenerated) may, according to the examples of those noble fathers—Washington, Jefferson, and Madison. We mean to remember that you are as good as we; that there is no difference between us, other than the difference of circumstances. We mean to recognize and bear in mind always, that you have as good hearts in your bosoms as other people, or as we claim to have, and treat you accordingly. We mean to marry your girls, when we have a chance—the white ones, I mean—and I have the honor to inform you that I once did have a chance in that way.

I have told you what we mean to do. I want to know, now, when that thing takes place, what you mean to do. I often hear it intimated that you mean to divide the Union whenever a Republican, or anything like it, is elected President of the United States. If that is so, I want to know what you are going to do with your half of it? Are you going to split the Ohio down through, and push your half off a piece? Or are you going to keep it right alongside of us outrageous fellows? Or

are you going to build up a wall some way, between your
country and ours, by which that movable property of
yours can't come over here any more, to the danger of
your losing it? Do you think you can better yourselves
on that subject, by leaving us here, under no obligation
whatever to return those specimens of your movable
property that come hither? You have divided the
Union, because we would not do right with you, as you
think, upon that subject; when we cease to be under
obligations to do anything for you, how much better off
do you think you will be? Will you make war upon us,
and kill us all? Why, gentlemen, I think you are as gal-
lant and as brave men as live; that you can fight as
bravely in a good cause, man for man, as any other people living; that you have shown yourselves capable of
this, upon various occasions; but, man for man, you are
not better than we are, and there are not so many of
you as there are of us. You will never make much of a
hand at whipping us. If we were fewer in numbers than
you, I think that you could whip us; if we were equal,
it would likely be a drawn battle; but being inferior in
numbers, you will make nothing by attempting to master
us.

ABRAHAM LINCOLN, with George Washington, will stand out in the pages of American history in exalted pre-eminence. Mr. Lincoln was suited to the epoch which rightly anticipated his advent to the Presidency; the *quality* of the man was the equivalent of the *perils* of the Chief Magistrate. Throughout his career, he displayed a character of perfect integrity, sincerity, undeviating rectitude and courage, while he exhibited, in rare combination, wisdom, gentleness and conciliation.

His "firmness in the right, as God gave him to see," was, to him, faith, courage, patience and boundless endurance in the cause of the right—to the American people, nationality restored, liberty and union vindicated, the dark stain of slavery erased, and free institutions preserved.

AUGUSTA, 1880.

EXTRACT FROM MR. LINCOLN'S SPEECH

AT JONESBORO, ILL., SEPTEMBER 15, 1858.

In so far as Judge Douglas has insisted that all the States have the right to do exactly as they please about all their domestic relations, including that of slavery, I agree entirely with him. I hold myself under constitutional obligations to allow the people in all the states, without interference, direct or indirect, to do exactly as they please; and I deny that I have any inclination to interfere with them, even if there were no such constitutional obligation.

I say, in the way our fathers originally left the Slavery question, the institution was in the course of ultimate extinction, and the public mind rested in the belief that it *was* in the course of ultimate extinction. I say, when this Government was first established, it was the policy of its founders to prohibit the spread of slavery into the new Territories of the United States, where it had not existed. All I have asked, or desired, anywhere, is that it should be placed back again upon the basis that the fathers of our govern-ment originally placed it upon. I have no doubt that it *would* become extinct, for all time to come, if we but re-adopted the policy of the fathers by restricting it to the limits it has already covered—restricting it from the new Territories.

IN the Autumn of 1859, I was residing in Cincinnati, and heard the late Stephen A. Douglas speak twice in that city or vicinity, and Mr. Lincoln speak once, from the steps of the Burnet House, I believe. I was impressed greatly with the contrast between them. Mr. Douglas was aggressive, confident in himself, and evidently bent on crushing his opponents. Mr. Lincoln seemed at first too modest and undemonstrative. But as he went on and forgot himself, and apparently his party, in his interest in grand principles, he rose in dignity, till he seemed more the embodiment of Justice, Freedom and Love of Humanity, than a mere man. He was lost in the grandeur of the cause, and stood unselfishly for the rights of all men, in all ages. And I have often thought that this idea of him then, gathered by me, best expresses the essence of his character, and inspired disregard of personal interests, and a complete self-surrender of everything to the welfare of all men, especially the humblest.

CARBONDALE, 1880.

EXTRACT FROM MR. LINCOLN'S ADDRESS

DELIVERED AT COOPER INSTITUTE, FEBRUARY 27, 1860.

Let all who believe that "Our fathers, who framed the Government under which we live, understood this . question just as well, and even better, than we do now," speak as they spoke, and act as they acted upon it. This is all Republicans ask—all Republicans desire—in relation to slavery. As those fathers marked it, so let it be again marked, as an evil not to be extended, but to be tolerated and protected only because of and so far as its actual presence among us makes that toleration and protection a necessity. Let all the guaranties those fathers gave it be, not grudgingly, but fully and fairly maintained.

It is exceedingly desirable that all parts of this great Confederacy shall be at peace, and in harmony, one with another. Even though much provoked, let us do nothing through passion and ill temper. Even though the Southern people will not so much as listen to us, let us calmly consider their demands, and yield to them if, in our deliberate view of our duty, we possibly can.

Wrong as we think slavery is, we can yet afford to let it alone where it is, because that much is due to the necessity arising from its actual presence in the nation; but can we, while our votes will prevent it, allow it to spread into the National Territories, and to overrun us here in these Free States? If our sense of duty forbids this, then let us stand by our duty, fearlessly and effectively. Let us be diverted by none of those sophistical contrivances wherewith we are so industriously plied and belabored—contrivances such as groping for some middle ground between the right and the wrong, vain as the search for a man who should be neither a living man nor a dead man—such as a policy of "don't care" on a question about which all true men do care—such as Union appeals beseeching true Union men to yield to Disunionists reversing the divine rule, and calling, not the sinners. but the righteous to repentance—such as invocations to Washington, imploring men to unsay what Washington said, and undo what Washington did. Neither let us be slandered from our duty by false accusations against us, nor frightened from it by menaces of destruction to the Government nor dungeons to ourselves. *Let us have faith, that right makes might, and in that faith let us, to the end, dare to do our duty as we understand it.*

ADDRESS OF ABRAHAM LINCOLN

TO THE CITIZENS OF SPRINGFIELD, ON HIS DEPARTURE
FOR WASHINGTON, FEBRUARY 11TH, 1861.

My Friends:

No one, not in my position, can appreciate the sadness I feel at this parting. To this people I owe all that I am. Here I have lived more than a quarter of a century; here my children were born, and here one of them lies buried. I know not how soon I shall see you again. A duty devolves upon me which is, perhaps, greater than that which has devolved upon any other man since the days of Washington. He never would have succeeded except by the aid of Divine Providence, upon which he at all times relied. I feel that I cannot succeed without the same Divine aid which sustained him, and on the same Almighty Being I place my reliance for support; and I hope you, my friends, will all pray that I may receive that Divine assistance, without which I cannot succeed, but with which success is certain. Again I bid you an affectionate farewell.

RESIDENCE OF ABRAHAM LINCOLN, SPRINGFIELD, ILL.—FROM 1836 TO 1861.

P. 145

IN 1834, I was a citizen of Springfield, Sangamon Co., Illinois. Mr. Lincoln lived in the country, fourteen miles from the town. He was a laborer, and a deputy surveyor, and at the same time a member of the legislature, elected the year previous. In 1835, he was a candidate for re-election. I had not seen him for the first six months of my residence there, but had heard him spoken of as a man of wonderful ability on the stump. He was a long, gawky, ugly, shapeless man. He had never spoken, as far as I know of, at the county seat, during his first candidacy. The second time he was a candidate, he had already made, in the legislature, considerable reputation; and on his renomination to the legislature, advertised to meet his opponents, and speak in Springfield, on a given day. I believe that that was the first public speech he ever made at the court-house. He was never ashamed, so far as I know, to admit his ignorance uqon any subject, or of the meaning of any word, no matter how ridiculous it might make him appear. As he was riding into town the evening before the speech, he passed the handsomest house in the village, which had just been built by Geo. Farquer; upon it he had placed a lightning-rod, the only one in the town or county. Some ten or twelve young men were riding with Lincoln. He asked them what that rod was for. They told him it was to keep off the lightning. "How does it do it?" he asked; none of them could tell. He rode into

town, bought a book on the properties of lightning, and
before morning knew all about it.   When he was ignorant on any subject, he addressed himself to the task of
being ignorant no longer.   On this occasion, a large
number of citizens came from a distance to hear him
speak.   He had very able opponents.   I stood near him
and heard the speech.   I was fresh from Kentucky
then, and had heard most of her great orators.   It struck
me then, as it seems to me now, that I never heard a
more effective speaker.   All the party weapons of
offense and defense seemed to be entirely under his
control.   The large crowd seemed to be swayed by him
as he pleased.   He was a Whig, and quite a number of
candidates were associated with him on the Whig ticket;
seven, I think, in number; there were seven Democrats
opposed to them.   The debate was a joint one, and Lincoln was appointed to close it, which he did as I have
heretofore described, in a most masterly style.   The
people commenced leaving the court-house, when Geo.
Farquer, a man of much celebrity in the State, rose, and
asked the people to hear him.   He was not a candidate,
but was a man of talents, and of great State notoriety.
as a speaker.   He commenced his speech by turning
to Lincoln and saying, "This young man will have
to be taken down; and I am truly sorry that the
task devolves upon me."   He then proceeded in a vein
of irony, sarcasm, and wit, to ridicule Lincoln in every way
that he could.   Lincoln stood, not more than ten feet
from him, with folded arms, and an eye flashing fire, and
listened attentively to him, without ever interrupting him
Lincoln then took the stand for reply.   He was pale and

his spirits seemed deeply moved. His opponent was one worthy of his steel. He answered him fully and completely. The conclusion of his speech I remember even now, so deep an impression did it make on me then. He said, "The gentleman commenced his speech by saying that this young man would have to be taken down, alluding to me; I am not so young in years as I am in the tricks and trades of a politician; but live long, or die young, I would rather die now, than, like the gentleman, change my politics, and simultaneous with the change receive an office worth three thousand dollars per year, and then have to erect a lightning-rod over my house, to protect a guilty conscience from an offended God." He used the lightning-rod against Farquer as he did everything in after life.

In 1837, after his return from the legislature, Mr. Lincoln obtained a license to practice law. He lived fourteen miles in the country, and had ridden into town on a borrowed horse, with no earthly goods but a pair of saddlebags, two or three law books, and some clothing which he had in the saddle-bags. He took an office, and engaged from the only cabinet-maker then in the village, a single bedstead. He came into my store (I was a merchant then), set his saddle-bags on the counter and asked me "what the furniture for a single bedstead would cost." I took slate and pencil and made calculation, and found the sum for furniture complete would amount to seventeen dollars in all. Said he, " It is probably cheap enough : but I want to say that, cheap as it is, I have not the money to pay. But if you will credit me until Christmas, and my experiment here as a lawyer is a success, I will pay you then.

10

If I fail in that I will probably never be able to pay you at all." The tone of his voice was so melancholy that I felt for him. I looked up at him, and I thought then, as I think now, that I never saw so gloomy and melancholy a face. I said to him, "The contraction of so small a debt seems to affect you so deeply, I think I can suggest a plan by which you will be able to attain your end, without incurring any debt. I have a very large room, and a very large double-bed in it; which you are perfectly welcome to share with me if you choose." "Where is your room?" asked he. "Up stairs," said I, pointing to the stairs leading from the store to my room. Without saying a word, he took his saddle-bags on his arm, went up stairs, set them down on the floor, came down again, and with a face beaming with pleasure and smiles, exclaimed: "Well, Speed, I'm moved." Mr. Lincoln was then twenty-seven years old, almost without friends, and with no property except the saddle-bags with the clothes mentioned, within. Now, for me to have lived to see such a man rise from point to point, and from place to place, filling all the places to which he was called with honor and distinction, until he reached the presidency, filling the presidential chair in the most trying time that any ruler ever had, seems to me more like fiction than fact. None but a genius like his could have accomplished so much; and none but a government like ours could produce such a man. It gave the young eagle scope for his wings; he tried it, and soared to the top!

In 1839 Mr. Lincoln, being then a lawyer in full practice, attended all the courts adjacent to Springfield. He was then attending court at Christiansburg, about thirty miles distant. I was there when the court broke up; quite a number of lawyers were coming from court to Springfield. We were riding along a country road, two and two together, some distance apart, Lincoln and Jno. J. Hardin being behind (Hardin was afterward made colonel and was killed at Buena Vista). We were passing through a thicket of wild plum and crab-apple trees, where we stopped to water our horses. After waiting some time Hardin came up and we asked him where Lincoln was. " Oh," said he, " when I saw him last" (there had been a severe wind storm) " he had caught two little birds in his hand, which the wind had blown from their nest, and he was hunting for the nest." Hardin left him before he found it. He finally found the nest, and placed the birds, to use his own words, " in the home provided for them by their mother." When he came up with the party they laughed at him; said he, earnestly : " I could not have slept to-night if I had not given those two little birds to their mother."

This was the flower that bloomed so beautifully in his nature, on his native prairies. He never lost the nobility of his nature, nor the kindness of his heart, by being removed to a higher sphere of action. On the contrary, both were increased. The enlarged sphere of his action developed the natural promptings of his heart.

Joshua F. Speed

· LOUISVILLE, 1882.

I FULLY concur with all that has ever been uttered—calculated to show that Abraham Lincoln was a pure and honest man, and possessor of very superior abilities.

Among those to whom I applied for biographical facts, while preparing the first edition of my Dictionary of Congress, was Mr. Lincoln; and his reply was so characteristic of the man, that I send the following: "Born in Hardin County, Kentucky, February 12, 1809; received a limited education; adopted the profession of law; was captain of volunteers in the Black Hawk war; was post-master of a small village; four times elected to the Illinois Legislature, and a Representative in Congress from 1847 to 1849." The several letters which he wrote to me, and two or three very pleasant interviews that I had with him, can never be forgotten; but what I cherish with peculiar pleasure, is the fact that he once suggested my appointment as Librarian of Congress; and when, through a distinguished friend, I suggested that Mr. A. R. Spofford was an applicant for the place, and better fitted for it than myself, the manner in which he commented on my suggestion was exceedingly gratifying.

Charles Lanman

WASHINGTON, 1882.

ABRAHAM LINCOLN AND THE CONVEN-
TION OF 1860.

NATIONS, like individuals, have turning-points in their lives. The United States has passed through one of them—her first crisis since she became a nation by the adoption of a constitution in 1789. No small amount of eloquent advocacy, as well as charitable compromise, were required to unite the different States together in one common bond in that early day, even though the glories of her Revolution were fresh in the minds of all. The only cause of this reluctance on the part of some of the States to enter into this compact grew out of a fear, that slavery might not be sustained after the national Union of the States had been consummated. And it is not improbable that some mental reservation existed as to the binding force of the constitution, on the part of some of the States at the time of signing it. When this union of all the States under one bond was accomplished we became, in the eyes of the world, a nation; and our patriotic pride and fidelity to a common interest seemed to give an assurance of perpetual harmony. This kindred feeling was not disturbed till slavery had assumed rights, which were con-

sidered hostile to the honor of the North, and dangerous
to the best interests of the nation. At this eventful
epoch, when everybody was intent on his calling, loath
to turn aside from his daily routine, the great issue was
forced upon the nation in no equivocal form at the convention of 1860. For the first time in the history of
presidential conventions, this issue completely transcended all others ; that of 1856 having been somewhat
vacillating.   A suspense now hung over the whole
country. Prophets harangued and everybody partook
of the general excitement. When the convention met it
was observable through a conviction that seemed to fill
the very air, that a new order of things was at hand ; that
new men and new measures would soon be brought to
the front by an irresistible influence that was gathering
force like the whirlwind.   And while (as is always the
case at such popular councils), noisy and thoughtless
demonstrations, like the froth that floats on deep waters,
were uppermost at times, yet the profound convictions of
political economists transcended them, whenever the
true issue came up for debate. It was the substance,
not the shadow, that this element of candor demanded ;
it asked no favors through a reciprocity of interest, but
challenged men to support principles according to their
merits. Political prestige weighed nothing. In vain, it
had oft been tried to bridge over the chasm ; heroic
treatment was demanded, and who should be the hero to
administer it, who could buffet the storm of indignation
ready to burst upon the head of him who accepted the
nomination of the anti-slavery party ? Who could step
into this arena impervious to the corruption of partisans ?

Who could become the political gladiator, in hand-to-hand conflict with the disciples of Calhoun, and the neophytes of the oligarchy of which he was father? Who could become the animated target at whose feet the shafts of malice should fall harmless? Who could be compromising without a letting down of principles? Who had firmness without arrogance, eloquence without pretension, charity without cupidity? Who had the virtues of the statesman without the vices of the partisan? He who had seen every phase of American life, and shared its wants, and felt its anxieties, and been taught in its school; and whose spotless record now beckoned to the lovers of justice to follow whither he might lead.

Abraham Lincoln. He was nominated, elected once, and again. His services wrung from the reluctant lips of his adversaries praise that they dared not refuse. The stickler for "blue blood" stood aghast, before the charm of his words—simple and potent, and fortified by the force of events; and last of all, the autocrats of the world obsequiously bowed before the bier which held the genius of America—a corpse, around which a halo of glory shone to the uttermost parts of the earth. Other rulers of nations had been assassinated, but none before had won such acknowledgments of that kind of grandeur which died in him to live again. Our country, in her youthful fecundity, stimulated into activity by the vastness of her wild domain, through which genius became the handmaiden of creative power, produced a Lincoln. It is not essential that heraldry or even conventionalism should accompany merit, it is a positive principle. All the more lustrous if unshackled with forms. Lincoln

SPEECH

TO THE MEMBERS OF THE LEGISLATURE OF INDIANA WHO WAITED UPON HIM AT HIS HOTEL.

" Solomon says there is ' a time to keep silence,' and when men wrangle by the mouth with no certainty that they *mean* the same *thing*, while using the same *word*, it perhaps were as well if they would keep silence."

" The words ' coercion ' and ' invasion' are much used in these days, and often with some temper and hot blood. Let us make sure, if we can, that we do not misunderstand the meaning of those who use them. Let us get the exact definitions of these words, not from dictionaries, but from the men themselves, who certainly deprecate the things they would represent by the use of the word. What then, is ' coercion'? What is ' invasion'? Would the marching of an army into South Carolina, without the consent of her people, and with hostile intent towards them, be invasion? I certainly think it would, and it would be ' coercion' also if South Carolinians were forced to submit. But if the United States should merely hold and retake its own forts and other property, and collect the duties on foreign importations, or even withhold the mails from places where they were habitually violated, would any or all these things be ' invasion' or ' coercion'? Do our professed lovers of the Union, but who spitefully resolve that they will resist coercion and invasion, understand that such things as these on the part of the United States would be coercion or invasion of a State? If so, their idea of means to preserve the object of their affection would seem exceedingly thin and airy. If sick, the little pills of the homœopathists would be much too large for it to swallow. In their view, the Union, as a family relation, would seem to be no regular marriage, but a sort of 'free love' arrangement, to be maintained only on 'passional attraction.' By the way, in what consists the special sacredness of a State? I speak not of the position assigned to a State in the Union by the Constitution ; for that, by the bond, we all recognize. That position, however, a State cannot carry out of the Union with it. I speak of that assumed primary right of a State to rule all which is *less* than itself, and ruin all which is larger than itself. If a State and a county, in a given case, should be equal in extent of territory, and equal in number of inhabitants—in what, as a matter of principle, is the State better than a county? Would an exchange of names be an exchange of *rights* upon principle? On what rightful principle may a State, being not more than one-fiftieth part of the nation in soil and population, break up the nation, and then coerce a proportionally larger subdivision of itself, in the most arbitrary way? What mysterious right to play tyrant is conferred on a district of country, with its people, by merely calling it a State? I am not asserting anything ; I am merely asking questions for you to consider."

SPEECH AT CINCINNATI, OHIO.

I have spoken but once before this in Cincinnati, that was a year previous to the late Presidential election. On that occasion, in a playful manner, but with sincere words, I addressed much of what I said to the Kentuckians. We mean to treat you as near as we possibly can, as Washington, Jefferson, and Madison treated you. We mean to leave you alone, and in no way to interfere with your institution, and, in a word, coming back to the original proposition, to treat you, so far as degenerated men (if we have degenerated) may, according to the examples of those noble fathers—Washington, Jefferson, and Madison. We mean to remember that you are as good as we; that there is no difference between us other than the difference of circumstances. We mean to recognize and bear in mind always that you have as good hearts in your bosoms as other people, or as we claim to have, and treat you accordingly.

Fellow-citizens of Kentucky! friends! brethren, may I call you in my new position? I see no occasion, and feel no inclination to retract a word of this. If it shall not be made good, be assured the fault shall not be mine.

HIS early term in Congress was while I was Speaker of the House of Representatives. Thirty-four years have elapsed since that Congress assembled, but I recall vividly the impressions I then formed, both as to his ability and his amiability. We were old Whigs together, and agreed entirely on all questions of public interest. I could not always concur in the policy of the party which made him President, but I never lost my personal regard for him. For shrewdness, sagacity and keen, practical sense, he has had no superior in our day and generation. His patience, perseverance, imperturbable good-nature and devoted patriotism, during the trying times of the civil war, were of inestimable value to the Union cause. Meantime, the forbearing and conciliatory spirit, which he manifested so signally in the last months of his presidency, rendered his death—quite apart from the abhorrent and atrocious manner in which it occurred—an inexpressible shock, even to those who had differed from his earlier views. His life, even at the moment it was taken away, as I said publicly at the time, was the most important and precious life in our whole land. I heartily wish success to the memorials of a career associated so prominently with the greatest event of our age, and which must ever have so exalted a place in American history.

Rob't C. Winthrop.

BOSTON, 1881.

PRIOR to his elevation to the Presidency of the United States I had never met Mr. Lincoln, although I was acquainted with the splendid reputation he had achieved in Illinois as a lawyer and statesman. His venerable father-in-law, Robert S. Todd, of Lexington, was one of my earliest friends, and his more distinguished relative, Hon. Daniel Breck, of this town, was my first law preceptor. From these gentlemen I had learned to admire his great character, and was not surprised, when, in 1860, the nomination for the chief magistracy of the republic was given him by the convention at Chicago over rivals so illustrious as Chase and Seward.

After his election, I met Mr. Lincoln often in Washington, and it will be always one of the pleasant memories of my life that I had this privilege and shared somewhat his regard and confidence. Great as were the men who constituted his cabinet—and in no administration were ever found three greater men than Chase, Seward and Stanton—I always thought, and still think, he was greater than any of them. Calm, courageous, generous, just; he was the impersonation of patriotism, and his labors to restore the Union by suppressing the rebel Confederacy, and by striking off the fetters from four million slaves, followed by his untimely death by the hand of an assassin, gave to him of all the men of this century the first place in the eyes of all mankind.

SPEECH AT SYRACUSE, N. Y.

I see you have erected a very fine and handsome platform here, for me, and I presume you expect me to speak from it. If I should go upon it, you would imagine that I was about to deliver you a much longer speech than I am. I wish you to understand that I mean no discourtesy to you by thus dealing. I intend discourtesy to no one. But I wish you to understand that, though I am unwilling to go upon this platform, you are not at liberty to draw any inference concerning any other platform with which my name has been, or is, connected. I wish you long life and prosperity, individually, and pray that with the perpetuity of those institutions under which we have all so long lived and prospered, our happiness may be secured, our future made brilliant, and the glorious destiny of our country established forever.

WHEN President Lincoln was killed, I was the acting United States Minister at Peking, and reported the assassination to His Imperial Highness, Prince Kung, then at the head of the government, from whom a suitable reply was received on the 8th of July, 1865. I sent the correspondence to the Secretary of State, with the following remarks: "The limits of a dispatch will hardly allow me more than to add my tribute of admiration to the character of Mr. Lincoln. His firm and consistent maintenance of the national cause, his clear understanding of the great questions at issue, and his unwearied efforts, while enforcing the laws, to deprive the conflict of all bitterness, were all so happily blended with a reliance on Divine guidance, as to elevate him to a high rank among successful statesmen. His name is hereafter identified with the cause of Emancipation, while his patriotism, integrity, and other virtues, and his untimely death, render him not unworthy of mention with William of Orange and Washington."

This was written seventeen years ago, since which time I have learned more of the inimitable blending in his character of mercy and firmness, and estimate him higher. He was tested in every way throughout the long struggle, and his rare virtues will endure him to the .American people the more they study his life.

S Wells Williams

YALE COLLEGE, 1882.
12

SPEECH

FROM THE STEPS OF THE CAPITOL, ALBANY, N. Y.

I AM notified by your Governor that this reception is given without distinction of party. I accept it the more gladly, because it is so. Almost all men in this country, and in any country where freedom of thought is tolerated, attach themselves to political parties. It is but ordinary charity to attribute this to the fact that in so attaching himself to the party which his judgment prefers, the citizen believes he thereby promotes the best interests of the whole country; but when an election is past, it is altogether befitting a free people that, until the next election, they should be as one people. The reception you have extended to me to-day, is not given to me personally. It should not be so, but as the representative, for the time being, of the majority of the nation. If the election had resulted in the selection of either of the other candidates, the same cordiality should have been extended to him, as is extended to me this day, in testimony of the devotion of the whole people to the Constitution and the whole Union, and of their desire to perpetuate our institutions, and to hand them down in their perfection, to succeeding generations.

T HE life of President Lincoln is written in imperishable characters in the history of the great American Republic.

J Bright

LONDON, 1880.

SPEECH IN THE ASSEMBLY HALL AT AL-BANY, N. Y.

I DO not propose to enter into an explanation of any particular line of policy as to our present difficulties, to be adopted by the incoming Administration. I deem it just to you, to myself, and to all, that I should see everything, that I should hear everything, that I should have every light that can be brought within my reach, in order that when I do so speak, I shall have enjoyed every opportunity to take correct and true grounds; and for this reason I don't propose to speak, at this time, of the policy of the Government. But when the time comes, I shall speak, as well as I am able, for the good of the present and future of this country—for the good both of the North and the South of this country—for the good of the one and the other; and of all sections of the country. In the meantime, if we have patience, if we restrain ourselves, if we allow ourselves not to run off in a passion, I still have confidence that the Almighty, the Maker of the Universe, will, through the instrumentality of this great and intelligent people, bring us through this, as he has through all the other difficulties of our country.

MORE fully than any other man, not excepting Washington, Abraham Lincoln embodied and exhibited our distinctive civilization. "From the people, of the people, and for the people," he inspired and directed them through the most trying ordeal that this government has passed, or ever can pass.

Geologists tell us, the lower stratum of the earth's crust is granite, and that the highest mountains are the upheaval of this granite, so granite is both base and crown. Mr. Lincoln was lifted by the force of his unrivaled genius from the mass of the people, the immutable basis, the granite of our civilization, to an elevation of solitary grandeur. Embracing all phases, from the humblest to the highest, his life bears all to a higher altitude where its influence falls in perpetual benediction.

G. De La Matyr

INDIANAPOLIS, 1882.

SPEECH AT POUGHKEEPSIE, N. Y.

I CANNOT refrain from saying that I am highly gratified, as much here indeed, under the circumstances, as I
have been anywhere on my route, to witness this noble
demonstration—made, not in honor of an individual, but
of the man who at this time humbly, but earnestly, represents the majesty of the Nation.   This reception, like all
others that have been tendered to me, doubtless ema-
nates from all the political parties, and not from one
alone.   As such, I accept it the more gratefully, since it
indicates an earnest desire on the part of the whole
people, without regard to political differences, to save
—not the country, because the country will save itself—
but to save the institutions of the country—those institutions under which, in the last three quarters of a century, we have grown to be a great, an intelligent, and a
happy people—the greatest, the most intelligent, and the
happiest people in the world.   These noble manifestations indicate, with unerring certainty, that the whole
people are willing to make common cause for this object ;
that if, as it ever must be, some have been successful in
the recent election, and some have been beaten—if some
are satisfied, and some are dissatisfied—the defeated party
are not in favor of sinking the ship, but are desirous of
running it through the tempest in safety, and willing, if
they think the people have committed an error in their
verdict now, to wait in the hope of reversing it, and set-

ting it right next time. I do not say that in the recent election the people did the wisest thing that could have been done; indeed, I do not think they did; but I do say, that in accepting the great trust committed to me, which I do with a determination to endeavor to prove worthy of it, I must rely upon you, upon the people of the whole country, for support; and with their sustaining aid, even I, humble as I am, cannot fail to carry the ship of state safely through the storm.

SPEECH AT PEEKSKILL, N. Y.

I WILL say in a single sentence, in regard to the difficulties that lie before me and our beloved country, that if I can only be as generously and unanimously sustained, as the demonstrations I have witnessed indicate I shall be, I shall not fail; but without your sustaining hands I am sure that neither I, nor any other man, can hope to surmount these difficulties. I trust that in the course I shall pursue, I shall be sustained not only by the party that elected me, but by the patriotic people of the whole country.

I LOOK upon A. Lincoln as a remarkable illustration of the important part which a sound social and moral character may play in a political career. While, in a lower sense, he opened up his own way to fortune by his own industry, in a higher sense, it was opened up for him by the moral forces at play about him. The ice-floe parts before the skillful sea-captain. Not by his own force chiefly, Lincoln threaded his narrow strip of open way, till at length he reached, and a great nation with him, the high-seas, by a shrewd intellect, and far more, by an honestly sympathetic heart. He was not a great man in intellect only, he was not a moral hero; but he possessed in an unusual degree, in an active, mobile form, humane sympathies; and these saved him and us. Abraham Lincoln was one of those few men, at the sight of whom, we trust God and take courage.

John Bascom

MADISON, 1880.

REPLY TO THE MAYOR OF NEW YORK.

In my devotion to the Union I hope I am behind no man in the nation. As to my wisdom in conducting affairs so as to tend to the preservation of the Union, I fear too great confidence may have been placed in me. I am sure I bring a heart devoted to the work. There is nothing that could ever bring me to consent—willingly to consent—to the destruction of this Union, unless it would be that thing for which the Union itself was made. I understand that the ship is made for carrying and preservation of the cargo; and so long as the ship is safe with the cargo it shall not be abandoned. This Union shall never be abandoned, unless the possibility of its existence shall cease to exist, without the necessity of throwing passengers and cargo overboard. So long, then, as it is possible that the prosperity and liberties of the people can be preserved within the Union, it shall be my purpose at all times to preserve it.

M R. LINCOLN was great in goodness, as well as good in greatness. Like the silent potent forces in nature, he was most powerful in the calm. He never shunned storms and tempests, but never courted them. His love of honesty and fair dealing was one of his most prominent characteristics; he never stooped to trickery. Let the following incident illustrate this trait in his character:

In the spring term of the Tazewell County Court, in 1847, which, at that time, was held in the village of Tremont, I was detained as witness an entire week. Lincoln was employed in several suits, and among them was one of Case *vs.* Snow Bros. The Snow Bros., as appeared in evidence (who were both minors), had purchased from an old Mr. Chase what was then called a "prairie team," consisting of two or three yoke of oxen and prairie plow, giving therefor their joint note for some two hundred dollars, but when pay-day came, refused to pay, pleading the minor act. The note was placed in Lincoln's hands for collection. The suit was called, a jury impaneled. The Snow Bros. did not deny the note, but pleaded, through their counsel, that they were minors, and that Mr. Case knew they were, at the time of the contract and conveyance. All this was admitted by Mr. Lincoln, with his peculiar phrase, "Yes, gentlemen, I guess that's so." The minor act was read, and its validity admitted, in the same manner. The counsel of the Snow Bros. were permitted, without question, to

state all these things to the jury, and to show by the stat-
ute that these minors could not be held responsible for
their contract.   By this time, you may well suppose that
I began to be uneasy.   "What!" thought I, "this good
old man, who confided in these boys, to be wronged in
this way, and even his counsel, Mr. Lincoln, to submit in
silence!"   I looked at the court, Judge Treat, but could
read nothing in his calm and dignified demeanor.   Just
then, Mr. Lincoln slowly got up, and in his strange, half
erect attitude, and clear, quiet accent began, " Gentlemen
of the jury, are you willing to allow these boys to begin
life with this shame and disgrace attached to their character?   If you are, *I* am not.   The best judge of human
character that ever wrote, has left these immortal words
for all of us to ponder :

> " ' Good name in man or woman, dear my lord,
>   Is the immediate jewel of their souls.
>   Who steals my purse, steals trash ; 'tis something, nothing :
>   'Twas mine, 'tis his ; and has been slave to thousands.
>   But he that filches from me my good name,
>   Robs me of that which not enriches him,
>   And leaves me poor, indeed.' "

Then rising to his full height, and looking upon the Snow
Bros. with the compassion of a brother, his long right arm
extended toward the opposing counsel, he continued :
" *Gentlemen of the Jury*, these poor, innocent boys would
never have attempted this low villainy, had it not been for
the advice of these lawyers."   Then, for a few minutes,
he showed how even the noble science of law may be
prostituted; with a scathing rebuke to those who thus

belittle their profession, and concluded: "And now, gentlemen, you have it in *your* power to set these boys right before the world." He plead for the young men only; I think he did not mention his client's name. The jury, without leaving their seats, decided that Snow Bros. must pay that debt; and they, after hearing Lincoln, were as willing to pay it as the jury were determined they should. I think the entire argument lasted not above five minutes.

I once heard Mr. Lincoln speak on the Tariff, and he illustrated it in this way; "I confess that I have not any very decided views on the question. A revenue we must have. In order to keep house, we must have breakfast, dinner and supper; and this tariff business seems to be necessary to bring them. But yet, there is something obscure about it. It reminds me of the fellow that came into a grocery down here in Menard County, at Salem, where I once lived, and called for a picayune's worth of crackers; so the clerk laid them out on the counter. After sitting awhile, he said to the clerk, 'I don't want these crackers, take them, and give me a glass of cider.' So the clerk put the crackers back into the box, and handed the fellow the cider. After drinking, he started for the door. 'Here, Bill,' called out the clerk, 'pay me for your cider.' 'Why,' said Bill, 'I gave you the crackers for it.' 'Well, then, pay me for the crackers.' 'But I haint had any;' responded Bill. 'That's so,' said the clerk. 'Well, clear out! It seems to me that I've lost a picayune somehow, but I can't make it out exactly.' "So," said Lincoln, after the

ABRAHAM LINCOLN, one of the grandest men this country or the world has ever produced, pure in life and motive, inflexible in his purpose to do right as he understood it, of undaunted courage in carrying out the principles he believed to be true, largehearted, and tender in his sympathy with human suffering—

> Bold as a lion and gentle as a child—
> He lived to bless the world.
> > He broke no promise, served no private end,
> > He gained no title, and he lost no friend.

John B. Gough

WORCESTER, 1880.

SPEECH TO VARIOUS REPUBLICAN ASSO· CIATIONS, NEW YORK.

It was not intimated to me that I was brought into the room where Daniel Webster and Henry Clay had made speeches, and where, in my position, I might be expected to do something like those men, or do something worthy of myself or my audience. I have been occupying a position since the Presidential election, of silence, of avoiding public speaking, of avoiding public writing; I have been doing so, because I thought upon full consideration that was the proper course for me to take. I have not kept silence since the Presidential election from any party wantonness, or from any indifference to the anxiety that pervades the minds of men about the aspect of the political affairs of this country. I have kept silence for the reason that I supposed it was peculiarly proper that I should do so until the time came when, according to the custom of the country, I could speak officially. I alluded to the custom of the Presidential-elect, at the time of taking the oath of office; that is what I meant by the custom of the country. I do suppose that, while the political drama being enacted in this country, at this time, is rapidly shifting its scenes— forbidding an anticipation, with any degree of certainty, to-day, what we shall see to-morrow—it was peculiarly fitting that I should see it all, up to the last minute, before I should take ground that I might be disposed (by the shifting of the scenes afterwards) also to shift. I have said several times, upon this journey, and I now repeat it to you, that when the time does come I shall then take the ground that I think is right, right for the North, for the South, for the East, for the West, for the whole country. And in doing so, I hope to feel no necessity pressing upon me to say anything in conflict with the Constitution; in conflict with the continued Union of these States, in conflict with the perpetuation of the liberties of this people, or anything in conflict with anything whatever that I have ever given you reason to expect from me.

13

LINCOLN was the truest friend I ever had and therefore my estimate of his character must be taken "cum grano salis." He was the most conscientious man I ever knew, and ranks with Washington in genius, public service, and patriotism. They will go down to posterity in equal love, admiration, and gratitude. After this I need not say that he was the man of his times : and such is the verdict of his contemporaries.

C M Clay

WHITE HALL, 1880.

SPEECH IN THE SENATE CHAMBER.

TRENTON, NEW JERSEY.

MAY I be pardoned if, upon this occasion, I mention that away back in my childhood, the earliest days of my being able to read, I got hold of a small book, such a one as few of the younger members have seen, "Weem's Life of Washington." I remember all the accounts there given of the battle-fields and struggles for liberties of the country, and none fixed themselves upon my imagination so deeply as the struggle here at Trenton, New Jersey. The crossing of the river, the contest with the Hessians ; the great hardships endured at that time, all fixed themselves on my memory, more than any single revolutionary event ; and you all know, for you have all been boys, how these early impressions last longer than any others. I recollect thinking then, boy even though I was, that there must have been something more than common that these men struggled for. I am exceedingly anxious that that thing which they struggled for ; that something even more than National Independence ; that something that held out a great promise to all the people of the world to all time to come —I am exceedingly anxious that this Union, the Constitution, and the liberties of the people shall be perpetuated in accordance with the original idea for which that struggle was made, and I shall be most happy indeed if

I shall be an humble instrument in the hands of the Almighty and of this, his most chosen people, as the chosen instrument—also in the hands of the Almighty—for perpetuating the object of that great struggle.

SPEECH AT TRENTON, NEW JERSEY.

DELIVERED IN THE HOUSE OF ASSEMBLY.

I SHALL endeavor to take the ground I deem most just to the North, the East, the West, the South, and the whole country. I take it, I hope, in good temper, certainly with no malice towards any section. I shall do all that may be in my power to promote a peaceful settle-ment of all our difficulties. The man does not live who is more devoted to peace than I am, none who would do more to preserve it, but it may be necessary to put the foot down firmly. And if I do my duty and do right you will sustain me, will you not? Received, as I am, by the members of a Legislature, the majority of whom do not agree with me in political sentiments, I trust that I may have their assistance in piloting the ship of State through this voyage, surrounded by perils as it is, for if it should suffer wreck now, there will be no pilot ever needed for another voyage.

H IS freedom from passion and bitterness—in his acute sense of justice—in his courageous faith in the right, and his inextinguishable hatred of wrong—in warm and heartfelt sympathy and mercy, in his coolness of judgment, in his unquestioned rectitude of intention——in a word, in his ability to lift himself for his country's sake above all mere partizanship, in all the marked traits of his character combined, he has had no parallel since Washington, and, while our republic endures he will live with him in the grateful hearts of his grateful countrymen.

SOUTH BEND, 1880.

ADDRESS TO THE MAYOR AND CITIZENS
OF PHILADELPHIA'

I DEEM it a happy circumstance that this dissatisfied position of our fellow-citizens does not point us to anything in which they are being injured, or about to be injured; for which reason I have felt all the while justified in concluding that the crisis, the panic, the anxiety of the country at this time, is artificial. If there be those who differ with me upon this subject, they have not pointed out the substantial difficulty that exists. I do not mean to say that an artificial panic may not do considerable harm; that it has done such I do not deny. I promise you, in all sincerity, that I bring to the work a sincere heart. Whether I will bring a head equal to that heart will be for future times to determine. It were useless for me to speak of details of plans now; I shall speak officially next Monday week, if ever. If I should not speak then, it were useless for me to do so now. If I do speak then it is useless for me to do so now. When I do speak, I shall take such ground as I deem best calculated to restore peace, harmony, and prosperity to the country, and tend to the perpetuity of the nation and the liberty of these States and these people. Your worthy Mayor has expressed the wish, in which I join with him, that it were convenient for me to remain in your city long enough to consult your merchants and manufacturers; or,

as it were, to listen to those breathings rising within the
consecrated walls wherein the Constitution of the United
States, and I will add, the Declaration of Independence,
were originally framed and adopted. I assure you and
your Mayor that I had hoped, on this occasion, and upon
all occasions during my life, that I shall do nothing inconsistent with the teachings of these holy and most
sacred walls. I never asked anything that does not
breathe from these sacred walls. All my political warfare
has been in favor of the teachings that came forth from
these sacred walls. May my right hand forget its cunning, and my tongue cleave to the roof my mouth, if ever
I prove false to those teachings.

SPEECH IN INDEPENDENCE HALL

AT PHILADELPHIA.

I HAVE never had a feeling, politically, that did not spring from the sentiments embodied in the Declaration of Independence. I have often pondered over the dangers which were incurred by the men who assembled here and framed and adopted that Declaration. I have pondered over the toils that were endured by the officers and soldiers of the army who achieved that independence. I have often inquired of myself what great principle or idea it was that kept this Confederacy so long together. It was not the mere matter of the separation of the colonies from the mother-land, but that sentiment in the Declaration of Independence which gave liberty not alone to the people of this country, but I hope to the world for all future time. It was that which gave promise that, in due time, the weight would be lifted from the shoulders of all men. This is the sentiment embodied in the Declaration of Independence. Now, my friends, can this country be saved on that basis? If it can, I shall consider myself one of the happiest men in the world if I can help to save it. If it cannot be saved upon that principle it will be truly awful. But if this country cannot be saved without giving up that principle, I was about to say *I would rather be assassinated on this spot than surrender it.*

ABRAHAM LINCOLN'S greatness and worth lay in his simple manhood. So that the excuse we offer for the faults and failings of some great men, "They were only human," was the very crown of his excellence. He was a whole man, human to the core of his heart.

Robert Collyer

NEW YORK, 1880.

SPEECH

BEFORE INDEPENDENCE HALL, PHILADELPHIA, FEB., 1861
WHILE HOISTING A NEW FLAG.

EACH additional star added to that flag has given additional prosperity and happiness to this country, until it has advanced to its present condition; and its welfare in the future, as well as in the past, is in your hands. Cultivating the spirit that animated our fathers, who gave renown and celebrity to this hall; cherishing that fraternal feeling which has so long characterized us as a nation; excluding passion, ill-temper, and precipitate action on all occasions, I think we may promise ourselves that additional stars shall from time to time be placed upon that flag, until we shall number, as was anticipated by the great historian, five hundred millions of happy and prosperous people.

ABRAHAM LINCOLN RAISING THE AMERICAN FLAG, AT INDEPENDENCE HALL, PHILA., FEB. 1861.

P. 204

I T would be difficult, in many words, and perhaps not more difficult in a few, to state my estimate of the " Life and Services of Abraham Lincoln." It was a hard life, a busy life, an American life, and a great life ; and it rendered services to the country which can hardly be over-estimated, and which it has been the fortune of, perhaps, only two other men to equal.

UTICA, 1880.

IT is not probable that the memory of Abraham Lincoln will perish from the earth, so long as "a government of the people, by the people, and for the people" shall stand. Nevertheless, I believe that anything which tends to bring the honest, true life of so grand a man nearer to the thoughts and hearts of each generation, is a worthy work.

IOWA CITY, 1882.

SPEECH

I HAVE already gone through one exceedingly interesting scene this morning, in the ceremonies at Philadelphia. Under the high conduct of gentlemen there, I
was for the first time allowed the privilege of standing
in old Independence Hall, to have a few words addressed
to me there, and opening up to me an opportunity of ex-
pressing, with much regret, that I had not more time to
express something of my own feelings, excited by the
occasion, somewhat to harmonize and give shape to the
feelings that had been really the feelings of my whole
life. Besides this, our friends there had provided a magnificent flag of our country; they had arranged so that
I was given the honor of raising it to the head of its
staff. And, when it went up, I was pleased that it went
to its place by the strength of my own feeble arm, when,
according to the arrangement, the cord was pulled, and
it floated gloriously to the wind, without an accident, in the
light, glowing sunshine of the morning. I could not help
hoping that there was, in the entire success of that beautiful ceremony, at least something of an omen of what is
to come. How could I help feeling, then, as I often
have felt? In the whole of that proceeding, I was a very
humble instrument. I had not provided the flag. I had

not made the arrangements for elevating it to its place; I had applied but a very small portion of my feeble strength in raising it. In the whole transaction, I was in the hands of the people who had arranged it, and, if I can have the same generous co-operation of the people of the nation, I think the flag of our country may yet be kept flaunting gloriously. It is not with any pleasure that I contemplate the possibility that a necessity may arise in this country for the use of the military arm. While I am exceedingly gratified to see the manifestation, upon your streets, of your military force here, and exceedingly gratified at your promise here, to use that force upon a proper emergency—while I make these acknowledgments, I desire to repeat, in order to preclude any possible misconstruction, that I do most sincerely hope that we shall have no use for them; that it will never become their duty to shed blood, and most especially, never to shed fraternal blood. I promise that, so far as I may have wisdom to direct, if so painful a result shall in any wise be brought about, it shall be through no fault of mine.

14

SPEECH

TO THE MAYOR AND COMMON COUNCIL OF WASHINGTON.

MR. MAYOR:

I thank you, and through you the municipal authorities of this city who accompany you, for this welcome. And as it is the first time in my life, since the present phase in politics has presented itself in this country, that I have said anything publicly within a region of country where the institution of slavery exists, I will take this occasion to say, that I think very much of the ill-feeling that has existed and still exists between the people in the sections from which I came and the people here, is dependent upon a misunderstanding of one another. I therefore avail myself of this opportunity to assure you, Mr. Mayor, and all the gentlemen present, that I have not now, and never have had, any other than as kindly feelings towards you as the people of my own section. I have not now, and never have had, any disposition to treat you in any respect otherwise than as my own neighbors. I have not now any purpose to withhold from you any of the benefits of the Constitution, under any circumstances, that I would not feel myself constrained to withhold from my own neighbors, and I hope, in a word, that when we shall become better acquainted —and I say it with great confidence—we shall like each other the more.

I have reached this city of Washington under circumstances considerably differing from those under which any other man has ever reached it. I hope that, if things shall go along as prosperously as I believe we all desire they may, I may have it in my power to remove something of this misunderstanding; that I may be enabled to convince you, and the people of your section of the country, that we regard you as in all things our equals, and in all things entitled to the same respect and the same treatment that we claim for ourselves; that we are in no wise disposed, if it were in our power, to oppress you, to deprive you of any of your rights under the Constitution of the United States, or even narrowly to split hairs with you in regard to these rights, but are determined to give you, as far as lies in our hands, all your rights under the Constitution—not grudgingly, but fully and fairly. I hope that, by thus dealing with you, we will become better acquainted, and be better friends.

PROCLAMATION,

APRIL 15, 1861.

Now, Therefore, I, ABRAHAM LINCOLN, President of the United States, by virtue of the power in me vested by the Constitution and the laws, have thought fit to call forth, and hereby do call forth, the militia of the several States of the Union to the aggregate number of 75,000, in order to suppress said combination and to cause the laws to be duly executed. The details for this object will be immediately communicated to the State authorities through the War Department.

I appeal to the loyal citizens to favor, facilitate and aid this effort to maintain the honor, the integrity, and the existence of our National Union, and the perpetuity of popular government, and to redress wrongs already long enough endured.

I deem it proper to say that the first service assigned to the force hereby called forth, will probably be to re-possess the forts, places and property which have been seized from the Union, and in every event the utmost care will be observed, consistent with the objects aforesaid, to avoid any devastation, any destruction of, or interference with property, or any disturbance of peaceful citizens in any part of the country; and I hereby command the persons composing the combination aforesaid, to disperse and retire peaceably to their respective abodes within twenty days from this date.

M Y personal recollection of Mr. Lincoln, and what
I have seen of him, in and about Springfield, dates
from about the year 1842, and was almost continuous
until he left for Washington, in February, 1861 ; and, of
course, I can say of, or concerning him, nothing but what
might be said by hundreds of others who knew him as
well, and much better, than I did. There was one trait
in Mr. Lincoln's character that I can never forget; that
was his great kindness and generous sympathy for the
young men, who were struggling night and day, to reach a
place at the bar, as lawyers. I well remember his coming
in the office of Col. Baker, where I studied and read law,
almost every afternoon ; and with his cheerful face, and
hearty greeting, to myself and other students, "How are
you this afternoon, boys ?" seat himself, and take up some
text-book, that some of us were reading, and give us a
close and rigid examination, laughing heartily at our answers, at times ; and always made the hour he spent with
us interesting and instructive ; occasionally relating, to
the great amusement of all present, an anecdote ; and,
after the hour so spent, he could go to a back yard, used
by the students, and join them in a game of ball, with as
much zest as any of us. But, when his watch told him
the hour was out, he would at once quit the game, and
bid us good-evening. Many years after, years that the
writer had spent in the active practice of law, I met Mr.
Lincoln, and was associated with him in about the last
case he had any connection with. This, I think, was in

the year 1859, and after his name had become a household word in all the land—after he had won imperishable renown as a political debater, with Senator Douglas; and while his great mind was full of the momentous questions then agitating the public mind—he could not, and did not, forget an old widow lady who had been, long years before, kind to him, while *he* was struggling, alone and unaided, in a new country, for the means to enable him to qualify himself for the high position afterward called upon, by his countrymen, to fill. This old widow lady, named Armstrong, known by almost every one in Menard Co. as Aunt Hannah, had a son—a wild boy of about twenty years of age—who, with others, became involved in a difficulty at a camp meeting, held in Mason Co., near Salt Creek, resulting in the killing of a man named Metzker. Young Armstrong, and another young man, were indicted for murder in the first degree. Aunt Hannah, young Armstrong's mother, employed the writer, and a lawyer named Dillworth, to defend her son. We obtained an order of court, allowing separate trials, and took a change of venue, on the part of Armstrong, to Cass Co., Illinois, in the spring of '59. Upon the writer reaching Beardstown, and while in consultation with my associate, at the hotel, Mr. Lincoln was announced. Upon entering, he gave us the gratifying information that he would, at the request of Aunt Hannah, assist us in the case of her son. This was agreeable news to us. We furnished Mr. Lincoln such facts as had come to our knowledge; he walked across the room two or three times, was again seated, and asked us for our line of defense, and the kind of jury we thought of taking. We were in favor of young men. He asked our reasons. We replied, the defendant being a young man, we thought the sympathies of young men could be more easily aroused in his behalf. Mr. Lincoln differed with us, and requested the privilege of making the challenges, which we accorded to him, and to me. The most remarkable-looking twelve men were sworn, that I had ever seen in a jury-box. All were past middle life, and the more strict the men were in enforcing obedience to the law, and the good order of society, the better pleased Mr. Lincoln was with them. The trial progressed, evidence heard and instructions given, and the State was heard from through its attorney. Mr. Lincoln made the closing argument for the defense. A grander, or a more powerful and eloquent speech, never, in my opinion, fell from the lips of man ; and when he closed, there was not a dry eye in the court-room. The young man was acquitted, for which Mr. Lincoln would not receive a cent. I have made this mention of some of my recollections of Mr. Lincoln, longer, perhaps, than I ought— but I could not well avoid it—for, taking him all in all, I think him one of the greatest men America has ever produced.

LEXINGTON, 1882.

REPLY

TO GOVERNOR HICKS AND MAYOR BROWN.

FOR the future, troops must be brought here, but I make no point of bringing them through Baltimore. Without any military knowledge myself, of course I must leave details to General Scott. He hastily said this morning, in the presence of these gentlemen, "March them around Baltimore and not through it." I sincerely hope the General, on fuller reflection, will consider this practical and proper, and that you will not object to it. By this, a collision of the people of Baltimore with the troops will be avoided, unless they go out of their way to seek it. I hope you will exert your influence to prevent this. Now and ever I shall do all in my power for peace, consistently with the maintenance of the government.

APRIL 20, 1861.

THE public services of Mr. Lincoln are well known to the world. But there is much of the man, the inner man and his real characteristics—familiar only to his neighbors and intimate friends, as they knew him, before he was so suddenly called to the Presidency of the United States, from a country village, where, and near which most of his life had been spent, to assume the "cares of state," and carry, Atlas-like, the destinies of the Western Continent upon his brawny and herculean shoulders. The world at large will never know as do those living neighbors and friends the real greatness of the man. Personally, I had but little intimate acquaintance with Mr. Lincoln, compared to what many others had, and what I observed of his character was mainly while sitting to me, prior to his nomination in 1860, for the clay model of his bust. But he impressed me, before I ever spoke with him, with a feeling akin to reverence—a feeling of affection. He was just the man to strike with favor every person who knew toil and privation—and what could be more natural ? for he himself had been a toiler at every drudgery, and experienced the severest privations from earliest boyhood to mature manhood. Its effect was plainly visible in his figure, in the form of the bones, muscle and sinew, in his motion and in his speech. He was a *plebeian* in the truest sense, and his prototype cannot be found among the great men of ancient or modern times. He has been compared with King Servius Tullius, but might with more propriety be compared with the Czar Alexander II. of Russia, who by his own personal will freed so many millions of serfs, in opposition to the wishes of his nobles; while the former freed no slaves, but granted some elective privileges to the plebeian claims, subject always to the approval of the patrician senators, and built a five-mile wall around Rome. But neither of these despots (one a King and the other an Emperor) possessed the characteristics of Abraham Lincoln. The fact that all three were assassinated does not signify much in making them resemblances of each other. In studying the marble and bronze portraits of the rulers and great men of ancient medieval and modern times, the writer has found none possessing any decided resemblance to Mr. Lincoln, whose features are distinctly in contrast with European types and may properly be designated as purely American. Our own brief history gives us the names of *five* distinctly remarkable men who were Presidents of the United States, greater than all others, more remarkable because they carved out and achieved their own immortality, and none but one of these five referred to was a college graduate, and he, by his own indomitable will, perseverance and industry, through extreme poverty, alone obtained a collegiate education. None of these five men were sons of presidents, nor did they possess wealthy and distinguished relatives (except, perhaps, the first) to advance and place them in high stations. No! they all earned their honors and promotion from stage to stage, from young boyhood, in the rough, rugged school of experience, toil and hardship, which ripened and fitted them for every station to which they were successively advanced up to the highest and proudest positions in the land. Nature had endowed these favorite sons with a wealth of ideas, a wealth of self-reliance, industry, honesty, patience and patriotism, far greater and more valuable than inherited riches, titles, or *class* privileges. Imagine Abraham Lincoln, as a sturdy youth in the depths of the primeval forests of the west, alone with his axe, felling the giant trees, lopping off the limbs, dividing the trunks in regular lengths, then, with beetle and wedges splitting them into rails, now and then wearily sitting on a stump or log, or lying on the ground to rest himself, and snatching a few moments to study a book, or perhaps contemplating the solitude of the forest, while watching the birds and listening to their wild songs. Then, in the grand moon-lit night, while floating silently down the mighty Mississippi on his flat-boat, he doubtless thought, planned and dreamed of his ambitious desire to rise in the world and get above his present lowly condition. Noble and ambitious resolves were weaving in his young brain. He, like the others of the immortal five, believed in himself to be able to grapple with the difficulties of life and take the responsibilities thrust upon him *by the people.* It was fortunate for the fame of these men that events of sufficient magnitude occurred, affording the opportunities to prove to the world their real fitness, talent and greatness to be imperishably engraved upon history's tablets among the immortal men of all ages. If the ambitious young men of the present and future generations will earnestly study and imitate these sublime characters, relying as they did upon their own honest, patient toil and privation of lux-

THERE is and can be but one opinion regarding the life and work performed by that *great man* Lincoln. He did more to perpetuate the existence of free institutions and a republican form of government than any man that has ever lived, and the debt mankind owes his memory can never be repaid.

He had but one fault. He was too sympathetic and tender-hearted. I well recollect one night about two o'clock A. M. in the early days of the war, that I was with him in the telegraph office at General McClellan's head-quarters. He arose from his chair to leave, straightened himself up and remarked, "To-morrow night I shall have a terrible headache." When asked the cause he replied, "To-morrow is hangman's day and I shall have to act upon death sentences," and I shall never forget the sad and sorrowful expression that came over his face. It is well known that Congress relieved him from the consideration of death sentences for desertion and other capital offenses, and conferred it upon army commanders.

George Stoneman

SAN GABRIEL, 1881.

MESSAGE TO CONGRESS

ASSEMBLED IN EXTRA SESSION, JULY 4, 1861.

I AM most happy to believe that the plain people understand and appreciate this. It is worthy of note that while in this, the Government's hour of trial, large numbers of those in the army and navy who have been favored with the offices, have resigned and proved false to the hand which pampered them, not one common soldier or common sailor is known to have deserted his flag. Great honor is due to those officers who have remained true despite the example of their treacherous associates, but the greatest honor and most important fact of all, is the unanimous firmness of the common soldiers and common sailors. To the last man, so far as known, they have successfully resisted the traitorous efforts of those whose commands but an hour before they obeyed as absolute law. This is the patriotic instinct of plain people. They understand without an argument that the destroying the Government which was made by Washington means no good to them. Our popular Government has often been called an experiment. Two points in it our people have settled: the successful establishing and the successful administering of it. One still remains: its successful maintenance against a formidable internal attempt to overthrow it. It is now for them to demonstrate to the world that those who can fairly carry an election, can also suppress a rebellion; that ballots are the rightful and peaceful successors of bullets, and that when ballots have fairly and constitutionally decided, there can be no successful appeal back to bullets; that there can be no successful appeal except to ballots themselves at succeeding elections. Such will be a great lesson of peace, teaching men that what they cannot take by an election, neither can they take by a war, teaching all the folly of being the beginners of a war.

As a private citizen the Executive could not have consented that these institutions shall perish, much less could he, in betrayal of so vast and so sacred a trust as these free people had confided to him. He felt that he had no moral right to shrink, nor even to count the chances of his own life in what might follow.

In full view of his great responsibility, he has so far done what he has deemed his duty. You will now, according to your own judgment, perform yours. He sincerely hopes that your views and your actions may so accord with his as to assure all faithful citizens who have been disturbed in their rights, of a certain and speedy restoration to them, under the Constitution and laws. and having thus chosen our cause without guile, and with pure purpose, let us renew our trust in God, and go forward without fear and with manly hearts.

PERSONAL CONFERENCE

WITH THE REPRESENTATIVES FROM THE BORDER STATES,
JULY 12, 1861.

AFTER the adjournment of Congress, now near, I shall have no opportunity of seeing you for several months. Believing that you of the Border States hold more power for good than any other equal number of members, I feel it a duty which I cannot justifiably waive to make this appeal to you. I intend no reproach or complaint when I assure you that, in my opinion, if you all had voted for the resolution in the gradual emancipation message of last March, the war would now be substantially ended. And the plan therein proposed is yet one of the most potent and swift means of ending it. Let the states which are in rebellion see definitely and certainly that in no event will the states you represent ever join their proposed Confederacy, and they cannot much longer maintain the contest. But you cannot divest them of their hope to ultimately have you with them so long as you show a determination to perpetuate the institution within your own states.

If the war continues long, as it must if the object be not sooner attained, the institution in your states will be extinguished by mere friction and abrasion—by the mere incidents of the war. It will be gone, and you will have nothing valuable in lieu of it. Much of its value is gone already. How much better for you and for your people to take the step which at once shortens the war, and secures substantial compensation for that which is sure to be wholly lost in any other event! How much better to thus save the money which else we sink forever in the war! How much better to do it while we can, lest the war, ere long, render us pecuniarily unable to do it! How much better for you as sellers, and the nation as buyer, to sell out and buy out that without which the war could never have been, than to sink both the thing to be sold and the price of it, in cutting one another's throats? I do not speak of emancipation at once, but of a decision at once to emancipate gradually.

Upon these considerations, I have again begged your attention to the message of March last. Before leaving the Capitol, consider and discuss it among yourselves. You are patriots and statesmen, and as such, I pray you to consider this proposition, and, at the least, commend it to the consideration of your states and people. As you would perpetuate popular government for the best people in the world, I beseech you that you do in no wise omit this. Our common country is in great peril, demanding the loftiest views and boldest action to bring a speedy relief. Once relieved, its form of government is saved to the world; its beloved history and cherished memories are vindicated, and its happy future fully assured and rendered inconceivably grand. To you, more than to any others, the privilege is given to assure that happiness, and swell that grandeur, and to link your own names therewith forever.

15

REPLY TO HORACE GREELEY.

My paramount object is to save the Union, and neither to save or destroy slavery.

If there be those who would not save the Union unless they could at the same time save slavery, I do not agree with them. If there be those who would not save the Union unless they could at the same time destroy slavery, I do not agree with them. *My paramount object is to save the Union, and not either to save or destroy slavery.* If I could save the Union without freeing any slave, I would do it. If I could save it by freeing all the slaves I would do it; and if I could do it by freeing some and leaving others alone, I would also do that. What I do about slavery and the colored race I do because I believe it helps to save the Union, and what I forbear, I forbear because I do not believe it helps to save the Union. I shall do less whenever I shall believe that what I am doing hurts the cause, and I shall do more whenever I believe doing more will help the cause.

THERE is but one opinion of the character of Abraham Lincoln, throughout the world. No living man can add anything to his fame. It will be polished by the wear of time, to a luster which will eclipse the glory of all men, not born as he was, to the boon of immortality.

R. J. Oglesby.

DECATUR, 1880.

REPLY TO A RELIGIOUS DELEGATION

WHO PRESENTED A MEMORIAL REQUESTING MR. LINCOLN TO ISSUE A PROCLAMATION OF UNIVERSAL EMANCIPATION.

I AM approached with the most opposite opinions and advice, and that by religious men, who are equally certain that they represent the divine will. I am sure that either the one or the other class is mistaken in that belief, and perhaps in some respects, both. I hope it will not be irreverent for me to say that if it is probable that God would reveal his will to others, on a point so connected with my duty, it might be supposed he would reveal it directly to me ; for, unless I am more deceived in myself than I often am, it is my earnest desire to know the will of Providence in this matter, and if I can learn what it is I will do it! These are not, however, the days of miracles, and I suppose it will be granted that I am not to expect a direct revelation. I must study the plain physical facts of the case, ascertain what is possible and learn what appears to be wise and right.

The subject is difficult, and good men do not agree. For instance, the other day four gentlemen of standing and intelligence from New York, called as a delegation on business connected with the war ; but before leaving two of them earnestly besought me to proclaim general emancipation, upon which the other two at once attacked them. I can assure you that the subject is on my mind, by day and night, more than any other. Whatever shall appear to be God's will I will do.

HIS wisdom, his accurate perceptions, his vigor of intellect, his humor and his unselfish patriotism are known to all. But what impressed me even more than these was the sweetness of his whole nature—his great loving heart. It was this, glorifying his other great qualities, that so endeared him to the people and caused his death to be mourned with such an unequaled depth of sorrow and abundance of tears. No man can take *his* place in the hearts of the American people.

Cyrus Northrop.

YALE COLLEGE, 1882.

INAUGURAL ADDRESS,

DELIVERED ON THE FOURTH DAY OF MARCH, 1861.

APPREHENSION seems to exist among the people of the Southern States that by the accession of a Republican administration their property and their peace and personal security are to be endangered. There has never been any reasonable cause for such apprehension. Indeed, the most ample evidence to the contrary has all the while existed and been open to their inspection. It is found in nearly all the published speeches of him who now addresses you. I do but quote from one of those speeches when I declare, that "I have no purpose, directly or indirectly, to interfere with the institution of slavery in the States where it exists. I believe I have no lawful right to do so, and I have no inclination to do so." Those who nominated and elected me did so with full knowledge that I had made this and many similar declarations, and had never recanted them.

Before entering upon so grave a matter as the destruction of our national fabric, with all its benefits, its memories and its hopes, would it not be wise to ascertain precisely why we do it? Will you hazard so desperate a step while there is any possibility that any portion of the ills you fly from have no real existence? Will you, while the certain ills you fly to are greater than all the real ones you fly from—will you risk the commission of so fearful a mistake?

Physically speaking, we cannot separate. We cannot remove our respective sections from each other, nor build an impassable wall between them. A husband and wife may be divorced, and go out of the presence and beyond the reach of each other, but the different parts of our country cannot do this. They cannot but remain face to face; and intercourse, either amicable or hostile, must continue between them. Is it impossible, then, to make that intercourse more advantageous or more satisfactory after separation than before? Can aliens make treaties easier than friends can make laws? Can treaties be more faithfully enforced between aliens than laws can among friends? Suppose you go to war, you cannot fight always; and when, after much loss on both sides, and no gain on either, you cease fighting, the identical old questions, as to terms of intercourse, are again upon you.

The Chief Magistrate derives all his authority from the people, and they have conferred none upon him to fix terms for the separation of the States. The people themselves can do this also if they choose; but the Executive, as such, has nothing to do with it. His duty is to administer the present government as it came to his hands, and to transmit it, unimpaired by him, to his successor.

Why should there not be a patient confidence in the ultimate justice of the people? Is there any better or equal hope in the world? In our present differences, is either party without faith of being in the right? If the Almighty Ruler of nations, with his eternal truth and justice, be on your side of the North, or yours of the

South, that truth and that justice will surely prevail, by the judgment of this great tribunal of the American people.

By the form of the government under which we live, the same people have wisely given their public servants but little power for mischief; and have, with equal wisdom, provided for the return of that little to their own hands at very short intervals. While the people retain their virtue and vigilance, no administration, by any extreme of wickedness or folly, can very seriously injure the government in the short space of four years.

My countrymen, one and all, think calmly and well upon this whole subject. Nothing valuable can be lost by taking time. If there be an object to hurry any of you in hot haste to a step which you would never take deliberately, that object will be frustrated by taking time; but no good can be frustrated by it. Such of you as are now dissatisfied still have the old Constitution unimpaired, and, on the sensitive point, the laws of your own framing under it; while the new administration will have no immediate power, if it would, to change either. If it were admitted that you who are dissatisfied hold the right side in the dispute, there still is no single good reason for precipitate action. Intelligence, patriotism, Christianity, and a firm reliance on Him who has never yet forsaken this favored land, are still competent to adjust, in the best way, all our present difficulty.

In your hands, my dissatisfied fellow-countrymen, and not in mine, is the momentous issue of civil war. The Government will not assail you.

You can have no conflict without being yourselves the aggressors. You have no oath registered in Heaven to

destroy the Government ; while I shall have the most
solemn one to " preserve, protect and defend " it.

I am loth to close. We are not enemies, but friends.
We must not be enemies. Though passion may have
strained, it must not break our bonds of affection.

The mystic chords of memory, stretching from every
battlefield and patriot grave to every living heart and
hearthstone all over this broad land, will yet swell the
chorus of the Union, when again touched, as surely they
will be, by the better angels of our nature.

I NEVER had personally an opportunity to know or study Mr. Lincoln, and my ideas of him are made up altogether from reading, and from conversations with prominent gentlemen who knew him well. From these sources, I have the impression firmly fixed, that Mr. Lincoln possessed great native good sense and a well-balanced head, what is generally called "common sense." He had an intuitive judgment of men, and he studied men closely; with these he combined a liberal and charitable judgment, and viewed the shortcomings of his fellows with leniency, mercy and goodness of heart. His intentions were good, and, as I think, on the side of his country at large, and I am of the opinion but few, very few, men would have passed through the ordeal of war, and such a war, as successfully as he did. The blow that struck him down inflicted a wound upon the whole country. His loss to the country was severe indeed, for I believe, had he lived, the work of pacification, or quieting the Southern States to practical relations with the Union —to use his own language—would have progressed more smoothly, and been consummated in less time, and with less expense, less bitterness and less loss to all parties.

In Mr. Lincoln's history there is as much profound stimulus to the young men of the country who desire to secure it, as in that of any man who has figured in our annals.

A H Garland

LITTLE ROCK, 1882.

FIRST ANNUAL MESSAGE

TO CONGRESS, DECEMBER 3, 1861.

THE war continues. In considering the policy to be adopted for suppressing the insurrection, I have been anxious and careful that the inevitable conflict for this purpose shall not degenerate into a violent and remorseless revolutionary struggle. I have, therefore, in every case thought it proper to keep the integrity of the Union prominent as the primary object of the contest on our part, leaving all questions which are not of vital military importance to the more deliberate action of the legislature.

In my present position, I could scarcely be justified were I to omit raising a warning voice against this approach of returning despotism.

It is not needed nor fitting here, that a general argument should be made in favor of popular institutions ; but there is one point, with its connections, not so hackneyed as most others, to which I ask a brief attention. It is the effort to place *capital* on an equal footing with, if not above *labor*, in the structure of government. It is assumed that labor is available only in connection with capital ; that nobody labors unless somebody else, owning capital, somehow, by the use of it, induces him to labor. This assumed, it is next considered whether it is best that capital shall *hire* laborers, and thus induce them to work by their own consent, or *buy* them, and drive them to it without their consent. Having proceeded so far, it is naturally concluded that all laborers are either *hired* laborers or what we call slaves. And further, it is assumed that whoever is once a hired laborer is fixed in that condition for life.

Now, there is no such relation between capital and labor as assumed; nor is there any such thing as a free man being fixed for life in the condition of a hired laborer. Both these assumptions are false, and all inferences from them are groundless.

Labor is prior to, and independent of capital. Capital is only the fruit of labor, and could never have existed if labor had not first existed. Labor is the superior of capital, and deserves much the higher consideration. Capital has its rights, which are as worthy of protection as any other rights. Nor is it denied that there is, and probably always will be, a relation between labor and capital, producing mutual benefits. The error is in assuming that the whole labor of a community exists within that relation. A few men own capital, and that few avoid labor themselves, and, with their capital, hire or buy another few to labor for them. A large majority belong to neither class—neither work for others, nor have others working for them. In most of the Southern States a majority of the whole people, of all colors, are neither slaves nor masters; while in the Northern a large majority are neither hirers nor hired. Men with their families—wives, sons, and daughters—work for themselves on their farms, in their houses, and in their shops, taking the whole product to themselves, and asking no favors of capital on the one hand, nor of hired laborers or slaves on the other. It is not forgotten that a considerable number of persons mingle their own labor with capital—that is, they labor with their own hands, and also buy or hire others to labor for them; but this is only a mixed, not a distinct, class. No principle stated is disturbed by the existence of this mixed class.

Again, as has already been said, there is not, of necessity, any such thing as the free hired laborer being fixed to that condition for life. Many independent men everywhere in these States, a few years back in their lives, were hired laborers. The prudent, penniless beginner in the world labors for wages awhile, saves a surplus with which to buy tools or land for himself; then labors on his own account another while, and at length hires another new beginner to help him. This is the just and generous, and prosperous system, which opens the way to all, gives hope to all, and consequent energy and progress, and improvement of condition to all. No men living are more worthy to be trusted than those who toil up from poverty—none less inclined to take, or touch, aught which they have not honestly earned. Let them beware of surrendering a politicial power which they already possess, and which, if surrendered, will surely be used to close the door of advancement against such as they, and to fix new disabilities and burdens upon them till all of liberty shall be lost.

The struggle *of* to-day is not altogether *for* to-day—it is for a vast future also. With a reliance on Providence, all the more firm and earnest, let us proceed in the great task which events have devolved upon us.

I WAS on duty in Washington in 1861, when Mr. Lincoln was inaugurated, and knew him quite well. But I never saw him after about the first part of February, 1862. In the short term of my acquaintance with him, I was always impressed with the great ability which he displayed in his view of the situation of the country at that time, with the patience which he showed in listening to the views of people of all shades of opinion in the discussion of various subjects, and with the good judgment which in my opinion he displayed in coming to a decision after hearing both sides of a question.

No one could have known him well at that time without coming to the conclusion that all of his energy and ability were devoted to bringing the country through the war successfully. All side issues were avoided, nothing but the one end of the preservation of the Union was kept in view. Beset by fanatics of all sides of the question, he steered clear of all extremes, and his patriotism and good sense enabled him to do the right things at the right times. In his appointment of leading general officers at this time, the fitness of the men guided him, and I know a case in which he appointed a man against the advice of his Cabinet, because he had given the man a promise that if he raised a brigade he should be made a Brigadier-General, believing that this man represented a class which it was important to conciliate. The condition having been fulfilled, he appointed the man notwithstand-

I KNEW Mr. Lincoln well and intimately. We were both members of the Thirtieth Congress, that is, from 1847 to 4th March, 1849. We both belonged to the Whig organization of that day, and were both ardent supporters of General Taylor to the Presidency in 1848. Mr. Lincoln, Mr. Wm. Ballard Preston, and Mr. Thos. S. Flournoy of Va., Mr. Toombs of Georgia, Mr. E. C. Cambell of Florida, and one or two others, and myself formed the first Congressional Taylor Club ; we were known as the Young Indians, who by our extensive correspondence organized the Taylor movement throughout the country, which resulted in his nomination at Philadelphia. Mr. Lincoln was careful as to his manners, awkward in his speech, but was possessed of a very strong, clear and vigorous mind. He always attracted the riveted attention of the House when he spoke ; his manner of speech as well as thought was original. He had no model. He was a man of strong convictions, and was what Carlyle would have called an earnest man. He abounded in anecdotes ; he illustrated everything that he was talking or speaking about by an anecdote ; his anecdotes were always exceedingly apt and pointed, and socially he always kept his company in a roar of laughter. In my last interview with him at the celebrated Hampton Roads Conference in 1865, this trait of his character seemed to be as prominent and striking as ever. He was a man of strong attachments, and his nature overflowed

16

ABRAHAM LINCOLN was the greatest President that ever occupied the Executive chair, and the best story-teller ever known to a free people.

Hugh J. Hastings

NEW YORK, 1881.

I COULD wish that fitting words would offer themselves to me to add to the multitude of tributes to the memory of Abraham Lincoln, but I fear that I should hardly find a phrase that eulogy has not applied or a sentiment to which patriotism has not given expression.

O. W. Holmes

BOSTON, 1882.

PROCLAMATION

RELATIVE TO GENERAL HUNTER'S ORDER DECLARING SLAVES
WITHIN HIS DEPARTMENT FREE.

I FURTHER make known, that whether it be competent
for me, as Commander-in-Chief of the Army and Navy,
to declare the slaves of any State or States free; and
whether, at any time or in any case, it shall have become
a necessity indispensable to the maintenance of the government to exercise such supposed powers, are questions
which, under my responsibility, I reserve to myself, and
which I cannot feel justified in leaving to the decision of
commanders in the field.

The United States ought to co-operate with any State
which may adopt a gradual abolishment of slavery, giving
to such State earnest expression to compensate for its
inconveniences, public and private, produced by such
change of system.

I beg of you a calm and enlarged consideration of
them, ranging, if it may be, far above partisan and personal politics. This proposal makes common object,
casting no reproaches upon any. It acts not the Pharisee.
The change it contemplates would come gently as the
dews of Heaven, not rending or wrecking anything.
Will you not embrace it? So much good has not been
done, by one effort, in all past time, as, in the providence
of God, it is now your high privilege to do. May the
vast future not have to lament that you have neglected it!

MAY 19th, 1862.

I KNEW him as a citizen, a lawyer and a politician, and I knew him afterwards as the President of the United States. His most striking characteristic was his simplicity, next to that was his independence of thought and self-reliance of reason. He had the heart of a child and the intellect of a philosopher. A patriot without guile, a politician without cunning or selfishness, a statesman of practical sense rather than finespun theory. The more I contemplate the history of his public life and services, the more I study his words, his works and the peculiarities of his character, the more I am inclined to believe that Abraham Lincoln was specially inspired, called and led by Providence to be the savior of our nation.

Andrew Shuman

CHICAGO, 1880.

LINCOLN READING THE EMANCIPATION PROCLAMATION TO HIS CABINET,

SEPTEMBER 22.

GENTLEMEN:—I have, as you are aware, thought a great deal about the relation of this war to slavery, and you all remember that several weeks ago I read to you an order I had prepared upon the subject, which, on account of objections made by some of you, was not issued. Ever since then my mind has been much occupied with this subject, and I have thought all along that the time for acting on it might probably come. I think the time has come now; I wish it was a better time. I wish that we were in a better condition. The action of the army against the rebels has not been quite what I should have best liked, but they have been driven out of Maryland, and Pennsylvania is no longer in danger of invasion.

When the rebel army was at Frederick, I determined, as soon as it should be driven out of Maryland, to issue a proclamation of emancipation, such as I thought most likely to be useful. I said nothing to any one, but I made a promise to myself and (hesitating a little), to my Maker. The rebel army is now driven out, and am going to fulfill that promise. I have got you together to hear what I have written down. I do not wish your advice about the main matter, for that I have determined for myself. This I say without intending anything but respect for any one of you. But I already know the views of each on this question. They have been heretofore expressed, and I have considered them as thoroughly and carefully as I can. What I have written is that which my reflections have determined me to say. If there is anything in the expressions I use, or in any minor matter which any one of you think had best be changed, I shall be glad to receive your suggestions. One other observation I will make. I know very well that many others might, in this matter as in others, do better than I can ; and if I was satisfied that the public confidence was more fully possessed by any one of them than by me, and knew of any constitutional way in which he could be put in my place, he should have it. I would gladly yield to him. But though I believe I have not so much of the confidence of the people as I had some time since, I do not know that, all things considered, any other person has more ; and, however this may be, there is no way in which I can have any other man put where I am. I am here ; I must do the best I can and bear the responsibility of taking the course which I feel I ought to take.

ON several occasions, during our unfortunate interne-
cine troubles, it fell to my lot to visit Washington
and have personal interviews with Abraham Lincoln, and
my impression of him then was, and still is, that
he possessed a heart, which, in its great humane
reach, would take in all mankind; that he was
a man of earnest, honest, single purpose; entirely
unostentatious, free from petty jealousy and ignoble
ambition; willing to live and labor for the good
of mankind; full of genuine sympathy; thinking of
everybody except himself; and who felt as if he were
sent to perform a mission on earth, that must hasten to
a completion in order that he might be removed to another scene of action. He was intellectual beyond most
men, with a grand reach of thought, which could grasp a
great subject and comprehend it in its entirety, and then,
with a few well-chosen words he could so simplify as to
make it plain and clear to the most ordinary understanding. Along with a gentle, tender, yearning sympathy, he
had the firmness of a rock and the courage of a lion.
No one in the right ever feared to meet him, and no one
in the wrong could stand unmoved before his deep,
searching gaze. He was evidently a man of destiny—
here for a purpose—to be removed with the end of his
mission. Simple, sincere, honest, earnest, upright, just,

ABRAHAM LINCOLN.

O HONORED name, revered and undecaying,
Engraven on each heart, O soul sublime !
That, like a planet through the heavens straying,
Outlives the wreck of time !

O rough strong soul, your noble self-possession
Is unforgotten. Still your work remains.
You freed from bondage and from vile oppression
A race in clanking chains.

O furrowed face, beloved by all the nation !
O tall gaunt form, to memory fondly dear !
O firm bold hand, our strength and our salvation !
O heart that knew no fear !

Lincoln, your manhood shall survive forever,
Shedding a fadeless halo round your name.
Urging men on, with wise and strong endeavor,
To bright and honest fame !

Through years of care, to rest and joy a stranger,
You saw complete the work you had begun,
Thoughtless of threats, nor heeding death or danger,
You toiled till all was done.

You freed the bondman from his iron master,
You broke the strong and cruel chains he wore,
You saved the Ship of State from foul disaster
And brought her safe to shore.

You fell ! An anxious nation's hopes seemed blighted,
While millions shuddered at your dreadful fall ;
But *God is good!* His wondrous hand has righted
And reunited all.

HE combined the integrity of Washington with the humanity of Wilberforce.

Geo. W. Julian

IRVINGTON, 1880.

NEXT to Washington, the Father of our Independence, stands Abraham Lincoln, the martyr of our Union, in the line of our Presidents.

Philip Schaff

NEW YORK, 1882.

TO THE SYNOD OF THE OLD SCHOOL PRESBYTERIANS OF BALTIMORE,

WHO WAITED UPON HIM IN A BODY.

I SAW, upon taking my position here, I was going to have an administration, if an administration at all, of extraordinary difficulty. It was without exception a time of the greatest difficulty this country ever saw. I was early brought to a lively reflection, that nothing in my power whatever, or others, to rely upon, would succeed, without direct assistance of the Almighty. I have often wished that I was a more devout man than I am; nevertheless, amid the greatest difficulties of my administration, when I could not see any other resort, I would place my whole reliance in God, knowing all would go well, and that he would decide for the right.

TO say that he was pre-eminently an honest man, a frank, sincere, outspoken man, who deceived no one, wronged no one, cajoled no one; that he was a great, strong, fearless man; that he was unselfishly patriotic, a worshiper of the constitution according to the old Whig interpretation of it, a devotee of the Union, an ardent lover of his whole country, hating no one, desiring to punish no one; yearning to see the Union restored, and the old good will and good humor return to bless the land—to say all this is only to say what is testified to by a cloud of witnesses, what no one anywhere will now not gladly admit. He occupied, I think, a larger place in the *affections* of the people than any of the great men who preceded him, and he will have it, I think, in the affection of the generations that are to come. He would have said, if questioned, that he greatly preferred to be so remembered. He endeared himself to the people by ways and practices and observances all worthy and honorable, generous and fair; and kindly memories of him are as general among those who, struggling to achieve political independence, owed chiefly to him their defeat, as they are among the men of the States whose armies obeyed orders and maintained the Union.

Albert Pike

WASHINGTON, 1882.

REPLY TO THE COMMITTEE OF THE LUTHERAN SYNOD OF 1862.

I WELCOME here the representatives of the Evangelical Lutherans of the United States. I accept with gratitude their assurances of the sympathy and support of that enlightened, influential, and loyal class of my fellow-citizens in an important crisis, which involves, in my judgment, not only the civil and religious liberties of our own dear land, but in a large degree the civil and religious liberties of mankind in many countries and through many ages. You well know, gentlemen, and the world knows, how reluctantly I accepted this issue of battle forced upon me, on my advent to this place, by the internal enemies of our country. You all know, the world knows the forces and the resources the public agents have brought into employment to sustain a government against which there has been brought not one complaint of real injury committed against society at home or abroad. You all may recollect that in taking up the sword thus forced into our hands, this government appealed to the prayers of the pious and the good, and declared that it placed its whole dependence upon the favor of God. I now humbly and reverently, in your presence, reiterate the acknowledgment of that dependence, not doubting that, if it shall please the Divine Being who determines the destinies of nations, that this shall remain a united people, they will, humbly seeking the divine guidance, make their prolonged national existence a source of new benefit and conditions of mankind.

ABRAHAM LINCOLN was essentially a thinker who had the courage of his convictions. He was a patriot who was ever willing to make personal sacrifices for his patriotism. He was, therefore, a man of action as well as of reflection. His character was based upon truth, and having been placed by fortune in the proper sphere of action, he showed he was a truly great man.

Abram S. Hewitt

NEW YORK, 1880.
17

SECOND ANNUAL MESSAGE

TO CONGRESS, DECEMBER 1, 1862.

PHYSICALLY speaking, we cannot separate. We cannot remove our respective sections from each other, nor build an impassable wall between them. A husband and wife may be divorced and go out of the presence and beyond the reach of each other; but the different parts of our country cannot do this. They cannot but remain face to face; and intercourse, either amicable or hostile, must continue between them. Is it possible, then, to make that intercourse more advantageous or more satisfactory *after* separation than *before?* Can aliens make treaties easier than friends can make laws? Can treaties be more faithfully enforced between aliens than laws can among friends? Suppose you go to war, you cannot fight always; and when, after much loss on both sides and no gain on either, you cease fighting, the identical old questions, as to terms of intercourse, are again upon you.

There is no line, straight or crooked, suitable for a national boundary, upon which to divide. Trace through, from east to west, upon the line between the free and slave country, and we shall find a little more than one-third of its length are rivers, easy to be crossed, and populated—or soon to be populated—thickly upon both sides; while nearly all its remaining length are merely surveyors' lines, over which people may walk back and forth without any consciousness of their presence. No part of this line can be made any more difficult to pass by writing it down on paper or parchment as a national boundary. The fact of separation, if it comes, gives up, on the part of the seceding section, the fugitive slave clause, along with all other Constitutional obligations upon the section seceded from, while I should expect no treaty stipulation would ever be made to take its place.

Is it doubted, then, that the plan I propose, if adopted, would shorten the war, and thus lessen its expenditure of money and of blood? Is it doubted that it would restore the national authority and national prosperity, and perpetuate both indefinitely? Is it doubted that we here —Congress and Executive—can secure its adoption? Will not the good people respond to a united and earnest appeal from us? Can we, can they, by any other means, so certainly or so speedily, assure these vital objects? We can succeed only by concert. It is not, "can *any* of us *imagine* better?" but "can we *all* do better?" Object whatsoever is possible, still the question recurs, "can we do better?" The dogmas of the quiet past are inadequate to the stormy present. The occasion is piled high with difficulty, and we must rise with the occasion. As our case is new, so we must think anew, and act anew. We must disenthrall ourselves, and then we shall save our country.

Fellow-citizens, *we* cannot escape history. We, of this Congress and this administration, will be remembered in spite of ourselves. No personal significance or insignificance can spare one or another of us. The fiery trial through which we pass will light us down, in honor or dishonor, to the latest generation. We *say* we are for the

Union. The world will not forget that we say this. We know how to save the Union. The world knows we do know how to save it. We—even *we here*—hold the power and bear the responsibility. In *giving* freedom to the *slave*, we *assure* freedom to the *free*—honorable alike in what we give and what we preserve. We shall nobly save, or meanly lose, the last, best hope of earth. Other means may succeed; this could not fail. The way is plain, peaceful, generous, just—a way which, if followed, the world will forever applaud, and God must forever bless.

A return to specie payments, however, at the earliest period compatible with due regard to all interests concerned, should ever be kept in view. Fluctuations in the value of currency are always injurious, and to reduce these fluctuations to the lowest possible point will always be a leading purpose in wise legislation. Convertibility—prompt and certain convertibility—into coin is generally acknowledged to be the best and surest safeguard against them; and it is extremely doubtful whether a circulation of United States notes, payable in coin and sufficiently large for the wants of the people, can be permanently, usefully and safely maintained.

LINCOLN was as evidently raised up of God for 1861, as Washington was for 1776. Two more unlike each other could hardly be produced in the history of a common country, among those who have identified themselves with its progress; but their common elements of character were those of the Anglo-Saxon race (so-called), a love of freedom and of law; perceptions of the right thing to do and of the right time to do it; all regulated by a sober faith in divine Providence, and a willingness to be His instrument for good to mankind.

A. Cleveland Coxe

BUFFALO, 1882.

EMANCIPATION PROCLAMATION,

JANUARY FIRST, 1863.

WHEREAS, on the 22d day of September, in the year of our Lord, 1862, a proclamation was issued by the President of the United States, containing, among other things, the following, to wit :   That on the first day of January, in the year of our Lord, 1863, all persons held as slaves, within any State or designated part of a State, the people whereof shall then be in rebellion against the United States, shall be thenceforth and forever free, and the Executive Government of the United States, including the military and naval authority thereof, will recognize and maintain the freedom of such persons, and will do no act or acts to repress such persons, or any of them, in any effort they may make for their actual freedom ; that the Executive will, on the first day of January aforesaid, issue a proclamation, designating the States and parts of States, if any, in which the people therein, respectively, shall then be in rebellion against the United States, and the fact that any State or the people thereof, shall, on that day, be in good faith represented in the Congress of the United States by members chosen thereto at elections wherein a majority of the qualified voters of such States shall have participated, shall, in the absence of strong countervailing testimony, be deemed conclusive evidence that such State and the people thereof are not in rebellion against the United States.

Now therefore, I, Abraham Lincoln, President of the United States, by virtue of the power vested in me as Commander-in-Chief of the Army and Navy, in a time of actual armed rebellion against the authority of the Government of the United States, as a fit and necessary war measure for suppressing said rebellion, do, on this first day of January, in the year of our Lord, 1863, and in accordance with my purpose so to do, publicly proclaimed for the full period of one hundred days from the date of the first above-mentioned order, designate as the States and parts of States therein, the people whereof, respectively, are this day in rebellion against the United States, the following, to wit : Arkansas, Texas and Louisiana (except the parishes of St. Bernard, Plaquemine, Jefferson, St. John, St. Charles, St. James, Ascension, Assumption, Terrebonne, La Fourche, St. Mary, St. Martin and Orleans, including the city of New Orleans), Mississippi, Alabama, Florida, Georgia, South Carolina, North Carolina and Virginia (except the forty-eight counties designated as West Virginia, and also the counties of Berkley, Accomac. Northampton, Elizabeth City, York, Princess Anne and Norfolk, including the cities of Norfolk and Portsmouth), which excepted parts are for the present left precisely as if this proclamation were not issued ; and by virtue of the power and for the purpose aforesaid, I do order and declare that all persons held as slaves within designated States, or parts of States, are, and henceforward shall be free, and that the Executive Government of the United States, including the military and naval authorities thereof, will recognize and maintain the freedom of the said persons ; and I hereby enjoin upon the people so declared to be free, to abstain from all violence, unless in necessary self-defense, and I recommend to them that, in all cases where allowed, they labor faithfully for reasonable wages ; and I further declare and make known that such persons of suitable condition will be received into the armed service of the United States, to garrison forts, positions, stations and other places, and to man vessels of all sorts in said service. And upon this, sincerely believed to be an act of justice, warranted by the Constitution upon military necessity, I invoke the considerate judgment of mankind, and the gracious favor of Almighty God.

In witness whereof, I have hereunto set my hand and caused the seal of the United States to be affixed.

Done at the City of Washington, this first day of January, in the year of our Lord, 1863, and of the Independence of the United States of America, the eighty-seventh.

Abraham Lincoln

A GREAT man, tender of heart, strong of nerve, of boundless patience and broadest sympathy, with no motive apart from his country, he could receive counsel from a child and give counsel to a sage. The simple approached him with ease, and the learned approached him with deference. Take him for all in all, Abraham Lincoln was one of the noblest, wisest and best men I ever knew.

Fred'k Douglass

WASHINGTON, 1880.

PRESIDENT LINCOLN excelled all his contemporaries, as he also excelled most of the eminent rulers of every time, in the humanity of his nature, in the constant assertion of reason over passion and feeling, in the art of dealing with men ; in fortitude, never disturbed by adversity, in capacity for delay when action was fraught with peril, in the power of immediate and resolute decision when delays were dangerous ; in comprehensive judgment, which forecasts the final and best opinion of nations and of posterity, and in the union of enlarged patriotism, wise philanthropy and the highest political justice, by which he was enabled to save a nation and to emancipate a race.

CHESTNUT HILLS FARM, 1880.

REPLY

TO AN ADDRESS FROM THE WORKINGMEN OF MANCHESTER, ENGLAND.

I KNOW, and deeply deplore, the sufferings which the workingmen at Manchester, and in all Europe, are called to endure in this crisis. It has been often and studiously represented that the attempt to overthrow this Government, which was built upon the foundation of human rights, and to substitute for it one which should rest exclusively on the basis of human slavery, was likely to obtain the favor of Europe. Through the action of our disloyal citizens, the workingmen of Europe have been subjected to severe trials, for the purpose of forcing their sanction to that attempt. Under these circumstances, I cannot but regard your decisive utterances upon the question as an instance of sublime Christian heroism, which has not been surpassed in any age or in any country. It is indeed an energetic and reinspiring assurance of the inherent power of truth, and of the ultimate and universal triumph of justice, humanity and freedom. I do not doubt that the sentiments you have expressed will be sustained by your great nation, and on the other hand I have no hesitation in assuring you that they will excite admiration, esteem, and the most reciprocal feelings of friendship among the American people. I hail this interchange of sentiment, therefore, as an augury, that, whatever else

I AM glad there is to be laid another block, perhaps I should say another course, upon the monument which the American people, year by year, are erecting to the memory of Abraham Lincoln. Every effort to perpetuate his name and make known his character engages my sympathy.

My personal acquaintance with Mr. Lincoln began shortly after his first inauguration as President of the United States. The perturbed condition of public affairs soon brought me much into his presence, and I saw more of him, by far, than is usual in the case of persons occupying places so widely apart. I have seen most of the great men of our country, my contemporaries, and have known them, more or less, it has so happened. It was easy to say Mr. Lincoln was the greatest of them all, but this would imperfectly express my conception of the truth. He was great in a different way from any other. He impressed me as no other man ever did. Never was the title Honest so expressive of character—honest not only in action and word, but also in thought and feeling and purpose. When he gave a reason for what he did, you felt instinctively that it was the real reason and not a mere attempt at justification. It was this profound truthfulness which gained for his words and actions the unquestioning confidence and support of the country.

Horace Maynard

KNOXVILLE, 1881.

I KNEW Mr. Lincoln very well, I may say somewhat intimately, before he was ever thought of in connection with the exalted station to which he was afterwards elected. In those years of his comparative obscurity, I knew him as preeminently a truthful man. His love of truth was conspicious in all his thinking. The object of his pursuit was truth, and not victory in argument or the triumph of his party, or the success of his own cause. This was always conspicuous in his conversation. It constituted the charm of his conversation. In his society one plainly saw, that his aim was so to use words to express and not conceal his real thoughts. This characteristic had formed his style, both of conversation and of writing. His habitual love of truth had led him successfully to cultivate such a use of language as would most clearly and accurately express his thoughts. His words were a perfectly transparent medium through which his thought always shone out with unclouded distinctness. No matter on what subject he was speaking, anyperson could understand him. This characteristic of his mind and heart gave a peculiar complexion to his speeches, whether at the bar, or in discussing the great political issues of the time. He always preferred to do more than justice rather than less to an opponent. It was often noticed, that he stated his opponent's argument with more force than his opponent himself had done. In the opening of his argument, his friends would often feel for the moment that he was surrendering the whole ground

18

in debate. They had no need to concern themselves on that subject, it would always turn out that he had only surrendered fallacious grounds, on which it was unsafe to rely, while the solid foundation on which his own faith rested was left intact, as the enduring basis on which he would build his argument. He was a very conscientious man; his anti-slavery opinions had their seat in no mere political expediency, but in the very depths of his moral nature. In the summer of 1856 he delivered a speech to a very large audience assembled on the public square in this city; the population of this county were at that time very largely of Southern origin, and had those views of slavery which prevailed in the States from which they came. His audience on that occasion were very largely of that character. Yet Mr. Lincoln made a very frank and explicit avowal of his opposition to slavery on moral grounds, and drew his argument against it from the deepest roots of natural justice; yet he presented the case with such irresistible eloquence that his speech was received with the greatest favor, and often with outbursts of very hearty applause. That speech went far in all this region to establish his reputation as a popular orator.

In a conversation I once had with him, at what was then his dingy office in Springfield, where I had gone for no other purpose than to enjoy the luxury of an hour's conversation with him, I spoke of the then recent anti-slavery excitement in St. Louis as proceeding entirely upon the ground of expediency for the white man. "I," said Mr. Lincoln, "must take into account the rights of the poor negro." That conscientious element is apparent in the whole course of his public policy. Conscience

constrained him to regard his oath to respect the constitution of the United States; and yet always to remember
the rights of the negro, and to do all for him which his constitutional powers permitted him to do. Had he not been
conscientious in both these directions, he would, in all
probability, have plunged his country in last anarchy.
Most admirably did his statesmanship combine in itself the
true conservative and the true radical. He was just such
a statesman as every nation needs in the great crisis of its
history. It is eminently an American phenomenon, that
a man was born in a log-cabin in the backwoods of Kentucky, who had precisely the intellectual endowments and
moral characteristics which his country would need in its
chief magistrate, in its hour of supreme necessity. Verily
there is a God in history! Mr. Lincoln's emotional character was one of the most kindly I have ever known.
The tenderness of his affections was almost womanly. I
confess I sometimes thought this trait in his character
was rather in excess, certainly, for the ruler of a great nation. He was not only incapable of malice, but I sometimes thought he was too much afraid of hurting anybody's feelings. If it was a fault, it was a fault of a great
and magnanimous soul, of which few men are capable. If
he had any vices they always leaned to virtue's side.
The wail of sorrow with which his foul taking-off was received throughout the civilized world was a spontaneous
tribute to the exalted and unique virtues of his character,
pointing him out as the man who, of all the great historic
names, had least deserved so sad a fate. There are remarkable analogies and equally remarkable contrasts between the careers of Mr. Lincoln and Gen. Garfield.

Both originated in obscurity and in the midst of the privations of frontier life; both were great in the natural endowments of the intellect, and greater still in the exalted moral characteristics in which they shone above most others of our statesmen. Both were cut off in the midst of their high career and in the very prime of life, by the hand of the merciless assassin. At the untimely and violent death of both, the civilized world put on mourning to an extent never before seen in history.

The contrast appears chiefly in this. Mr. Lincoln was born and reared in a community in which the advantages of education had been little enjoyed, and consequently the spirit of liberal learning had been little diffused. He had none to encourage and help him. He must find his way out into the light of knowledge by his own unassisted efforts. As a consequence, he did not acquire the first rudiments of an education till he had reached mature manhood. Mr. Garfield was born in a community in which education had been universal from its very origin, and where men built the school-house in every neighborhood simultaneously with their own log cabins. The whole people was, as the consequence, imbued with the spirit of liberal learning, and as soon as young Garfield began to show the superiority of his talents in the common school, the suggestion came from every quarter, you should have a collegiate education. An educated community bore him onward towards his great destiny from his very boyhood. This made the task a comparatively easy one. At the time of life when Mr. Lincoln was just beginning to acquire the first rudiments, Mr. Garfield was already a graduate of one of our most renowned colleges. Such is the advantage of being born in a community in which the first rudiments of knowledge are universally diffused by the ubiquitous common school.

That Mr. Lincoln succeeded in surmounting the obstacles which hemmed him in on every side, is wonderful indeed. Few men, certainly, have ever risen to greatness, purely by the force of intellectual and moral excellence, by a road so hard as that by which he traveled; yet he accomplished the mighty task without one of the arts of the demagogue, or one of the vices of the corrupt politician; and transferred his residence from the obscure log-cabin in the wilderness, to the executive mansion of a mighty nation, in his fifty-third year. Dying by violence in his fifty-seventh year, he left a name behind to be forever spoken with honor and reverence in the halls of the great and in the palaces of kings, and to be cherished with imperishable affection in the humble dwellings of the poor and lowly.

J. M. Sturtevant

JACKSONVILLE, 1882.

RESPONSE TO A SERENADE,

July, 1863.

I AM very glad indeed to see you to-night, and yet I will not say I thank you for this call ; but I do most sincerely thank Almighty God for the occasion on which you have called. How long ago is it ?—eighty odd years —since, on the Fourth of July, for the first time in the history of the world, a nation, by its representatives, assembled and declared as a self-evident truth, "that all men are created equal." That was the birthday of the United States of America. Since then the Fourth of July has had several very peculiar recognitions. The two men most distinguished in the framing and support of the Declaration were Thomas Jefferson and John Adams— the one having penned it, and the other sustained it the most forcibly in debate—the only two of the fifty-five who signed it, and were elected Presidents of the United States. Precisely fifty years after they put their hands to the paper, it pleased Almighty God to take both from this stage of action. This was indeed an extraordinary and remarkable event in our history. Another President five years after was called from this stage of existence on the same day and month of the year ; and now on this last Fourth of July just passed, when we have a gigantic rebellion, at the bottom of which is an effort to overthrow the principle that all men were created equal, we have the surrender of a most powerful position and army on that very day. And not only so, but in a succession of battles in Pennsylvania, near to us, through three days, so rapidly fought that they might be called one great battle, on the first, second and third of the month of July; and on the fourth the cohorts of those who opposed the declaration that all men are created equal, "turned tail" and run. Gentlemen, this is a glorious theme and the occasion for a speech, but I am not prepared to make one worthy of the occasion. I would like to speak in terms of praise due to the many brave officers and soldiers who have fought in the cause of the Union and liberties of their country from the beginning of the war. These are trying occasions, not only in success, but for the want of success. I dislike to mention the name of one single officer, lest I might do wrong to those I might forget. Recent events bring up glorious names, and particularly prominent ones : but these I will not mention. Having said this much, I will now take the music.

H E was one whom responsibility educated, and he showed himself more and more nearly equal to duty as year after year laid on him ever fresh burdens. God-given and God-led and sustained, we must ever believe him.

Wendell Phillips

Boston, 1880.

T HUS saith the Lord, In an acceptable time have I heard thee, and in a day of salvation have I helped thee . . . . That thou mayest say to the prisoners, go forth ; to them that are in darkness, show yourselves.—Isaiah xlix. 8, 9.

Noah Porter

Yale College, 1880.

PROCLAMATION.

THE year that is drawing towards its close has been filled with the blessings of fruitful fields and healthful skies. To these bounties, which are so constantly enjoyed that we are prone to forget the source from which they come, others have been added which are of so extraordinary a nature that they cannot fail to penetrate and soften even the heart which is habitually insensible to the ever-watchful providence of Almighty God. In the midst of a civil war of unequaled magnitude and severity, which has sometimes seemed to invite and provoke the aggressions of foreign states, peace has been preserved with all nations, order has been maintained, the laws have been respected and obeyed, and harmony has prevailed everywhere except in the theater of military conflict, while that theater has been greatly contracted by the advancing armies and navies of the Union. The needful diversion of wealth and strength from the fields of peaceful industry to the national defense, have not arrested the plow, the shuttle, or the ship. The axe has enlarged the borders of our settlements, and the mines as well of iron and coal as of the precious metals, have yielded even more abundantly than heretofore. Population has steadily increased, notwithstanding the waste that has been made in the camp, the siege and the battle-field; and the country, rejoicing in the consciousness of augmented strength and vigor, is permitted to expect a continuance of years with large increase of freedom. No human counsel hath devised, nor hath any mortal hand worked out these great things. They are the gracious gifts of the Most High God, who, while dealing with us in anger for our sins, hath nevertheless remembered mercy. It has seemed to me fit and proper that they should be solemnly, reverently, and gratefully acknowledged, as with one heart and voice, by the whole American people. I do, therefore, invite my fellow-citizens in every part of the United States, and also those who are at sea, and those who are sojourning in foreign lands, to set apart and observe the last Thursday of November next as a day of thanksgiving and prayer to our beneficent Father, who dwelleth in the heavens. And I recommend to them that, while offering up the ascriptions justly due to Him for such singular deliverances and blessings, they do also, with humble penitence for our national perverseness and disobedience, commend to his tender care all those who have become widows, orphans, mourners or sufferers in the lamentable civil strife in which we are unavoidably engaged, and fervently implore the interposition of the Almighty Hand to heal the wounds of the nation, and to restore it, as soon as may be consistent with the divine purposes, to the full enjoyment of peace, harmony, tranquillity, and union.

Abraham Lincoln

OCTOBER 3, 1863.

REPLY TO COMMITTEE OF THE PRESBY-
TERIAN CHURCH (NEW SCHOOL),.

PHILADELPHIA, 1863.

IN my administration I might have committed some errors. It would be indeed remarkable if I had not. I have acted according to my best judgment in every case. As a pilot I have used my best exertions to keep afloat our ship of state, and shall be glad to resign my trust at the appointed time to another pilot more skillful and successful than I may prove. In every case, and at all hazards, the Government must be perpetuated. Relying, as I do, upon the Almighty Power, and encouraged, as I am, by these resolutions which you have just read, with the support which I receive from Christian men, I shall not hesitate to use all the means at my control to secure the termination of this rebellion, and will hope for success.

MY FIRST SIGHT OF MR. LINCOLN.

H E was riding into the city of New York with
military and civic escort, on his way to Washington to be inaugurated for the first time to the Presidency of the United States. The country was at that
moment in the first throes of the great rebellion. Millions of hearts were beating anxiously in view of the advent to power of this untried man. Had he been called
of God to the throne of power at such a time as this to
be the leader and deliverer of the people?

As the carriage in which he sat passed slowly by me
on the Fifth avenue, he was looking weary, sad, feeble
and faint. My disappointment was excessive, so great,
indeed, as to be almost overwhelming. He did not look
to me to be the man for the hour. The next day I was
with him and others in the Governor's room in the City
Hall, when the Mayor of the city made to Mr. Lincoln an
official address. Of this speech I will say nothing; but
the reply by Mr. Lincoln was so modest, firm, patriotic
and pertinent, that my fears of the day before began to
subside, and I saw in this new man a promise of great
things to come. It was not boldness nor dash, nor high-
sounding pledges; nor did he, in office, with the mighty
armies of a roused nation at his command, ever assume
to be more than he promised in that little upper chamber
in New York, on his journey to the seat of government,

to take the helm of the ship of state then tossing in the storm. During the war, I was dining with a party of which Gen. Burnside was one. A gentleman expressed surprise and regret that the war had not brought to the front in civil service some man of such commanding force of character, will-power and genius as to compel his countrymen to accept him as the born statesman for the hour. Gen. Burnside said : "We are drifting, and it is better so. I think Mr. Lincoln is just the man to keep the ship on its course. One more headstrong, willful and resolute might divide and weaken the counsels of the nation. We shall go through and come out all right." It did not please God to spare him until the people were settled in peace in the redeemed and reunited land. But he saw from the mount of vision the goodly sight afar, and died in faith.

S. Irenaeus Prime

New York, 1882.

M R. LINCOLN'S life was one of true patriotism, and his character one of honesty and of the highest type of religious sentiment.

Alx. Ramsey

St. Paul, 1882.

———

W HEN history crystallizes that the events of a century shall be recorded in a sentence, then will the administrations of Washington and Lincoln be the epochal marks of this age. The former founded a republic, the latter was the great emancipator of the nineteenth century.

C. E. Pratt

Brooklyn, 1880.

LETTER TO GENERAL GRANT.

MAJOR-GENERAL GRANT.—My Dear General: I do not remember that you and I ever met personally. I write this now as a grateful acknowlegement for the almost inestimable service you have done the country. I write to say a word further. When you first reached the vicinity of Vicksburg, I thought you should do what you finally did—march the troops across the neck, run the batteries with the transports, and thus go below; and I never had any faith, except a general hope that you knew better than I, that the Yazoo Pass expedition, and the like, could succeed. When you got below, and took Port Gibson, Grand Gulf and vicinity, I thought you should go down the river and join General Banks; and when you turned northward, east of the Big Black, I feared it was a mistake. I now wish to make the personal acknowledgment that you were right and I was wrong.

Abraham Lincoln

THERE can be, I think, but one opinion among those competent to form a judgment of the general character and services of Abraham Lincoln. His native genius, the solidity of his understanding, his common sense and remarkable sagacity, his patience and courage, and above all, his incorruptible integrity and steadfast faith in God, gave him eminent administrative ability, made him a noble man, a great statesman and the second Father of his Country. This will, I doubt not, be the judgment of history.

Ray Palmer

NEWARK, 1882.
19

A PROCLAMATION.

JULY 15, 1863.

IT has pleased Almighty God to hearken to the supplication and prayers of an afflicted people, and to vouchsafe to the army and the navy of the United States, on the land and on the sea, victories so signal and so effective as to furnish reasonable grounds for augmented confidence that the Union of these States will be maintained, their constitution preserved, and their peace and prosperity permanently secured. But these victories have been accorded not without sacrifice of life, limb, and liberty, incurred by brave, patriotic and loyal citizens. Domestic affliction, in every part of the country, follows in the train of these fearful bereavements. It is meet and right to recognize and confess the presence of the Almighty Father; and the power of his hand equally in these triumphs and these sorrows.

Now, therefore, be it known, that I do set apart Thursday, the sixth day of August next, to be observed as a day for national thanksgiving, praise and prayer; and I invite the people of the United States to assemble on that occasion in their customary places of worship, and, in the form approved by their own conscience, render the homage due to the Divine Majesty, for the wonderful things he has done in the nation's behalf, and invoke the influence of his holy Spirit, to subdue the anger which has produced, and so long sustained, a

NATIONAL LINCOLN MONUMENT AT SPRINGFIELD, ILLINOIS.

Unveiled and dedicated, October 15, 1874. Dimensions 72½ by 119½ feet square, and 100 feet high. Designed and modeled by Larkin G. Mead. Cost, $212,000.

Emblematical of the Constitution of the United States. President Lincoln standing above the coat of arms, with the Infantry, Navy, Artillery, and Cavalry marshalled around him, wields all for holding the States together in a perpetual bond of Union, without which he could never hope to effect the great enemy of human freedom. The grand climax is indicated by President Lincoln with his left hand holding out as a golden sceptre, the Emancipation Proclamation, while in his right he holds the pen with which he had just written it. The right hand is resting on another badge of authority, the American Flag, thrown over the *fasces*. At the foot of the *fasces* lies a wreath of laurel with which to crown the President as the victor over slavery and rebellion.

I HAVE no capacity to do justice to the greatness, purity and honesty of Abraham Lincoln, nor to the immense value of his service to our country. The great heart of the nation alone is equal to a work of such magnitude. He touched the manacles of four millions of men and women, and in the twinkling of an eye they dropped off forever. He wrote a word, and slavery, which had hung like a mill-stone around the neck of the nation, compelling it to bow its head in shame and disgrace, sunk into oblivion. The possibilities of his life were grand ; how grandly were they realized ! The glory and luster of his name will stand in the history of the nation "more lasting than a monument of brass."

LEWISTON, 1882.

LETTER TO JAMES C. CONKLING,

AUGUST, 1863.

THE signs look better. The Father of Waters again goes unvexed to the sea. Thanks to the great Northwest for it; nor yet wholly to them. Three hundred miles up they web New England, Empire, Keystone and Jersey, hewing their way right and left. The sunny South, too, in more colors than one, also lent a helping hand. On the spot, their part of the history was jotted down in black and white. The job was a great national one, and let none be slighted who bore an honorable part in it. And while those who have cleared the great river may well be proud, even that is not all. It is hard to say that anything has been more bravely and well done than at Antietam, Murfreesboro, Gettysburg, and on many fields of less note. Nor must Uncle Sam's wet feet be forgotten. At all the watery margins they have been present. Not only on the deep sea, the broad bay, and the rapid river, but also up the narrow, muddy bayou, and wherever the ground was a little damp, they have been and made their tracks. Thanks to all. For the great republic—for the principle it lives by and keeps alive—for man's vast future—thanks to all. Peace does not appear so distant as it did. I hope it will come soon and come to stay; and so come as to be worth the keeping in all future time. It will then have been proved that among freemen there can be no successful appeal from the ballot to the bullet, and that they who take such appeal are sure to lose their case and pay the cost. And there will be some black men who can remember that with silent tongue, and clinched teeth, and steady eye, and well-poised bayonets, they have helped mankind on to this great consummation, while I fear there will be some white ones unable to forget that with malignant heart and deceitful speech they have striven to hinder it. Still, let us not be over-sanguine of a speedy, final triumph. Let us be quite sober. Let us diligently apply the means, never doubting that a just God, in his own good time, will give us the rightful result.

Abraham Lincoln

HE was not only the head of an administration which shaped events the mightiest of the century, but its balance-wheel also. The American people owe it to him that the important steps in the war for the preservation of the Union were taken just at the fitting moment.

Eugene Hale

ELLSWORTH, 1880.

"BE just and fear not."

Albert J. Myer

U. S. SIGNAL SERVICE, 1880.

ADDRESS ON THE BATTLE-FIELD OF GETTYSBURG,

NOVEMBER 19, 1863.

FOURSCORE and seven years ago our fathers brought forth upon this continent a new nation, conceived in Liberty, and dedicated to the proposition that all men are created equal. Now we are engaged in a great civil war, testing whether that nation, or any nation so conceived and so dedicated, can long endure. We are met on a great battle-field of that war. We are met to dedicate a portion of it as the final resting-place of those who here gave their lives that that nation might live. It is altogether fitting and proper that we should do this.

But, in a larger sense, we cannot dedicate, we cannot consecrate, we cannot hallow this ground. The brave men, living and dead, who struggled here, have consecrated it far above our power to add or detract. The world will little note, nor long remember, what we say here, but it can never forget what they did here. It is for us, the living, rather, to be dedicated here to the unfinished work that they have thus far so nobly carried on. It is rather for us to be here dedicated to the great task remaining before us—that from these honored dead we take increased devotion to the cause for which they here gave the last full measure of devotion—that we here highly resolve that the dead shall not have died in vain— that the nation shall, under God, have a new birth of freedom, and that the government of the people, by the people, and for the people, shall not perish from the earth.

ARTILLERY GROUP OF STATUARY.   NATIONAL LINCOLN MONUMENT.

Representing three artillerymen, one, an officer standing on a dismounted cannon in an attitude of defiance, while below him is a prostrate soldier, wounded by the same shot that disabled his gun, and a boy in an attitude of sympathy and horror, springing forward as if to succor his wounded comrade.

GREAT men are divinely called to great missions. As certainly as God called Abraham to be the human founder of his church, or Moses to lead his people out of bondage into liberty, or "girded" Cyrus for his beneficent work, though unknown by that famous commander, or commissioned Paul to be the leader of an evangelistic host, to open the gates of gospel day to heathen nations, or inspired Luther and Wesley to rekindle the fires of religion on the altars of a faithless church, so certainly does it appear to thoughtful minds that he called Abraham Lincoln to rise from the log-cabin in the wilderness, through difficulties and obstacles that would have appalled a weaker man, to take the helm of the new American nation in its crisis hour, to strike the shackles from an enslaved race, and thence to ascend to a victor's throne and a martyr's crown.

C. A. Payne,

DELAWARE, 1880.

M R. LINCOLN was certainly a most remarkable man. He was undoubtedly well fitted for the times in which he lived, and the emergency that confronted him. He began with a very moderate degree of public confidence and sympathy. A large proportion of the community had, at the time of his first election, and for a considerable period afterwards, a painful sense of distrust as to his qualifications for the position to which he had been called. This distrust was slow to yield. Good things were done, but they were all attributed, on account of this preconceived opinion of his ability, to the excellence of his advisers, while the evils and the mistakes were all laid to him. His physical organization must not be overlooked as one of the sources of his success. The great practical men of the world have been, not necessarily of large, but of strong bodily frames. To the heathen philosopher, a sound mind in a sound body seemed the greatest good: "*Mens sana in corpore sano.*" The discipline of his early life prepared his frame for the laborious duties which were to devolve upon him. It is true that this discipline did not develop his form into a beautiful and graceful one—his warmest friends could not claim that for him—but they could declare that "his large eyes in their softness and beauty expressed nothing but benevolence and gentleness," and that a pleasant smile frequently brought out more vividly the earnest cast of his features, which were serious even to sadness. He has been called by one of his best friends "a wiry, awkward giant." He was six feet four inches high ; his arms were long, almost disproportionately so ; his mouth and nose were both exceedingly large ; his features were coarse, and his large hands exhibited the traces of toil. He was not specially attentive to dress, though by no means slovenly. The formal politeness of fashionable life he had not, though the gentleness of the unspoiled child of nature he had. He said once that he had never studied the art of paying compliments to women. Yet they never received a grander one than he paid when he declared : "If all that has been said by orators and poets since the creation of the world, in praise of women, were applied to American women, it would not do them justice for their conduct doing the war." It has been stated that he had none of the grossness of life. He was not a licentious man. He was not addicted to the use of profane language. He did not gamble. He was temperate, and he did not use tobacco in any form. Only those who have known the fearful extent to which these habits prevail among our public men can appre-. ciate the honor which the absence of them confers upon the late President. His honesty passed into a proverb, and his integrity was beyond reproach. It was not called in question, even in the height of political excitement and vituperation. His qualities of heart were such as commended him to all men. He was naturally disposed to think well of his race. His prepossessions were generally in favor of a man. He would rather love than hate him ; in fact, he seemed as if he could not hate him if he would. The entire absence of vindictiveness, either personal or political, was one of the ripe fruits of his native tenderness. Was he ever heard to have said a hard thing of his opponents, or known to have uttered a single word showing personal hate or even personal feeling? Between him and his predecessors no parallel can be drawn, for no other President ever held the reins of power through four years of virulent rebellion. It is therefore impossible to say how much better or how much worse others would have done. Not graceful nor refined, not always using the English language correctly, he proved to be a meet and proper man for the times. He had the greatness of goodness; not a powerful nor a brilliant intellect, but plain, practical good sense; a sincere purpose to do right; an eminent Catholic spirit that was ready to listen to all sides, and a firm, unshaken belief in the expediency of justice. When others with higher and more profound faculties might have failed, he succeeded, guided by his matchless sagacity and prudence and common sense and native shrewdness. His thoughts were his own; they were fresh and original, and were clothed with a quaintness, a directness, a simplicity of style, peculiar to himself. He had a vein of humor which marked him from all other men in his position, and lost him, perhaps, the reputation of official dignity; and yet this very humor, which in most important emergencies could not refrain from making the witty repartee or telling the pointed anecdote, undoubtedly helped him to endure those fatigues and cares under which he would otherwise have sunken.

In the words of Daniel Webster on the death of President Taylor: "He has left on the minds of the country a strong impression; first, of his absolute honesty

MY acquaintance with the lamented President Lincoln began in the winter of 1832–3, during the session of the Legislature of this State, of which I was a member, and warmly interested in procuring an act for the construction of the Illinois and Michigan Canal, for which I had introduced a bill, which was defeated. I then introduced a bill for a railroad, instead of a canal, which passed the House, lost in the Senate by the casting vote of the Speaker, Zadoc Casey. At the next session Mr. Lincoln was a member. I, as a lobbyist, attended that and the successive sessions until the passage of the act to construct the canal. Mr. Lincoln, in and out of the Legislature, favored its construction at the earliest possible moment, by his advice, and rendered efficient aid. Indeed, I very much doubt if the bill could have passed as early as it did without his valuable help. We were thrown much together, our intimacy increasing. I never had a friend to whom I was more warmly attached. His character was nearly faultless. Possessing a warm, generous heart, genial, affable, honest, courteous to his opponents, persevering, industrious in research, never losing sight of the principal point under discussion, aptly illustrating by his stories, always brought into good effect; he was free from political trickery or denunciation of the private character of his opponents; in debate firm and collected; with "charity towards all, malice towards none," he won the confidence of the public, even of his political opponents.

20

His elevation to the highest honor within the gift of the people did not alter his feelings or deportment towards his acquaintances, however humble. The poor and ignorant, the wealthy and educated, were met with the same cordiality and frankness. This manly and noble course pre-eminently distinguished him; he had a heart full of tenderness for his fellow-man, wholly void of selfish pride, vanity or cringing adulation. If he, by industry and perseverance, gifted by a superior mind, advanced himself in social position, he did not lose sight of the great principle ever guiding him, that "all men were created equal."

I called on him in Washington the year of his inauguration; was alone with him for an hour or more; found him greatly changed, his countenance bearing an expression of great mental anxiety, and the whole topic of our conversation was the then existing civil war, which affected him deeply, though he spoke with confidence of the suppression of the rebellion, rejoicing that so large a portion of the people were for using the resources of our country to bring back the rebellious States into the Union. Examining the map hanging on the wall, pointing out the points most strong in the rebel district, he said: "Douglas and myself have studied this map very closely. I am indebted to him for wise counsel. I have no better adviser, and feel under great obligations to him." I left Washington with a feeling our nation had not misplaced its confidence in choosing him as its President. Two years after I again visited Washington and went to the White House to pay my respects to him; in the ante-

room was my friend Thos. L. Forrest; sending in our
cards, and waiting nearly two hours without seeing him,
conversing by the window opening upon the fine grounds
and garden at the rear of the White House. About six
o'clock the band from the navy yard appeared and began
to play, when Mr. Forrest said: "This is Saturday,
when the grounds are open to the public; the President
will present himself on the balcony below; let us join the
crowd." So we adjourned and filed in with the crowd.
The President, with Adjutant-Gen. Thomas, were seated
on the balcony. The crowd was great, marching com-
pactly past the President, the men raising their hats in
salutation. As my friend and myself passed he said to me:
"The President seems to notice you—turn toward him."
"No," I said, "I don't care to be recognized." At that
instant Mr. Lincoln started from his seat, advancing
quickly to the iron railing, and leaning over, beckoning
with his long arm, called: "Hubbard! Hubbard! come
here." I left the ranks and ascended the stone steps to
the gate of the balcony, which was locked, Gen. Thomas
saying: "Wait a moment, I will get the key." "Never
mind, General," said Mr. Lincoln, "Hubbard is used to
jumping—he can scale that fence." I climbed over and
for about an hour we conversed and watched the large
crowd, the rebel flag being in sight on Arlington
Heights. This was the last time I ever saw his face in
life, little thinking at the time I should be one of the
escorts of his honored remains from this city to his last
resting-place amid the tears of a sorrowing nation. I
simply mention the circumstance of his calling me to sit

I F "by his works he be known," he was the greatest
statesman America ever produced. In less than a
hundred years his name will be honored and revered above
that of any other American name. He was a great man
of the people, and the greatest advocate of universal liberty—the first President who believed in the letter and
spirit of the Declaration of Independence.

E. B. Martindale

WASHINGTON, 1880.

SPEECH AT A LADIES' FAIR IN WASH-INGTON,

MARCH 21, 1864.

LADIES AND GENTLEMEN :—I appear to say but a word. This extraordinary war in which we are engaged falls heavily upon all classes of people, but the most heavily upon the soldiers. For it has been said, "All that a man hath will he give for his life," and, while all contribute of their substance, the soldier puts his life at stake, and often yields it up in his country's cause. *The highest merit, then, is due to the soldier.*

In this extraordinary war, extraordinary developments have manifested themselves, such as have not been seen in former wars ; and, among these manifestations, nothing has been more remarkable than these fairs for the relief of suffering soldiers and their families, and the chief agents in these fairs are the women of America !

I am not accustomed to the use of language of eulogy I have never studied the art of paying compliments to women ; but I must say, that, if all that has been said by orators and poets since the creation of the world in praise of women were applied to the women of America, it would not do them justice for their conduct during the war. I will close by saying, God bless the women of America.

I HAD only a slight personal acquaintance with Mr. Lincoln, but yield to no one in veneration for his memory, or admiration for his grand qualities of head and heart.

Levi P. Morton

LEGATION DES ETATS-UNIS D'AMERIQUE,
    PARIS, 1881.

MR. LINCOLN'S history will be "of all time," and he will be recalled as one of the grandest figures of the world's history.

Winfd. S. Hancock

GÓVERNOR'S ISLAND, 1881.

LETTER WRITTEN TO A. G. HODGES,

APRIL 4, 1864.

I ATTEMPT no compliment to my own sagacity. I claim not to have controlled events, but confess plainly that events have controlled me. Now, at the end of three years' struggle, the nation's condition is not what either party or any man devised or expected. God alone can claim it. Whither it is tending seems plain. If God now wills the removal of a great wrong, and wills, also, that we of the North, as well as you of the South, shall pay fairly for our complicity in that wrong, impartial history will find therein new causes to attest and revere the justice and goodness of God.

Abraham Lincoln

When clos'd years since the fratricidal strife,
One latest victim offer'd up his life,
That plain, good man, who, with life's parting tone,
Breath'd charity for all, and malice toward none ;
So kind, so truthful, modest and sincere,
Prompt to forgive the injury and the sneer ;
Brimming with gracious love, for all a smile,
In whose big heart there was no taint of guile,
Lamented Lincoln, sacred be his rest !
With all his mourning country's honors blest !
Long will the land his tragic end deplore,
The noblest martyr when the war was o'er.

He freed the slave !   No chains now bind his hand,
All disenthrall'd he proudly walks the land ;
'Twas Lincoln's voice emancipation gave,
That snapt the gyves and fetters of the slave,
Bade him that was a slave be slave no more,
Free as God's blessed beams from heaven that pour.

Isaac McLellan

SHELTER ISLAND, 1880.

SPEECH

AT THE OPENING OF A FAIR IN BALTIMORE, FOR THE BENE-
FIT OF THE UNITED STATES SANITARY COMMIS-
SION, APRIL, 1864.

CALLING it to mind that we are in Baltimore, we cannot fail to note that the world moves. Looking upon
these many people I see assembled here to serve, as they
best may, the soldiers of the Union, it at once occurs to
me that three years ago the same soldiers could not so
much as pass through Baltimore. The change from then
till now is both great and gratifying. I would say, blessings upon the men who have wrought the change, and
the fair women who strive to reward them for it!

When the war began, three years ago, neither party nor
any man expected it would last till now. Each looked for
the end, in some way, long ere to-day. Neither did any
anticipate that domestic slavery would be much affected
by the war. But here we are; the war has not ended,
and slavery has been much affected—how much need not
now be recounted. So true it is that man proposes and
God disposes.

The world has never had a good definition of the
word liberty, and the American people, just now, are
much in want of one. We all declare for liberty, but in
using the same *word* we do not all mean the same thing.
With some the word liberty may mean for each man to do
as he pleases with himself, and the product of his labor;

while to others the same word may mean for some men to do as they please with other men, and the product of other men's labor. Here are two, not only different, but incompatible things, called by the same name, liberty. And it follows that each of these things is, by the respective parties, called by two different and incompatible names—liberty and tyranny.

The shepherd drives the wolf from the sheep's throat, for which the sheep thanks the shepherd as a *liberator*, while the wolf denounces him for the same act, as the destroyer of liberty, especially as the sheep was a black one. Plainly, the sheep and the wolf are not agreed upon a definition of the word liberty, and precisely the same difference prevails to-day among us human creatures, even in the North, and all professing to love liberty.

HE was the true American, at one with the people in his origin, his simplicity of character, his rugged manliness, and his stern devotion to the cause of civil liberty. While he lived, he was the friend of his country, and when he died the sense of personal bereavement darkened every American home. In the supreme crisis of American history, his faith in the ultimate triumph of popular institutions never failed him. By that faith he saved the nation, he widened the bounds of human freedom, and he rendered forever sacred those principles of government which rest upon justice and the equal rights of man. His real epitaph cannot be written. It has received its truest expression in the silent memory of those great historic deeds with which his name is associated, and which can never, as long as liberty is cherished by man, be effaced from the records of time.

William C. Morey

UNIVERSITY OF ROCHESTER, 1880.

RESPONSE TO A DELEGATION OF THE NATIONAL UNION LEAGUE.

I CAN only say, in response to the kind remarks of your chairman, as I suppose, that I am very grateful for the renewed confidence which has been accorded to me both by the Convention and by the National League. I am not insensible at all to the personal compliment there is in this, and yet I do not allow myself to believe that any but a small portion of it is to be appropriated as a personal compliment; that really ‹the Convention and the Union League assembled with a higher view—that of taking care of the interests of the country for the present and the great future—and that the part I am entitled to appropriate as a compliment is only that part which I may lay hold of as being the opinion of the Convention and of the League, that I am not entirely unworthy to be intrusted with the place which I have occupied for the last three years. But I do not allow myself to suppose that either the Convention or the League have concluded to decide that I am either the greatest or best man in America, but rather they have concluded that it is not best to swap horses while crossing the river, and have further concluded that I am not so poor a horse that they might not make a botch of it in trying to swap.

A BRAHAM LINCOLN'S cheerfulness and wit were invaluable to him in the trying years of our civil war. Cheerfulness to a good man or woman is always a mighty sustaining power. Mr. Lincoln's unwavering faith that good would finally overcome evil buoyed his spirits through the darkest hours. Of Mr. Lincoln's inflexible honesty of purpose, there is but one opinion throughout the world. He was a noble, whole-souled, tender-hearted man. He was a model President of this model Republic. His fame is justly immortal.

P. T. Barnum

BRIDGEPORT, 1880.

SPEECH AT THE PHILADELPHIA FAIR,

JUNE 16, 1864.

WAR, at the best, is terrible, and this war of ours, in its magnitude and in its duration, is one of the most terrible. It has deranged business totally in many localities, and partially in all localities. It has destroyed property and ruined homes; it has produced a national debt and taxation unprecedented, at least in this country; it has carried mourning to almost every home, until it can almost be said that the "heavens are hung in black." Yet the war continues, and several relieving coincidents have accompanied it from the very beginning, which have not been known, as I understand, or have any knowledge of, in any former wars in the history of the world. The Sanitary Commission, with all its benevolent labors; the Christian Commission, with all its Christian and benevolent labors, and the various places, arrangements, so to speak, and institutions, have contributed to the comfort and relief of the soldiers.

It is a pertinent question, often asked in the mind privately, and from one to the other, "When is the war to end?" Surely I feel as deep an interest in this question as any other can, but I do not wish to name a day, a month, or a year when it is to end. I do not wish to run any risk of seeing the time come, without our being ready for the end, for fear of disappointment because the time has come and not the end. We accepted this war for an object, a worthy object, and the war will end when that object is attained. Under God, I hope it never will end until that time. Speaking of the present campaign, General Grant is reported to have said, " I am going through on this line, if it takes all summer." This war has taken three years; it was begun or accepted upon the line of restoring the national authority over the whole national domain, and for the American people, as far as my knowledge enables me to speak, I say we are going through on this line, if it takes three years more.

I have never been in the habit of making predictions in regard to the war, but I am almost tempted to make one. If I were to hazard it, it is this: That Grant is this evening, with General Meade and General Hancock, and the brave officers and soldiers with him, in a position from whence he will never be dislodged until Richmond is taken. And I have but one single proposition to put now, and, perhaps, I can best put it in the form of an interrogative—If I shall discover that General Grant and the noble officers and men under him can be greater facilitated in their work by a sudden pouring forward of men and assistance, will you give them to me? Are you ready to march? [Cries of "yes."] Then, I say, stand ready, for I am watching for the chance.

21

SPEECH

TO A SERENADING CLUB OF PENNSYLVANIANS ON THE NIGHT OF HIS SECOND ELECTION, 1864.

EVEN before I had been informed by you that this compliment was paid me by loyal citizens of Pennsylvania friendly to me, I had inferred that you were of that portion of my countrymen who think that the best interests of the nation are to be subserved by the support of the present administration. I do not pretend to say that you, who think so, embrace all the patriotism and loyalty of the country; but I do believe, and I trust without personal interest, that the welfare of the country does require that such support and indorsement be given. I earnestly believe that the consequences of this day's work, if it be as you assume and as now seems probable, will be to the lasting advantage, if not to the very salvation, of the country. I cannot, at this hour, say what has been the result of the election; but whatever it may be, I have no desire to modify this opinion: that all who have labored to-day in behalf of the Union organization have wrought for the best interest of their country and the world, not only for the present, but for all future ages. *I am thankful to God for this approval of the people; but while deeply grateful for this mark of their confidence in me, if I know my heart, my gratitude is free from any taint of personal triumph. I do not impugn the motives of any one opposed to me. It is no pleasure to me to triumph over any one, but I give thanks to the Almighty for this evidence of the people's resolution to stand by free government and the rights of humanity.*

MR. LINCOLN A STATESMAN.

THERE is a popular impression that the wise states-manship displayed by our national government during the late civil war, in its foreign relations, was almost wholly due to the direction of the intellect and judgment of Secretary Seward. It is attested, on the contrary, by persons supposed to have knowledge of some of the secrets of the Cabinet of President Lincoln, that some of the wisest acts of statesmanship that marked the career of Mr. Seward in his intercourse with foreign governments, during the administration of Mr. Lincoln, were inspired by the suggestions of the President. In support of the latter position, a single incident may suffice, which came under the observation of the writer. It had relation to perhaps the most delicate question of right which arose between the United States and Great Britain during that war. The incident was the surrender of Mason and Slidell, Confederate ambassadors to European courts.

The writer was in Washington when the news reached there of the capture of those two arch-conspirators against the life of the republic, by Captain Wilkes, commander of the national steam sloop-of-war *San Jacinto*, whom he had forcibly taken from the British mail steamer *Trent*. The act of Captain Wilkes was universally applauded by all loyal Americans, and the land was filled with rejoicings because two of the most mischievous men among the enemies of the Government were in custody. For the moment, men did not stop to consider the law or the expediency involved in the act. Public honors were tendered to Captain Wilkes, and resolutions of thanks were passed by public bodies. The Secretary of the Navy wrote him a congratulatory letter on the "great public services" he had rendered in "capturing the rebel emissaries, Mason and Slidell," and assured him that his conduct had "the emphatic approval of the department." The House of Representatives tendered him their thanks for the service he had done. But there was one thoughtful man in the nation, in whom was vested the tremendous executive power of the republic at that time, and whose vision was constantly endeavoring to explore the mysteries of the near future, who had indulged calmer and wiser thoughts than most men at that critical moment, because his feelings were kept in subjection to his judgment by a sense of heavy responsibility. That man was Abraham Lincoln.

The writer was in the office of the Secretary of War when the telegraphic dispatch announcing the capture of Mason and Slidell was brought in and read. He can never forget the scene that ensued. Led by Secretary Stanton, who was followed by Governor Andrew of Massachusetts, and others who were present, cheer after cheer was heartily given by the company. A little later, the writer, accompanied by the late Elisha Whittlesey, then the venerable First Comptroller of the Treasury, was favored with a brief interview with the President, when the clear judgment of that far-seeing and sagacious statesman uttered through his lips the words which formed the suggestion of and the key-note to the judicious action of the Secretary of State afterwards.

"I fear the traitors will prove to be white elephants," said Mr. Lincoln. "We must stick to American principles concerning the rights of neutrals," he continued. "We fought Great Britain for insisting, by theory and practice, on the right to do just what Captain Wilkes has just done. If Great Britain shall now protest against the act and demand their release, we must give them up, apologize for the act as a violation of our doctrines, and thus forever bind her over to keep the peace in relation to neutrals, and so acknowledge that she has been wrong for sixty years."

Great Britain did protest and make the demand, also made preparations for war against the United States at the same moment. On the same day when Lord John Russell sent the protest and demand to Lord Lyons, the British minister at Washington, Secretary Seward forwarded a dispatch to Minister Adams in London, informing him that this Government disclaimed the act of Captain Wilkes, and giving assurance that it was ready to make a satisfactory arrangement of all difficulties arising out of the unauthorized act. These dispatches passed each other in mid-ocean.

The Government, in opposition to popular sentiment, decided at once to restore Mason and Slidell to the protection of the British flag. It was soon afterwards done, war between the two nations was averted, and, in the language of President Lincoln, the British Government was "forever bound to keep the peace in relation to neutrals."

THE right man in the right place was never more clearly seen than in the story of President Lincoln. His simplicity and humor, his patient wisdom and hopeful courage, his conspicuous integrity and universal charity made him by all odds the most impressive figure of our dark days. And coming years can only make more tender the affection and more profound the reverence which his own age has been proud to give to the savior of his country.

S. G. Barnes.

1880.

IT must be confessed that Mr. Lincoln's early life gave no promise of the power he showed at the head of the nation ; but I believe he was born for the emergency, and when it came I am confident that of the three interested—the emergency, Mr. Lincoln, and the American public—the emergency was the most completely astonished. It is my humble judgment that in all the positions the great crisis forced him into he was a perfect fit.

J. M. Bailey.

DANBURY, 1882.

ADDRESS TO THE POLITICAL CLUBS.

It has long been a grave question whether any government not too strong for the liberties of its people can be strong enough to maintain its existence in great emergencies.

On this point the present rebellion has brought our republic to a severe test, and a presidential election occurring in regular course during the rebellion, has added not a little to the strain. If the loyal people, united, were put to the utmost of their strength by the rebellion, must they not fail when divided and partially paralyzed by a political war among themselves.?

But the election was a necessity. We cannot have a free government without elections; and if the rebellion could force us to forego or postpone a national election, it might fairly claim to have already conquered and ruined us.

The strife of the election is but human nature practically applied to the facts in the case. What has occurred in this case must ever recur in similar cases. Human nature will not change. In any future great national trial, compared with the men who have passed through this, we shall have as weak and as strong, as silly and as wise, as bad and as good. Let us therefore study the incidents of this as philosophy to learn wisdom from, and none of them as wrongs to be revenged.

While I am deeply sensible to the high compliment

M Y first visit with Mr Lincoln was a few days before he issued his Emancipation Proclamation, when I was introduced by the Hon. John Covode. The President was walking his room, apparently under great excitement, and spoke to Mr. Covode in nearly the following words, which made a deep impression on my mind: "I have studied that matter well; my mind is made up—it *must be done.* I am driven to it. There is to me no other way out of our troubles. But although my duty is plain, it is in some respects *painful*, and I trust the people will understand that I act not in anger, but in expectation of a greater good." These few words revealed to me some of the noble attributes of his nature. "I do it not in anger, but in expectation of a greater good." Nothing but the honest sense of duty could have induced him to issue that proclamation, and this he desired the people to know, that his motives might not be misunderstood. No man was ever more free from the spirit of revenge or more conscientious in the discharge of his duties. President Lincoln was also remarkably tolerant. He was the friend of all, and never, to my knowledge, gave the influence of his great name to encourage sectarianism in any of its names or forms; he had "charity for all and malice toward none."

The following is in proof. Immediately after the earliest battles of the war most of the sick and wounded were brought to the Philadelphia hospitals for treatment, and I was in daily receipt of letters from my denominational friends soliciting me to visit husbands and brothers who were among the sick and wounded. As much of my time was thus occupied, and at considerable expense, it was suggested by the Hon. Henry D. Moore that application be made for the position of hospital chaplain, and it was on the recommendation of Mr. Moore and Governor Curtin that the President made the nomination. Soon as it was announced in the papers that my name had been sent to the Senate for confirmation a self-constituted committee of " Young Christians "(?) consulted with a few others, as bigoted as themselves, and volunteered their services to visit Washington and try to induce the President to withdraw the name. It so happened that when these gentlemen called on the President Mr. Covode was present and made known the interview to a reporter, and it thus became public. It was in substance as follows :

THE INTERVIEW.

" We have called, Mr. President, to confer with you in regard to the appointment of Mr. Shrigley, of Philadelphia, as hospital chaplain."

The President responded : " Oh, yes, gentlemen ; I have sent his name to the Senate, and he will no doubt be confirmed at an early day."

One of the young men replied : " We have not come to ask for the appointment, but to solicit you to withdraw the nomination."

" Ah," said Lincoln, " that alters the case ; but on what ground do you wish the nomination withdrawn ?"

The answer was, " Mr. Shrigley is not sound in his theological opinions."

The President inquired: "On what question is the gentleman unsound?"

Response.—"He does not believe in endless punish. ment; not only so, sir, but he believes that even the rebels themselves will finally be saved."

"Is that so?" inquired the President.

The members of the committee both responded, "Yes," "Yes."

"Well, gentlemen, if that be so, and there is any way under heaven whereby the rebels can be saved, then, for God's sake and their sakes, let the man be appointed."

And he *was appointed*, and served until the war closed. In relation to this matter the Hon. John Covode wrote Hon. Henry D. Moore as follows:

"WASHINGTON, 29th January, 1863.

"DEAR SIR: Your friend Mr. Shrigley's appointment was sent to the Senate on the 22d inst. It gives me pleasure to think that I have been able to aid you in this matter.

"Truly yours, JOHN COVODE.

"P. S.—Believing that both you and I, after our long public services, will be benefited by our friend's prayers, I hope we shall have them.

"J. C."

James Shrigley.

PHILADELPHIA, 1882.

22

LETTER TO MRS. ELIZA P. GURNEY.

I HAVE not forgotten, probably never shall forget, the very impressive occasion when yourself and friends visited me on a Sabbath forenoon two years ago. Nor shall your kind letter, written nearly a year later, ever be forgotten. In all it has been your purpose to strengthen my reliance in God. I am much indebted to the good Christian people of the country for their constant prayers and consolations, and to no one of them more than to yourself. The purposes of the Almighty are perfect and must prevail, though we erring mortals may fail to accurately perceive them in advance. We hoped for a happy termination of this terrible war long before this, but God knows best, and has ruled otherwise. We shall yet acknowledge his wisdom and our own errors therein ; meanwhile we must work earnestly in the best light he gives us, trusting that so working still conduces to the great ends he ordains. Surely he intends some great good to follow this mighty convulsion, which no mortal could make, and no mortal could stay. Your people, the Friends, have had, and are having, very great trials, on principles and faith opposed to both war and oppression, they can only practically oppose oppression by war. In this hard dilemma, some have chosen one horn and some the other. For those appealing to me on conscientious grounds I have done and shall do the best I could and can in my own conscience, under my oath to the law. That you believe this I doubt not, and believe I shall still receive for my country and myself your earnest prayers to our Father in heaven.

SEPTEMBER, 1864.

A S the best contribution which I can make, is the following extract from a letter by the late Rt. Rev.
Charles P. McIlvaine, D.D., D.C.L., who knew Mr. Lincoln well, and was brought into official relations with him.
He mourned for him, not only as I do for a great president, but for a personal friend.

"The *man*, so wise, so pure, of such simplicity, such
inflexible determination to the right, who had done so
well in duties and times beyond precedent difficult; who
had gone on winning the confidence, admiration and love
of all classes, till there seemed no more to gain; just finishing his great work, just about to reap the harvest of
all his toil, just showing how moderate and wise and tender he was going to be, cut down by an assassin! Oh,
how it has smitten the nation's heart!"

Responding with all my heart to such an estimate of
the character of President Lincoln.

G. T. Bedell

CLEVELAND, 1882.

I ONCE had a long day's talk about Abraham Lincoln with a friend in Kentucky, Joshua F. Speed, who had lived in intimate relation with Lincoln when he was a young lawyer in Springfield, just beginning business. He said that every case he had took his whole interest and attention. Once he had to argue a case in which all depended on finding the right boundary for a piece of land on the prairie. There are no stones there for boundaries, and few trees, so the surveyors were in the habit of fixing the corners of the lots by shoveling up a little heap of earth. But it happened that a prairie squirrel, or gopher, does the same thing. Hence it becomes important to distinguish between the mounds made by the surveyor and those made by the gopher. Lincoln sent to New York to get books to tell him of the habits of the gopher, brought them into court, showed the judge and jury how the gopher built his mound, how it differed from that of the surveyor, and after he had won his case, sat up late in the night still studying about the gopher, so as to be sure he knew all about him.

J. F. Clarke

BOSTON, 1882,

I FIRST made Mr. Lincoln's acquaintance in 1860, while in Springfield, Ill., on professional business. We met in the studio of my friend Mr. Thomas Jones, the sculptor, who was at that time modeling Mr. Lincoln's bust. The circumstances were favorable to a conversation on literary subjects, and I was charmed with the earnestness and originality exhibited in Mr. Lincoln's remarks and criticisms. His clear insight into characterization was apparent in the expression of his conception of the personalities of Falstaff and old Weller, who seemed to be especial favorites with him. He regarded old Weller as a sort of stage-coach embodiment or type of the Fat Knight, the latter being a tavern reflection, as it were, of the velvet-and-brocade or court side of wit and humor, and the other the familiar or road-side phase or expression of it; but both suggestive of "*the cap-and-bells,*" and furnishing the materials for wholesome merriment. Speaking of Dickens, he said that his works of fiction were so near the reality that the author seemed to him to have picked up his materials from actual life as he elbowed his way through its crowded thoroughfares, after the manner, in a certain sense, of Shakespeare himself. As there was but little of the metaphysical or speculative element in Mr. Lincoln's mind, though strong in practical philosophy, common sense, and clear moral intuitions, it was not difficult to understand and appreciate the preference he expressed, on this occasion, for the speech of King Claudius: "Oh! my offense is rank and smells to heaven," over Hamlet's philosophical " To be or not to be." He expressed a wonder that actors should have laid so much stress on the thought contained in the latter soliloquy, and passed with such comparative indifference over the soul-searching expressions of the king, uttered under the stings of self-accusation. " The former," said Mr. Lincoln, " is merely a philosophical reflection on the question of life and death, without actual reference to a future judgment; while the latter is a solemn acknowl-edgment of inevitable punishment hereafter, for the in-fraction of divine law. Let any one reflect on the moral tone of the two soliloquies, and there can be no mistak-ing the force and grandeur of the lesson taught by one, and the merely speculative consideration in the other, of an alternative for the ills that flesh is heir to." It was very plain how such a mind as his could not fail to be forcibly struck with the truth and grandeur of the follow-ing lines :

> " In the corrupted currents of this world,
>   Offense's gilded hand may shove by justice ;
>   And oft 'tis seen, the wicked prize itself
>   Buys out the law.   But 'tis not so above ;
>   There is no shuffling ; there the action lies
>   In his true nature ; and we ourselves compelled,
>   Even to the teeth and forehead of our faults,
>   To give in evidence."

The conversation turned upon the political condition of the country (it was at the troubled period just previous to Mr. Lincoln's inauguration) and he spoke upon the sub-ject plainly and without hesitation. So deeply was I im-pressed with his hope and faith for the future of the

country and the ultimate triumph of right and justice in
its affairs, that glowed in the fervor of his simple and un-
affected language, and beamed from his benevolent
features, that I lost sight of all the previous impressions
that his reputed story-telling proclivities and his broad
witticisms had made upon me ; I saw only the man—as the
whole world learned to know him—in whom the sacred
principles of eternal justice and human rights were to find
an honest and unflinching champion in the bitter hours
of trial and affliction.

I will simply add a few words in this connection
with regard to the mirthful element of Mr. Lincoln's
character. It has too frequently been misunderstood and
unjustly censured. The following anecdote furnishes us
an instance of the slight ground upon which rested many
of the charges made against Mr. Lincoln, of undignified
conduct and heartless expressions upon serious and
even solemn occasions. The incident was related to me
by one who stood at the President's side at the time of
its occurrence. One day, a detachment of troops was
marching along the avenue singing the soul-stirring
strain of "John Brown." They were walled in on either
side by throngs of citizens and strangers, whose voices
mingled in the roll of the mighty war-song. In the midst
of this exciting scene, a man had clambered into a small
tree, on the side-walk, where he clung, unmindful of the
jeers of the passing crowd, called forth by the strange
antics he was unconsciously exhibiting in his efforts to
overcome the swaying motion of the slight stem which
bent beneath his weight. Mr. Lincoln's attention was
attracted for a moment, and he paused in the serious

conversation in which he was deeply interested and in an abstracted manner, yet with a droll cast of the eye, and a nod of the head in the direction of the man, he repeated, in his dry and peculiar utterance, the following old-fashioned couplet :

> " And Zaccheous he, did climb a tree,
> His Lord and Master, for to see—"

Amid the laughter of those who had observed the incongruity of the scene, Mr. Lincoln resumed the serious tone of his remarks, as if nothing unusual had happened. And yet, said my informant, I have heard him charged, in connection with this incident, with a want of proper feeling, and even with turning sacred subjects into ridicule. It was evident, said he, that Mr. Lincoln did not employ the quotation in a spirit of levity. It was but an unconscious exhibition of the mirthful tendency—or, perhaps, more correctly speaking—necessity of the man's nature. He seemed, as it were, to instinctively select the old-time, ballad-like couplet, from among the mass of quaint and home-spun verse with which his memory was stored, more from the sing-song tone of its jingling rhyme, which perhaps suggested a likeness to the swinging motion of the man before him, than from any intent to ridicule the verses or its allusion to sacred history. It may be that such freaks of fancy were the unpremeditated make-weights by which an over-strained mental activity was prevented from taxing the brain too constantly.

He who can, for a moment, believe that Mr. Lincoln gave utterance to such an expression in a spirit of levity, or could utter a heartless jest, in the midst of a scene calculated to arouse all the interest and enthusiasm of the mind, and stir every deep and impassioned feeling of the heart, by its grandly solemn surroundings, and inevitably terrible consequences, does not understand the character of Abraham Lincoln. Those soldiers and their imperiled lives ; the destinies of the cause they were thronging to the front to defend ; the fortunes of the families they left behind ; the bloodshed, misery and suffering in store for the nation ; all this was crowding upon his brain and throbbing in his heart, with as much intensified sympathy and soul-harrowing foreboding as ever wrung the heart of wife or mother, when called upon to surrender a loved son or a husband to the cause of freedom.

The following incident is but one of many instances of his personal sufferings in the general cause. Having called upon Mr. Lincoln on one occasion during the war, by special appointment, at 9 o'clock in the morning, I was shown into a private room. When the President appeared I was surprised to find him in a state of intensified grief and nervous excitement, the very embodiment of woe, the alternate fever and cold of his hand, and his whole physical being, indicating an overstrained condition, attendant upon mental and physical agitation and suffering. After a few passing remarks the cause of his condition was explained, when I learned from his lips, for the first time, the news of our defeat at Chancellorville. I shall never forget the kindly and grateful expression of his face when I stated the fact that, not being aware of the disaster when I came, I felt the propriety of deferring the occasion of our interview to some more fitting time. Receiving an earnest pressure of the hand, and a fervent "God bless you," I left the presence of one whom I felt to be indeed bowed down under the burden of a nation's affliction. And yet, strange as it may appear to those of a different temperament, Mr. Lincoln could, as he certainly did on many an occasion, by force of will, subdue the heart-throb, crush back the rising tear, and turn his thoughts in other channels, molding his features to expression of indifference or mirth. This same "levity," as some white-haired sinners of his day called it, was often the "nice fence," with which he foiled the more serious thrusts made by his opponents, and as such served his purpose, perhaps better than other means might have done.

Those who knew Mr. Lincoln and loved the man had cause to look through and over such peculiarities, content with an appreciation of the more sterling qualities which generously and thoroughly pervaded his nature. What was said of Thomas Fuller, the facetious, though devout old preacher, who lived in the troublous times of Charles the First, may be as truly said of Mr. Lincoln: "He was endowed with that happy buoyancy of spirit which, next to religion itself, is the most precious possession of man." Untiring humor seemed the ruling passion of his soul; quaintly and facetiously he thought, wrote and spoke, preferring ever a jocose expression even in his gravest moments.

With a heart open to all innocent pleasure and purged from the leaven of malice and uncharitableness, it was as natural that he should be as full of mirth as it is for the grasshopper to chirp, or bees to hum, or birds to warble in the spring breeze and the bright sunshine.

James E. Murdoch

CINCINNATI, 1882.

23

SPEECH TO THE 148TH OHIO REGIMENT.

IT is vain and foolish to arraign this man or that for the part he has taken or has not taken, and to hold the Government responsible for his acts. In no administration can there be perfect equality of action and uniform satisfaction rendered by all.

But this Government must be preserved in spite of the acts of any man or set of men. It is worthy your every effort. Nowhere in the world is presented a Government of so much liberty and equality. To the humblest and poorest amongst us are held out the highest privileges and positions. The present moment finds me at the White House, yet there is as good a chance for your children as there was for my father's. Again I admonish you not to be turned from your stern purpose of defending our beloved country and its free institutions by any arguments urged by ambitious and designing men, but stand fast to the Union and the old flag.

ABRAHAM LINCOLN'S name ranks with the purest of men, the wisest of statesmen, the most sincere and devoted patriot, the loveliest character of American statesmen.

Chas Foster

COLUMBUS, 1880.

" JUSTUM ac tenacem propositi virum
Non civium ardor prava jubentium
Non vultus instantis tyranni,
Mente quatit solida."

HORACE.

"With malice toward none, with charity to all, with firmness in the right."

LINCOLN.

Hamilton Fish

NEW YORK, 1880.

REMARKS TO A SERENADING PARTY AT THE WHITE HOUSE.

I AM notified that this is a compliment paid to me by the loyal Marylanders resident in this District. I infer that the adoption of the new Constitution for the State furnishes the occasion, and that, in your view, the extirpation of slavery constitutes the chief merit of the new Constitution.

Most heartily do I congratulate you and Maryland, and the nation, and the world upon the event. I regret that it did not occur two years sooner; which, I am sure, would have saved to the nation more money than would have met all the private loss incident to the measure. But it has come at last, and I sincerely hope its friends may fully realize all their anticipations of good from it, and that its opponents may, by its effects, be agreeably and profitably disappointed. A word upon another subject. Something said by the Secretary of State, in his recent speech at Auburn, has been construed by some into a threat that, if I shall be beaten at the election, I will, between then and the end of my constitutional term, do what I may be able to ruin the Government. Others regard the fact that the Chicago Convention adjourned not *sine die*, but to meet again, if called to do so by a particular individual, as the intimation of a purpose that if their nominee shall be elected he will at once seize the control of the Government. I hope the good people will permit themselves to suffer no uneasiness on this point.

I am struggling to maintain the Government, not to overthrow it; I am struggling especially to prevent others from overthrowing it. I therefore say that, if I shall live, I shall remain President until the fourth of next March, and that whoever shall be constitutionally elected therefor, in November, shall be duly installed as President on the fourth of March, and that, in the interval, I shall do my utmost that whoever is to hold the helm for the next voyage shall start with the best possible chance to save the ship. This is due the people both on principle and under the Constitution. Their will, constitutionally expressed, is the ultimate law for all. If they should deliberately resolve to have immediate peace, even at the loss of their country and their liberties, I have not the power or the right to resist them. It is their own business, and they must do as they please with their own; I believe, however, they are still resolved to preserve their country and their liberty; and, in this office or out, I am resolved to stand by them. I may add, that in this purpose to save the country and its liberties no class of people seem so nearly unanimous as the soldiers in the field and seamen afloat. Do they not have the hardest of it? Who should quail while they do not? God bless the soldiers and seamen, with all their brave commanders!

OCTOBER 19, 1864.

OBSERVANCE OF THE SABBATH.

THE President, Commander-in-Chief of the Army and Navy, desires and enjoins the orderly observance of the Sabbath by the officers and men in the military and naval service. The importance to man and beast of the prescribed weekly rest, the sacred rights of Christian soldiers and sailors, a becoming deference to the best sentiment of Christian people, and a due regard for the Divine Will, demand that Sunday labor in the army and navy be reduced to the measure of strict necessity. The discipline and character of the national forces should not suffer, nor the cause they defend be imperiled, by the profanation of the day or name of the Most High. "At the time of public distress," adopting the words of Washington in 1776, "men may find enough to do in the service of their God and their country without abandoning themselves to vice and immorality." The first general order issued by the Father of his Country after the Declaration of Independence indicates the spirit in which our institutions were founded and should ever be defended: "*The General hopes and trusts that every officer and man will endeavor to live and act as becomes a Christian soldier defending the dearest rights and liberties of his country.*"

Abraham Lincoln

NOVEMBER 16, 1864.

THE name of Abraham Lincoln will not grow dim with age, like many names brilliant in their own day, yet fading with the lapse of time. But that name will shine with ever-increasing luster, as the results of his public life and services shall be more clearly manifested in the increasing greatness of his country, which, without his wise leadership, aided by faithful counselors, would have been dissolved into clusters of insignificant states, forever at war and forever weak.

Henry S. Frieze.

1880.

LINCOLN—the statesman, the emancipator, the martyr, whose services to his country will be remembered with those of Washington.

Cyrus W. Field.

NEW YORK, 1880.

LETTER TO MRS. BIXBY OF BOSTON.

I HAVE been shown on the file of the War Department a statement of the Adjutant-General of Massachusetts, that you are the mother of five sons who have died gloriously on the field of battle. I feel how weak and fruitless must be any word of mine which should attempt to beguile you from the grief of a loss so over whelming; but I cannot refrain from tendering to you the consolation that may be found in the thanks of the republic they died to save. I pray that our Heavenly Father may assuage the anguish of your bereavements, and leave only the cherished memory of the loved and lost, and the solemn pride that must be yours to have laid so costly a sacrifice upon the altar of freedom.

Abraham Lincoln

NOVEMBER 21, 1864.

NO man has so happily blended in his character child-like simplicity with true greatness and nobility, and combined so great a degree of tenderness with lofty and unflinching courage, as the lamented Lincoln. The energy and perseverance that enabled him to overcome the poverty and obscurity which enshrouded his youth eminently qualified him to encounter and surmount the colossal difficulties that environed his administration. His strong common sense, undaunted patriotism, and wise statesmanship have left an impress on our institutions which will never be effaced so long as this is freedom's home; and their influence shall not be felt here alone, but throughout the civilized world, for centuries to come.

He has taken and will hold rank in history with the purest and most illustrious of mankind. Admiring countrymen have erected a noble shaft to mark his last resting-place, while in their heart of hearts they have builded a mausoleum that will successfully defy the devouring tooth of time; but surpassing these is the monument erected by his philanthropic statesmanship, of manacles torn from the limbs of four million slaves.

W. O. Bradley

LANCASTER, 1882.

REMARKS TO A DELEGATION FROM OHIO.

I AM very much obliged to you for this compliment. I have just been saying, and as I have just said it, I will repeat it: The hardest of all speeches which I have to answer is a serenade. I never know what to say on such occasions. I suppose that you have done me this kindness in connection with the action of the Baltimore Convention, which has recently taken place, and with which, of course, I am very well satisfied. What we want still more than Baltimore Conventions or Presidential Elections is success under General Grant. I propose that you constantly bear in mind that the support you owe to the brave officers and soldiers in the field is of the very first importance, and we should, therefore, bend all our energies to that point. Now, without detaining you any longer, I propose that you help me to close up what I am now saying with three rousing cheers for General Grant and the officers and soldiers under his command.

FROM our official and social relations, for over four years, I had abundant opportunity to know Mr. Lincoln well. I have been a student of human nature and character all my life, and of all the men that have ever challenged my attention, I have never found Mr. Lincoln's equal; possessing the simplicity of a child, and the tenderness of a woman, he combined, in his make-up, all the sterner qualities of a perfect man. A close observer of men, measures and events, and with a discriminating mind that led to a correct judgment, was added a conscientiousness of the right and a moral courage to do it, that enabled him to execute his honest convictions of all the political and social duties that were required of him as a man and a magistrate.

JACKSONVILLE, 1881.

FOURTH ANNUAL MESSAGE

TO CONGRESS, DECEMBER 6TH, 1864.

THE most remarkable feature in the military opera-
tions of the year is General Sherman's attempted march
of three hundred miles directly through the insurgent
region.   It tends to show a great increase of our relative
strength that our General-in-Chief should feel able to
confront and hold in check every active force of the enemy,
and yet to detach a well-appointed large army to move
on such an expedition.   The result not yet being known,
conjecture in regard to it is not here indulged.

Important movements have also occurred during the
year to the effect of molding society for durability in
the Union.   Although short of complete success, it is
much in the right direction that twelve thousand citizens
in each of the States of Arkansas and Louisiana have
organized loyal State governments, with free constitu-
tions, and are earnestly struggling to maintain and administer them.   The movements in the same direction—
more extensive, though less definite—in Missouri,
Kentucky, and Tennessee should not be overlooked.
But Maryland presents the example of complete success.
Maryland is secure to Liberty and Union for all the
future.   The genius of rebellion will no more claim
Maryland.   Like another foul spirit, being driven out, it
may seek to tear her, but it will woo her no more.

In presenting the abandonment of armed resistance to

the national authority, on the part of the insurgents, as the only indispensable condition to ending the war on the part of the Government, I retract nothing heretofore said as to slavery. I repeat the declaration made a year ago, that "while I remain in my present position I shall not attempt to retract or modify the emancipation proclamation, nor shall I return to slavery any person who is free by the terms of that proclamation, or by any of the acts of Congress." If the people should, by whatever mode or means, make it an executive duty to re-enslave such persons, another, and not I, must be their instrument to perform it.

In stating a single condition of peace, I mean simply to say that the war will cease on the part of the Government whenever it shall have ceased on the part of those who began it.

**INFANTRY GROUP OF STATUARY. NATIONAL LINCOLN
MONUMENT.**

Representing a body of infantry soldiers on the march. They are fired
upon from some covert place, and the color-bearer killed. The captain
raises the colors with one hand, and with the other points to the enemy
and orders a bayonet charge, which the private on his right is in the act of
executing. The drummer-boy becomes excited, loses his cap, throws
away his haversack, puts one drumstick in his belt, draws a revolver and
engages in the conflict. The exploded shell indicates that they are on
ground that has been fought over before.

[EXTRACT.]

I KNOW, when I left him, that I was more than ever impressed by his kindly nature, his deep and earnest sympathy with the afflictions of the whole people, resulting from the war, and by the march of hostile armies through the South ; and that his earnest desire seemed to be to end the war speedily, without more bloodshed or devastation, and to restore all the men of both sections to their homes. In the language of his second inaugural address he seemed to have " charity for all, malice toward none," and, above all, an absolute faith in the courage, manliness, and integrity of the armies in the field. When at rest or listening, his legs and arms seemed to hang almost lifeless, and his face was care-worn and haggard; but the moment he began to talk his face lightened up, his tall form, as it were, unfolded, and he was the very impersonation of good-humor and fellowship. The last words I recall as addressed to me were that he would feel better when I was back at Goldsboro'. We parted at the gang-way of the *River Queen* about noon of March 28th, and I never saw him again. Of all the men I ever met, he seemed to possess more of the elements of greatness, combined with goodness, than any other.

W. T. Sherman

WASHINGTON, 1880.

A PRIVATE soldier from my congressional district having been convicted of knocking down his captain, was sentenced to two years' labor on the Dry Tortugas. With some of his neighbors I called upon President Lincoln to solicit a pardon. He appeared completely worn out, and complained of weariness ; said he was unable to look after details, and we must go to Stanton. I told him we had been there, but he declined to interfere. "Then, said the President, "attend to it yourselves at the Capitol." I inquired what Congress could do in the matter, and quick as thought he said : " Pass a law that a private shall have a right to knock down his captain." But after the wit came the pardon.

Glenni W. Scofield

WARREN, 1880.
24

SECOND INAUGURAL ADDRESS,

DELIVERED MARCH 3, 1865.

"FELLOW COUNTRYMEN: At this second appearing to take the oath of the presidential office, there is less occasion for an extended address than there was at the first. Then a statement somewhat in detail of a course to be pursued seemed fitting and proper. Now, at the expiration of four years, during which public declarations have been constantly called forth on every point and phase of the great contest which still absorbs the attention and engrosses the energies of the nation, little that is new could be presented. The progress of our arms, upon which all else chiefly depends, is as well known to the public as to myself, and it is, I trust, reasonably satisfactory and encouraging to all. With high hope for the future, no prediction in regard to it is ventured.

"On the occasion corresponding to this, four years ago, all thoughts were anxiously directed to an impending civil war. All dreaded it; all sought to avert it. While the inaugural address was being delivered from this place, devoted altogether to saving the Union without war, insurgent agents were in the city seeking to destroy it without war—seeking to dissolve the Union and divide its effects by negotiation. Both parties deprecated war; but one of them would make war rather than let the nation survive, and the other would accept war rather than let it perish. And the war came.

"Both could not be answered—those of neither have been answered fully. The Almighty has his own purposes. Woe unto the world because of offenses! for it must needs be that offenses come; but woe to that man by whom the offense cometh.

"If we shall suppose that American slavery is one of those offenses which, in the providence of God, must needs come, but which, having continued through his appointed time, he now wills to remove, and that he gives to North and South this terrible war, as the woe due to those by whom the offense came, shall we discern therein any departure from those Divine attributes which the believers in a living God always ascribe to him? Fondly do we hope, fervently do we pray, that this mighty scourge of war may soon pass away. Yet, if God wills that it continue until all the wealth piled by the bondsman's two hundred and fifty years of unrequited toil shall be sunk, and until every drop of blood drawn by the lash shall be paid by another drawn with the sword, as was said three thousand years ago, so still it must be said: 'The judgments of the Lord are true and righteous altogether.'

"With malice toward none, with charity for all, with firmness in the right, as God gives us to see the right, let us strive on to finish the work we are in; to bind up the nation's wounds; to care for him who shall have borne the battle, and for his widow and for his orphan; to do all which may achieve and cherish a just and lasting peace among ourselves, and with all nations."

Abraham Lincoln

"BESIDES .... he hath borne his faculties so meek,
   Hath been so clean in his great office
That his virtues will plead like angels, trumpet-tongued,
Against the deep damnation of his taking off.
And Pity, like a naked, new-born babe, striding the blast,
Or Heaven's cherubim, horsed on the sightless couriers of
   the air,
Shall blow the horrid deed in every eye,
That tears shall drown the wind."

Lawrence Barrett.

COHASSET, 1880.

I BELIEVE in Divine inspiration for good, and that
   God sometimes intervenes in the affairs of man.
Abraham Lincoln, in my view, was charged with a Divine
mission, which he executed wisely and well, and is justly
entitled to the reverence, gratitude and love of all loyal
citizens of our great republic.

Neal Dow

PORTLAND, 1882.

A VERBAL MESSAGE GIVEN BY MR. LIN-COLN TO HON. SCHUYLER COLFAX, FOR THE MINERS OF THE FAR WEST,

APRIL 14, 1865.

MR. COLFAX :—I want you to take a message from me to the miners whom you visit. I have very large ideas of the mineral wealth of our nation. I believe it practically inexhaustible. It abounds all over the western country, from the Rocky Mountains to the Pacific, and its development has scarcely commenced. During the war, when we were adding a couple of millions of dollars every day to our national debt, I did not care about encouraging the increase in the volume of our precious metals. We had the country to save first. But, now that the rebellion is overthrown, and we know pretty nearly the amount of our national debt, the more gold and silver we mine makes the payment of that debt so much the easier. Now, I am going to encourage that in every possible way. We shall have hundreds of thousands of disbanded soldiers, and many have feared that their return home in such great numbers might paralyze industry by furnishing suddenly a greater supply of labor than there will be a demand for. I am going to try and attract them to the hidden wealth of our mountain ranges, where there is room enough for all. Immigration, which even the war has not stopped, will land upon our shores hundreds of thousands more per year from over-crowded Europe. I intend to point them to the gold and silver that waits for them in the West. Tell the miners from me that I shall promote their interests to the utmost of my ability, because their prosperity is the prosperity of the nation ; and we shall prove, in a very few years, that we are, indeed, the *treasury of the world.*

Mr. Lincoln went to the opera, saying :—" People may think strange of it, but I *must* have some relief from this terrible anxiety, or it will kill me."

APRIL 14TH, 1865.

FORD'S THEATRE,

TENTH STREET, WASHINGTON, D. C.

FRIDAY EVENING, APRIL 14th, 1865.

THIS EVENING
the performance will be honored by the presence of
PRESIDENT LINCOLN.

Benefit and last night of MISS

LAURA KEENE,

The distinguished Manageress, Authoress and Actress, supported by
Mr. JOHN DYOTT and Mr. HARRY HAWK.

Tom Taylor's celebrated Eccentric Comedy as originally produced in
America by Miss Keene, and performed by her upwards of
ONE THOUSAND NIGHTS

ENTITLED

OUR AMERICAN COUSIN.

FLORENCE TRENCHARD	Miss LAURA KEENE.
Abel Murcott	John Dyott.
Asa Trenchard	Harry Hawk.
Sir Edward Trenchard	T. C. Gourlay.
Lord Dundreary	E. A. Emerson.
Mr. Coyle, Attorney	J. Mathews.
Lieut. Vernon, R. N	W. J. Ferguson.
Captain De Boots	C. Byrnes.
Binney	G. G. Spear.
Buddicomb, a valet	J. H. Evans.
John Whicker, a gardner	J. L. De Bonay
Rasper, a groom	
Bailiffs	G. A. Parkhurst and L Johnson.
Mary Trenchard	Miss J. Gourlay.
Mrs. Mountchessington	Mrs. H. Muzzey.
Augusta	Miss H. Truman.
Georgiana	Miss M. Hart.
Sharpe	Mrs. J. H. Evans.
Skillet	Miss M. Gourlay.

THE PRICES OF ADMISSION :

Orchestra,	$1 00	Dress Circle and Parquette,	$ 75
Family Circle	25	Private Boxes,	$6 00 and $10 00

J. R. FORD, Business Manager.

H. POLKINHORN & SON, Printers, Washington, D. C.

ABRAHAM LINCOLN is the purest man of the people known to history. In his public career he was as incorruptible as Aristides the Just, as sagacious as William the Silent, as brave as Cromwell, and as unselfish as Codrus the Athenian, who fell in the forefront of the battle, that by the sacrifice of his life he might be the preserver of his country.

Martin L. D'Ooge

UNIVERSITY OF MICHIGAN, 1880.

HE was a patriot and a wise man. The fundamental ideas of the American republican system controlled his mind and dictated his action. His wisdom carried the United States safely through the war of secession and abolished slavery. His death was a calamity for the country, but it left his fame without a fault or criticism.

Charles A. Dana.

NEW YORK, 1881.

PERHAPS no quality in the character of the late President Lincoln was more conspicuous or more engaging than his broad and deep humanity—the interest he felt in every human being—and the unostentatious and beautiful manifestations of it which were visible to all who had intercourse with him.

No person of much sentiment or sensibility ever looked into his wonderful eyes without feeling the spell which they exerted, or without knowing that they were the windows through which a great soul was looking upon the problems of life and the actors in them, with a calm, philosophic and loving sympathy. This was one of the secrets of the magical power of Lincoln's presence.

He was mirthful, talkative and sad by turns ; fond of superficial anecdotes, and invented and used them at convenience or pleasure, to furnish amusement, to parry a bore, or to point an argument. He was familiar and companionable in ordinary intercourse, always neglectful of assuming any unreal dignity, and apparently unconscious of the greatness of his office, except only the greatness of its responsibilities. To a casual observer, he was homely in person and awkward in manners; and yet he was a man with whom no one could presume to trifle. and before whom, even in his playful moods, every one was impressed by his greatness of spirit.

We have had no man in our history like Lincoln in his leading characteristics, and they cannot be imitated. He had not much of the serene and contemplative gravity which belongs to our traditional Washington ; none of the imperious personality of Jackson ; none of the winsome and chivalric dash of Henry Clay ; none of the ponderous eloquence of Webster, and but little of that polite learning which gives high ornament to literature and statesmanship ; but he had a subtle and comprehensive intellect, wonderful power of intuition, and a transparency of soul through which the truth shone into affairs and gave them an interpretation almost divine.

Nobody ever feared that Lincoln would do a mean or wrong thing ; no one dreaded a foolish thing from him ; and the country came, finally, to expect from him the wisest and best that could be done in every case and on every subject.

It is doubtful if any man born and reared under the civilization of the older States could ever have become a characteristic Lincoln. To produce him the rough simplicity of frontier life was necessary ; its needs, its privations, its efforts, its self-reliance—that whole sphere of experience in which the daily life, though simple, is yet full of problems such as can be, and must be, solved ; and which are but the epitome of those larger problems which, later on, demand the strongest and most versatile powers in their solution. In that simple life the facts and uses of knowledge, rather than its verbiage, are acquired and appreciated; all the faculties are quickened and toughened a more quiet contact with nature is enjoyed ; and out of that contact often comes the consciousness of a mysterious Power greater than nature, between which and men a communion more or less palpable is possible, a communion which gives to human actions the elements of dignity and power that extend far above and beyond the realm and the period of earthly existence. Lincoln was a man of profound spirituality. All this, and much that might be added, was essential to the development of a man like Abraham Lincoln.

But I intended to speak especially and almost wholly of the humanity of Lincoln—of his love for the whole race of men, and of his sympathy with individuals in their trials and distresses. Passing by those great public acts, his Proclamation of Emancipation and the like, which have become historic, and which have modified the laws and institutions and even the civilization of the country, let me give a few personal incidents which have never been published.

While officially resident in Washington, during the late war, I once had occasion to call upon President Lincoln with the late Senator Henry Wilson, upon an errand of a public nature in which we were mutually interested. In the recognized order of precedence a member of the House of Representatives, as I then was, could not times of pressure for audience with the President gain admittance so long as there were Cabinet Ministers, members of the Diplomatic Corps, Senators or Justices of the Supreme Court desiring audience with him, and all civilians must wait their opportunity until after members of Congress and officers of the Army and Navy, and of the Civil Service and others, had had their turns respectively. Having a joint errand with Senator Wilson, I could avail of his privilege of earlier admission ; but we were obliged to wait some time in the anteroom before we could be received, and when at length the door was opened to us, a small lad, perhaps ten or twelve years old, who had been waiting for admission several days without success, slipped in between us, and approached the President in advance. The latter gave the Senator and myself a cordial but brief salutation, and turning immediately to the lad, said: "And who is the little boy?" During their conference the Senator and myself were apparently forgotten. The boy soon told his story, which was in substance that he had come to Washington seeking employment as a page in the House of Representatives, and he wished the President to give him such an appointment. To this the President replied that such appointments were not at his disposal, and that application must be made to the door-keeper of the House at the Capitol. "But, sir," said the lad, still undaunted, "I am a good boy, and have a letter from my mother, and one from the supervisors of my town, and one from my Sunday-school teacher, and they all told me that I could earn enough in one session of Congress to keep my mother and the rest of us comfortable all the remainder of the year." The President took the lad's papers, and ran his eye over them with that penetrating and absorbing look so familiar to all who knew him, and then took his pen and wrote upon the back of one of them: "If Captain Goodnow can give a place to this good little boy, I shall be gratified," and signed it "A. Lincoln."

The boy's face became radiant with hope, and he walked out of the room with a step as light as though all the angels were whispering their congratulations.

Only after the lad had gone did the President seem

to realize that a Senator and another person had been some time waiting to see him.

Think for a moment of the President of a great nation, and that nation engaged in one of the most terrible wars ever waged among men, himself worn down with anxiety and labor, subjected to the alternations of success and defeat, racked by complaints of the envious, the disloyal and the unreasonable, pressed to the decision of grave questions of public policy, and encumbered by the numberless and nameless incidents of civil and martial responsibility, yet able so far to forget them all as to give himself up for the time being to the errand of a little boy who had braved an interview uninvited, and of whom he knew nothing, but that he had a story to tell of his widowed mother, and of his ambition to serve her.

On another occasion I had an interview with President Lincoln on behalf of a captain in one of our Massachusetts regiments, a brave man, who, after most valiant service, had been captured by the rebels, and was then held a prisoner at Richmond. I asked that he might be exchanged. The President replied with much kindness that such cases were so numerous that he could not deal with them individually, but must classify and decide them in considerable numbers. This was obviously so true as scarcely to admit of reply; yet I ventured to say that if he could but hear this case, I thought it so remarkable that he would be glad to make it an exception. "Well, state it," he said, and I did so; and immediately on my closing, the President said, "I wish you would go over to the War Department and tell Gen. —— that story, just as you have told it to me, and say from me that if it be possible for him to effect the exchange of Captain —— without compromising the cases of other prisoners of his rank, I wish him to do so." "But," I said, "for a technical misdemeanor Captain —— has, since his capture, been deprived of his commission and reduced to the ranks, and probably the rebels will not exchange him for a private soldier." "Well," said the President, "if Gen. —— raises that point, say to him that if he can arrange the exchange part, I can take care of the rank part, and I will do so." The captain was in Washington in about ten days afterwards.

Again, a boy from one of the country towns of Massachusetts, who had entered a store in Boston, and become dazzled by the apparent universal distribution of wealth, without any definite idea of how it was acquired, fell into the fault of robbing his employer's letters as he took them to and from the post-office, and, having been convicted of the offense, was serving out his sentence in jail. The father of this boy came to Washington to obtain a pardon for his son, and I accompanied him to the White House and introduced him. A petition signed by a large number of respectable citizens was presented. The President put on his spectacles and stretched himself at length upon his arm-chair while he deliberately read the document, and then he turned to me and asked if I met a man going down the stairs as I came up. I said that I did. "Yes," said the President; "he was the last person in this room before you came, and his errand was to get a man pardoned out of the penitentiary ; and now you have come to get a boy out of jail !" Then, with one of those bursts of humor which were both contagious and irresistible, he said : " I'll tell you what it is, we must abolish those courts, or they will be the death of us. I thought it bad enough that they put so many men in the penitentiaries for me to get out ; but if they have now begun on the boys and the jails, and have roped you into the delivery, let's after them ! And they deserve the worst fate," he soon continued, " because, according to the evidence that comes to me, they pick out the very best men and send them to the penitentiary ; and this present petition shows they are playing the same game on the good boys, and sending them all to jail. The man you met on the stairs affirmed that his friend in the penitentiary is a most exemplary citizen, and Massachusetts must be a happy State if her boys out of jail are as virtuous as this one appears to be who is in. Yes ; down with the courts and deliverance to their victims, and then we can have some peace !"

During all this time the President was in a most merry mood. Then his face assumed a sad and thoughtful expression, and he proceeded to say that he could quite understand how a boy from simple country life might be overcome by the sight of universal abundance in a large city, and by a full supply of money in the pockets of almost everybody, and be led to commit even such an offense as this one had done, and yet not be justly put into the class of hopeless criminals ; and if he could be satisfied that this was a case of that kind, and that the boy would be placed under proper influences, and probably saved from a bad career, he would be glad to extend the clemency asked for. The father explained his purpose in that respect, the Congressmen from the State in which he belonged united in the petition, and the boy was pardoned.

Such examples as these, varying in character, but all springing from the same tender and noble qualities of heart, might be multiplied almost indefinitely; but they all found culmination in that grandest utterance of modern eloquence, at the consecration of the battle-field of Gettysburg, when, the promptings of his soul having summoned his intellect to the point of supreme exaltation, he spoke to all mankind those words of patriotism, admonition and pathos which will continue to sound through the ages as long as the flowers shall bloom or the waters flow.

BOSTON, 1882.
25

I HAVE always had the greatest admiration for the amiable, simple and honest traits of Mr. Lincoln's character. I believe that, under the providence of God, he was, next to Washington, the greatest instrument for the preservation of the Union and the integrity of the country; and this was brought about chiefly through his strict and faithful adherence to the Constitution of his country.

New York, 1880.

IN the revolutionary struggle George Washington was raised up to be our great leader in the achievement of national independence ; and in the rebellion Abraham Lincoln was placed in the Presidential chair to preserve the Union from dissolution and destruction.   Each of these great men seems to have been chosen of God for his special work, and the names of Washington and Lincoln will forever be united in the memory and love of the American people.

Israel Ward Andrews.

MARIETTA COLLEGE, 1880.

ABRAHAM LINCOLN was the man for the times ; and in the great work he accomplished for his country, and in the cause of human rights, he has not been surpassed by any of the greatest and best men of our land.

P. A. Chadbourne

WILLIAMS COLLEGE.

IN the broadest and best sense of the term, Abraham Lincoln was America's great "Commoner." Possibly he builded wiser than he knew, for while

> "He carved his name on time as on a rock,
> And stood thereon as on a monument,"

he was apparently unconscious as an infant-giant of his own high possibilities. A patriot without pretense, and a statesman by intuition, he could still descend to the level of the humblest, ever ready with a jest to point a moral, and with a story to confound a sophist.

At the time when bloody treason flourished and he fell, the Southern people, unjustly accused of sympathy with his assassin, were just beginning to appreciate his sterling qualities and the wisdom of his acts. His death was to the North a bereavement and a grief; to the South it was a dire calamity which hindered the consummation of that "more perfect union" for which all good people prayed; and to-day the men and women of the South, without distinction of race or color, cherish the memory of the Martyr-President as that of a Deliverer.

> *He*, whom the people honored; *he*, the wise,
>   Who fought for honor's prize;
> He, whom the armies reverenced—the good,
>   Who every lure withstood;
> He, whom the ransomed worshiped; HE, the blest,
>   Has gone to his great rest!

A BRAHAM LINCOLN. AN AMERICAN, I
find all the characteristics of the ideal American
embodied in this great, good MAN. Coming ages alone
can properly estimate the value of his services to this
country and to human freedom in all lands.

Jas. Marvin

LAWRENCE, 1880.

N O other statesman in the world's history has ever
won from so many men their personal affection,
thorough confidence and enthusiastic admiration, as
Abraham Lincoln.

C. M. Mead.

ANDOVER THEOLOGICAL SEMINARY, 1880.

M Y first acquaintance with Abraham Lincoln commenced on his arrival at New Salem, Sangamon
County, Illinois, on a flat-boat, about the year 1830, in
company with one Denton Offeit, who had a store.
Lincoln clerked for him some time, after which he went
to work at anything that could be found to do, such as
cutting and splitting rails, etc. He had worked but a
short time when he was appointed deputy-sheriff, and
after a time became county-surveyor under one Calhoun,
of Springfield, which business he followed for some time.
Lincoln was poor; but it was soon discovered that he
possessed a very high order of intellect, and therefore
he was helped and encouraged, and soon had a host of
friends in New Salem. About this time he went into the
family grocery business, but left the business principally
in charge of his partner, while he devoted his time to
other business and at the same time studying to make
something of himself. When at work he was in the
habit of carrying a book about with him, and when
stopping to rest would devote the time to reading, and
what he read he remembered. I recollect of his saying
that "A fool could learn about as well as a wise man,
but after he had learned, it did not do him any good."

Lincoln said he did not believe in total depravity,
and, although it was not popular to believe it, it was
easier to do right than wrong; that the first thought
was: what was right? and the second —what was wrong?
Therefore it was easier to do right than wrong, and

easier to take care of, as it would take care of itself. It took an effort to do wrong, and a still greater effort to take care of it ; but do right, and it would take care of itself. Then you had nothing to do but to go ahead and do right and nothing to trouble you.

He was a very close observer. Speaking of a prayer he once heard a very pious man make, in which he prayed very earnestly for the "widowers," he said he "did not know but what it might be an improvement on prayer ; that he did not know but the widows had about as hard a time as the widowers, but believed that God did all things right."

Lincoln, during his residence in New Salem, was a candidate for the Legislature. There were nine who wanted to be elected, and he said : "They let him off with 700 votes—a little behind the ninth man." After this some of the talented, big men induced him to move to Springfield. The next time he was a candidate he was elected to the Legislature, where he distinguished himself by taking a prominent part in favor of internal improvements and other important measures. In politics he was a Whig, and so was I ; and when the Whig party had worn itself out in honorable age he and I joined the Republican party. After leaving New Salem for Springfield, Mr. Lincoln and myself petitioned for a new county. He looked out the lines of the proposed new county, and the result was the county of Menard was set off. At this time he was an able lawyer, and stood very high in the profession. He was always kind to his friends, and attended to some law business for me, frequently gave me advice ; and I do not recollect of his ever charging me anything for it. He was not only kind to his friends, but possessed a large share of humanity and was kind to all.

I was acquainted with him a long time, and I never knew him to do a wrong act. While he had a host of friends, I would not say that he had no enemies. In this connection I will quote in substance what he said at the funeral of one Boling Green, of Menard county, an old citizen and friend of Mr. Lincoln. The arrangements for the funeral were that Dr. McNeal, of Springfield, was to preach the funeral sermon and Mr. Lincoln was to speak of the character of the deceased. Dr. McNeal, in his introductory remarks, said that in relation to the character of the deceased he would say nothing, as that was left to better and abler hands. At the conclusion of the sermon Mr. Lincoln arose and said that Mr. Green, the deceased, had a great many friends, and had always been a true friend to him, but he would not say that he, Green, had no enemies. There was, however, one consolation in that, for he read in Sacred Writ, a woe was pronounced on that man that all men spoke well of, and in that his deceased friend got rid of that "woe;" and so I would say of Mr. Lincoln, he will get rid of that woe. As is well known, Mr. Lincoln volunteered and went into the Black Hawk War, as captain of a company of Illinois troops, and, as I recollect, did well and was liked by all. The "boys" would get discouraged, but Lincoln would cheer them up by cracking his jokes, telling amusing stories and appearing always cheerful.

It may not be generally known, but Mr. Lincoln surveyed and laid out the town of Petersburg, which is now a city. He was also elected to Congress, the well-known Peter Cartwright, a Methodist preacher, being his opponent in the canvass. The records of the country show what he did in opposition to the Kansas-Nebraska bill, when he took issue with Stephen A. Douglas, agreed upon a joint discussion, and made a canvass of the State.

At one of their public discussions—I believe it was at Havana—after the discussion had been somewhat prolonged and it was thought that Mr. Douglas had exhausted his argument, Mr. Lincoln came forward and told a story. He said: There were large poplar trees in Kentucky, and he knew a man who had a very large one, and nothing near to pile upon it, so as to burn it, and it was so large that it could not be hauled away; and he then asked if any one could tell what they did about it? No one answering, he told them: "They went around it." "Just so," said Mr. Lincoln, "Mr. Douglas will have to do with his Kansas-Nebraska bill, just go around it." The well-known remark of Mr. Lincoln, that the Government could not exist half free and half slave, and that a house divided against itself could not stand. My opinion is, there never was a better man than Abraham Lincoln, and I came to this conclusion from a long acquaintance with him.

William McNeely

Petersburg, 1882.

ABRAHAM LINCOLN.

OUR country's Titan! on her mighty rivers,
  Her trackless plains, in virgin forests growing,
That strength was nurtured which a land delivers,
  And reaps the harvest of a century's sowing.

Harvest of blood and death: Oh! hapless nation,
  Into that gulf her best and bravest throwing !
Rome gave her Curtius for an expiation—
  Our sealed abyss was thy great heart's outflowing.

Louisa Parsons Hopkins

NEW BEDFORD, 1882.

I T would be a difficult matter for any one to give a proper idea of Abraham Lincoln and his services during the years he was engaged in the most stupendous labor that has perhaps fallen to the lot of a statesman. He can be better judged by his works than by anything I could say. I was intimately associated with Mr. Lincoln during a period of two or three weeks when the war of the rebellion was drawing to a close, and my remembrance of him is of a man whose mind was oppressed with care and whose body was almost broken down with the magnitude of his labors ; whose days and nights were passed in sleepless anxiety for the preservation and welfare of the Union. I knew nothing, personally, of Mr. Lincoln's trials in the Cabinet, where I am sure he had much to contend with, or of the dissensions with politicians who, amid the ruins of their country, were working for their own aggrandizement. I only knew the President as an honest, faithful worker in his country's cause, who did the best he could to bring the war to a speedy close, while at the same time he showed a determined spirit to yield nothing that would militate against the Republic of which he was the head. Although painted by his enemies in the blackest colors, President Lincoln had a heart capable of the greatest sympathy and the keenest emotions for the carnage and destruction he saw going on in every direction, and if necessary he would have sacrificed his life to avert these horrors. If Mr. Lincoln had never done more than the one act of abolishing slavery and wiping out that blot on our civilization, it would have been enough to immortalize him ;

but if his biography is publicly written when prejudices are laid aside, so that the man can be seen in his greatness and integrity, no nobler character will adorn the pages of American history. The last days of President Lincoln's life, except the two final ones, were passed in my company and mostly on board my flag-ship, and I take great satisfaction in the knowledge that he considered them the happiest days of his administration. He came to City Point, unaccompanied by any of his Cabinet, to witness what he knew was about to take place in the downfall of the Confederate stronghold. He was anxious for peace and was willing to extend the most liberal terms to those who had made war upon us. I kept from the President all those who would have annoyed him or disturbed the tranquillity he enjoyed on ship-board, and I think he was grateful for my consideration. It would take a large volume to contain a true story of Lincoln's administration. He was the central figure in the Cabinet, and without him it would have been nothing. He was the opposing power against political schemers who wished to put this or that general at the head of our armies, and when left to his own judgment he always selected the right man. Take him altogether, Abraham Lincoln was one of the most remarkable men this country has produced, and will be revered in the future more than any other President except Washington. The two names will go down together to posterity.

Davd D Porter

Washington.

NAVY GROUP OF STATUARY. NATIONAL LINCOLN MONUMENT.

Representing a scene on the deck of a ship of war. The mortar is properly poised, the gunner as rolled up a shell ready to be elevated into the mortar, the boy, whose duty it is to carry cartridges the piece, and who in nautical phrase is called the powder monkey, has elevated himself to the ighest position. The two latter believing they are about to enter upon an engagement, are peering into the distance with manifest indications of excitement. The Commander, however, having taken n observation through his telescope, finds there is no cause to apprehend danger, and is calmly editating.

THE VISIT OF PRESIDENT LINCOLN TO RICHMOND,

THE ABANDONED CONFEDERATE CAPITAL, ON THE 4TH OF APRIL, 1865.

THE abandoned and burning city was occupied, the day previous, by General Weitzel's command, consisting of a division of white troops under General Devins and a colored division which I commanded. The President, accompanied by Admiral Porter, had landed early in the afternoon from the gun-boat *Malvern*, which came up from City Point, and leading his little son Tad, the three walked up from the landing to General Weitzel's quarters, in the house occupied two days before by the Confederate President. By the time he reached it, the streets were almost impassable, being obstructed mostly by negroes struggling to get sight of the man whom they regarded as their savior. A reception was held immediately, that lasted some hours, and then a ride was proposed, and, accompanied by a number of general officers, the party, filling two ambulances, drove through the city and Capitol grounds until sundown. The same evening, Mr. Campbell, of the Confederate Cabinet, and some other prominent Confederates, interviewed Mr. Lincoln with propositions for the restoration of Virginia to the Union. The President remained until the 7th without agreeing upon any plan that was accepted. This was the last time

26

ABRAHAM LINCOLN.

FEBRUARY 12, 1809.

NO minster bells' loud pæan
  Proclaimed the moment when
He came to earth to be an
  Uncrowned king of men;
No purple to enfold him,
  Our country's royal guest;
But loving arms to hold him.
  Silence ! God knoweth best !

APRIL 15, 1865.

The way was long and cheerless,
  But dawn succeeded night;
That soul, so brave and fearless,
  Dwells evermore in light !
No shadows dim his glory,
  Our hearts his praise resound,
And history tells his story,—
  Our nation's king is crowned !

Sophie E. Eastman.

SOUTH HADLEY, 1882.

THE most conspicuous victim of our nation's rise and progress has been Abraham Lincoln. The long and cruel war of the rebellion was over. The first glad days of peace had come. The waters of the flood of wrath were disappearing, and the long-tossed ark of the national life had just rested upon solid ground. The dove was returning from the redeemed world with a branch of olive, when the hand of the assassin struck down the emancipator of the race of slaves. To those of us who remember vividly the war days, who cannot recall the awful shock of that event? The brave patriot's life, covered, as it had been, with contumely and abuse, derided, scorned, criticised, condemned, stood at the last far above all his compeers, and we understood at the last why it was that the leadership of this elect nation had been committed to his patient, suffering keeping through the storm of the civil war, and not to his companions, a Seward, a Chase or a Stanton, since in the light of his death we beheld the divine meaning of his choice, and felt that, like Saul among the elder brethren of his father's house, the horn of the prophetic people, like that of Samuel of old, had anointed with holy oil that man of the people whom God had unmistakably called and chosen to be the leader through the crisis of the rebellion.

Wm Wilberforce Newton

BOSTON, 1882.

ABRAHAM LINCOLN I regard as belonging to the same class with the judges in Israel. He was raised up by Divine Providence to be the deliverer of this nation in a time of great peril. His work done, God permitted him to be removed without conscious suffering, by the bullet of a most cowardly and wicked assassin. His name will stand on the roll of fame next to that of Washington as a benefactor of his race.

L. Scott

1880.

THE life and services of President Lincoln must ever be regarded as one of the most beneficent gifts which an ever-willing Providence has ever conferred upon this much-favored country. He seems to have been raised up for the times in which he lived—times as critical as it is possible to conceive—and for those times he was exactly fitted. Perhaps it is too much to say no other man could have done the noble work which he did in saving the Union, but I know of no other that in my judgment could have done so well. An ardent patriot, shrewd, with large common sense, far-reaching foresight, firmness and tenacity of purpose, possessing the largest sympathies, "with malice for none and charity for all," I cannot hope ever to see his like again.

W. Strong

WASHINGTON, 1880.

N O admirer who speaks in his praise must pause to conceal a stain upon his good name. No true man falters in his affection at the remembrance of any mean action or littleness in the life of Lincoln. The purity of his reputation ennobles every incident of his career and gives significance to all the events of his past."

W. D. Howells

BELMONT, 1880.

———

M R. LINCOLN will be known in history, first, as an honest man; second, as a statesman in the truest and best meaning of the word; third, as a humanist with a sincere love of his whole country, and a heart large enough to take in the whole human race; fourth, as the great martyr to the cause of Liberty throughout the world.

John Gibbon

U. S. ARMY, 1882.

THE Martyr President seals with his blood the emancipation of a race, and grasping four millions of broken coffles, ascends to the bosom of his God, thus consecrating the land of Washington as the home of the emigrant and the asylum of the oppressed of every clime and of all races of men.

Galusha A. Grow

PHILADELPHIA, 1880.

ABRAHAM LINCOLN was the right man in the right place, at the right time. The whole country owes him a debt of endless gratitude.

W. W. Goodwin

CAMBRIDGE, 1880.

LINCOLN came so aptly to the need of his times, and was so exactly fitted for the burden of his greatness, that probably he impressed few of his casual acquaintances with his transcendent qualities. Now that he has gone from the world, which he did so much to make better, those who have a definite knowledge of the crisis in which he was the greatest actor can see and wonder at his greatness. Others were divided upon abstract questions, which, by unkindly discussion, seemed to have grown into causes of sectional hate. Even many of the leaders of the party which made Lincoln President forgot their love of country in their hatred of slavery, and would have accepted disunion even, that they might fight slavery more earnestly. They made the mistake which history shows has been made so often. They fancied that excessive philanthropy might take the place of patriotism. Lincoln first and above all loved his country. Every other love, opinion, principle was in utter subordination to his patriotism. That was his strength. That made him the representative and the worthy leader of all patriots of every sort of opinion. He was the leader of all the patriotic people; he was the leader of the war. He was the incarnation of a nation's love of country. In his grave he remains the exemplar and the idol of patriotism.

C. E. Lippincott

CHANDLERVILLE, 1881.

THE grand legacy of American freedom, bequeathed to us by the Father of his Country, and which a wicked rebellion would have squandered, was saved, we trust, for all coming time, by that noble martyr, *Abraham Lincoln.*

Geo. B. Griffith

EAST LEMPSTER, 1881.

ABRAHAM LINCOLN at all times impressed me as a man of native good sense, singleness of motive and integrity of purpose. His life has been of great good to this nation, because he "desired to be on the Lord's side," gave his voice for the freedom of the oppressed and his life for the Union of the States. No better legacy can be left to the youth of our land than the example of great men and women—great in goodness of heart and character.

John G. Fee

BEREA COLLEGE, 1882.

THE possibility of such a man as Abraham Lincoln is a standing argument in favor of a Government which unites freedom with strength, and has strength without tyranny. Courts and kingdoms might be searched in vain for a prince who, by tradition or culture, had attained such wisdom in the government of men as had the son of the backwoods. What gentleness, wisdom, patience! What wit! What skill in argument! What power of persuasion! What sublime faith! These were qualities which bound him to the hearts of his countrymen and made him worthy to be a martyr to liberty.

Frederick Smyth

MANCHESTER, 1880.

IN February, '63, I went to Washington, so much prejudiced against President Lincoln that I was with difficulty persuaded to attend a reception, and would only go on condition that I should not be presented. I went into his presence with a feeling of scorn for the man who had tried to save the Union and slavery—the man who had rescinded the orders of Gen. Fremont and Gen. Hunter, emancipating the slaves of rebels in arms against the Government. I had no respect for the man who had emancipated a nation of slaves, not as an act of justice, but as a means to an end; and, was no little startled to find a chill of awe pass over me as my eyes rested upon him. It was as if I had suddenly passed a turn in a road and come into full view of the Matterhorn; as if I had stepped from a close room into a mountain breeze.

I have always been sensitive to the atmosphere of those I met, but have never found that of any one impress me as did that of Mr. Lincoln, and I know no word save "grandeur" which expresses the quality of that atmosphere. I think that to me no familiarity, no circumstance, could have made him other than grand. The jests, the sallies, with which he amused small people and covered his own greatness, were the shrubs on the mountain side, the flowers which shot up in the crevices of the rocks! They were no part of the mountain. Grandly and alone he walked his way through this life; and the world had no honors, no emoluments, no reproaches, no shames, no punishments which he could not have borne without swerving or bias.

Washington was to Lincoln what St. Peter's is to the Matterhorn. He was a fine combination of good material, worked into form by high art; but art had nothing to do in making Lincoln; only God, and His elements, could effect the equipoise or outline of this rugged, thoroughly balanced nature.

I stood for some time watching him receive his guests and getting back my own breath and circulation; not realizing · the full measure of the effect his presence had on me, but fully impressed by a conviction of his honesty. Whatever he had done, or left undone, was the result of conviction. He had done what he believed to be right, and stood ready to bear every responsibility of his acts.

He could never dodge or prevaricate, and his policy was that of the teacher who seeks to lead his pupils to the highest plane, and by the best means known to himself. His simplicity and self-forgetfulness, his total lack of that weakness which finds strength in rank, were evident at a glance. To himself he was no greater as Commander-in-chief than he would have been as corporal or private. His aims were all his country's, his ambition to render her the best service in his power; and this he would have done in any position, with as much pride as he commanded his armies.

His evident weariness, and the patience with which he stood shaking hands, as one might pump on a sinking ship, made me angry with the senseless custom. Were there not enough demands on his time and strength, without this unreasonable drain? I hesitated about being presented, because it would be another hand for him to shake, but felt I could not go away without yielding what was counted a token of respect and protesting against the custom. So when he took my hand I said: "May the Lord have mercy on you, poor man; for the people have none!"

He threw up his head and laughed pleasantly, and those around him joined the laugh; but I went off angry, indignant, that he should be sacrificed to a false social custom—an insolent demand of thoughtless people, and vain people, who added this burden to that of an already cruelly overtaxed public servant.

Jane Grey Swisshelm

CHICAGO, 1882.

THE life and services of a public man can only be impartially estimated when he has passed from active duty. Washington was largely reviled while living; his memory is now universally revered. In public life Lincoln was a second Washington, and his memory occupies a corresponding position in the hearts of his loyal countrymen. Side by side their names will go down in history to the end of time, the one as the instrument that secured independence, and the other as the instrument that preserved our Union and gave freedom to four million slaves. He was sacrificed, but his martyrdom gave emphasis to the living principles embodied in our amended Constitution; as the lifting up of Christ elevated the principles it was his mission to establish. These are now almost universally acknowledged. These are the beacon lights which moderate despotisms and are the hope of people who seek liberty for the sake of the human race.

CINCINNATI, 1880.

A FEW months after the inauguration of President
Lincoln I received a letter from the Hon.
Charles Sumner, requesting me to come to Washington
at my earliest convenience.   The day after my arrival in
Washington I was introduced to the President.   Mr.
Lincoln received me very cordially, and invited me to
dine with him.   Assembled at the President's table were
several prominent gentlemen, to whom Mr. Lincoln
introduced me as "a red-hot abolitionist from Canada."
One of the guests, a prominent member of Congress,
from Indiana, said, in a slurring manner : "I wish the
negroes of the United States would emigrate to Canada,
as the Canadians are so fond of their company."   Mr.
Lincoln said : "It would be better for the negroes, that's
certain."   "Yes," I replied a little warmly, "it would be
better for the negroes ; for, under our flag, the blackest
negro is entitled to and freely accorded every right and
privilege enjoyed by native Canadians.   We make no
distinction in respect to the color of a man's skin.   It is
true, we live under a monarchical form of government,
but every man and woman, white, black, or brown, have
equal rights under our laws."   Mr. Lincoln, in a jocular
way, said to the member of Congress : "If you are not
careful, you will bring on a war with Canada ; I think we
have got a big enough job on hand now."   The conversation then turned on the attitude of England toward
the free States in their contest with the slave-holders.
One gentleman remarked that he was surprised to see so

many manifestations of unfriendliness on the part of the English and Canadian people, and asked me how I accounted for it. I replied: "How can you expect it otherwise, when there exists in your Northern States so much diversity of opinion as to the justness of your cause? The unfriendly expressions of an English statesman, or the avowed hostility of a few English and Canadian papers, are noted by you with painful surprise; while the treasonable utterances and acts of some of your own political leaders and people are quite overlooked. Besides, you cannot expect the sympathy of the Christian world in your behalf, while you display such an utter disregard for the rights and liberties of your own citizens, as I witnessed in this city yesterday." Mr. Lincoln asked to what I alluded. I replied: "A United States marshal passed through Washington yesterday, having in his charge a colored man, whom he was taking back to Virginia under your Fugitive Slave Law. The man had escaped from his master, who is an open rebel, and fled to Wilmington, Delaware, where he was arrested and taken back into slavery."

After dinner Mr. Lincoln led me to a window, distant from the rest of the party, and said: "Mr. Sumner sent for you at my request; we need a confidential person in Canada to look after our interests, and keep us posted as to the schemes of the Confederates in Canada. You have been strongly recommended to me for the position. Your mission shall be as confidential as you please; no one here but your friend Mr. Sumner and myself shall have any knowledge of your position. Your communications may be sent direct to me under cover to Major ——.

Think it over to-night, and if you can accept the mission
come up and see me at nine o'clock to-morrow morning."
When I took my leave of him, he said : " I hope you will
decide to serve us." The position thus offered was one
not suited to my tastes, but, as Mr. Lincoln appeared very
desirous that I should accept it, I concluded to lay aside
my prejudices and accept the responsibilities of the
mission. I was also persuaded to this conclusion by the
wishes of my friend, Mr. Sumner.

At nine o'clock next morning, I waited upon the
President, and announced my decision. He grasped my
hand in a hearty manner, and said, " Thank you, thank
you ; I am glad of it." I said, " Mr. Lincoln, if the object
of your Government is the liberation from bondage of
the poor slaves of the South, I should feel justified in
accepting any position where I could best serve you ; but
when I see so much tenderness for that vile institution
and for the interests of slave-holders, I question whether
your efforts to crush the rebellion will meet with the
favor of Heaven." He replied : " I sincerely wish that
all men were free, and I especially wish for the complete
abolition of slavery in this country ; but my private wishes
and feelings must yield to the duties of my position. My
first duty is to maintain the integrity of the Union.
With that object in view, I shall endeavor to save it,
either with or without slavery. I have always been an
anti-slavery man. Away back in 1839, when I was a
member of the Legislature of Illinois, I presented a
resolution asking for the emancipation of slavery in the
District of Columbia, when, with but few exceptions, the
popular mind of my State was opposed to it. If the

institution of slavery is destroyed, and the slaves set free, as a result of this conflict which the slave-holders have forced upon us, I shall rejoice as heartily as you. In the meantime, help us to circumvent the machinations of the rebel agents in Canada. There is no doubt they will use your country as a communicating link with Europe, and also with their friends in New York. It is quite possible, also, that they may make Canada a base to harass and annoy our people along the frontier."

After a lengthy conversation relative to private matters connected with my mission, I rose to leave, when he said: "I will walk down to Willard's with you; the hotel is on my way to the Capitol, where I have an engagement at noon."

Before we reached the hotel, a man came up to the President and thrust a letter into his hand, at the same time applying for some office in Wisconsin. I saw that the President was offended at the rudeness, for he passed the letter back without looking at it, saying: "No, sir! I am not going to open shop here." This was said in a most emphatic manner, but accompanied by a comical gesture which caused the rejected applicant to smile. As we continued our walk, the President spoke of the annoyances incident to his position, saying: "These office-seekers are a curse to this country; no sooner was my election certain, than I became the prey of hundreds of hungry, persistent applicants for office, whose highest ambition is to feed at the government crib." When he bid me good-by, he said: "Let me hear from you once a week at least." As he turned to leave me a young army officer stopped him and made some request, to which the

President replied with a good deal of humor: " No, I can't do that ; I must not interfere ; they would scratch my eyes out, if I did. You must go to the proper department."

As I watched the President wending his way towards the Capitol, I was deeply impressed with the dreadful responsibility that rested upon him. The hopes of millions of Republicans throughout the world were fixed upon him ; while twenty millions of his own people looked to him for the salvation of the Republic, and four millions of poor, down-trodden slaves in the South looked to him for freedom. Mr. Lincoln was no ordinary man. He had a quick and ready perception of facts, a retentive memory, and a logical turn of mind, which patiently and unwaveringly followed every link in the chain of thought on every subject which he investigated. He was honest, temperate and forgiving. He was a good man, a man of noble and kindly heart. I never heard him speak unkindly of any man ; even the rebels received no word of anger from him.

MY SECOND VISIT TO WASHINGTON.

On my arrival there (about midnight) I went direct to the Executive Mansion, and sent my card to the President, who had retired to bed. In a few minutes the porter returned and requested me to accompany him to the President's office, where, in a short time, Mr. Lincoln would join me. The room into which I was ushered was the same in which I had spent several hours with the President on the occasion of my first interview with him. Scattered about the floor, and lying open on the table, were several military maps and documents, indicating recent use. On the wall hung a picture of that noble friend of freedom, John Bright, of England.

In a few minutes the President came in and welcomed me in the most friendly manner; I expressed my regret at disturbing him at such an hour. He replied in a good-humored manner, saying: "No, no; you did right; you may waken me up whenever you please. I have slept with one eye open ever since I came to Washington; I never close both, except when an office-seeker is looking for me. I am glad," referring to a letter I had sent him, "you are pleased with the Emancipation Proclamation, but there is work before us yet. We must make that proclamation effective by victories over our enemies; it is a paper bullet, after all, and of no account, except we can sustain it." I expressed my belief that God would aid the cause of the Union now that justice had been done to the poor negro. He replied: " I hope so; the suffering and misery that attends this conflict is killing me by inches; I wish it was over."

I then laid before the President the "rebel mail." He carefully examined the address of each letter, making occasional remarks. At length he found one addressed to Franklin Pierce, ex-President of the United States, then residing in New Hampshire, and another to ex-Attorney-General Cushing, a resident of Massachusetts. He appeared much surprised, and remarked, with a sigh, but without the slightest tone of asperity: "I will have these letters inclosed in official envelopes, and sent to these parties." When he had finished examining the addresses, he tied up all those addressed to private individuals, saying : " I won't bother with them, but these look like official letters ; I guess I'll go through them now." He then opened them, and read their contents, slowly and carefully. While he was thus occupied, I had an excellent opportunity of studying this extraordinary man. A marked change had taken place in his countenance since my first interview with him. He looked much older, and bore traces of having passed through months of painful anxiety and trouble. There was a sad, serious look in his eyes that spoke louder than words of the disappointments, trials and discouragements he had encountered since the war began. The wrinkles about the eyes and forehead were deeper ; the lips were firmer, but indicative of kindness and forbearance. The great struggle had brought out the hidden riches of his noble nature, and developed virtues and capacities which surprised his oldest and most intimate friends. He was simple, but astute ; he possessed the rare faculty of seeing things just as they are ; he was a just, charitable and honest man.

Having finished reading the letters, I rose to go, saying that I would go to "Willard's," and have a rest. "No, no," said the President, "it is now three o'clock ; you shall stay with me while you are in town ; I'll find you a bed," and leading the way, he took me into a bedroom, saying : "Take a good sleep ; you shall not be disturbed." Bidding me "good-night" he left the room to go back and pore over the rebel letters until daylight, as he afterwards told me.

If ever an individual was raised up by the Almighty to perform a special service, that person was Abraham Lincoln. No parent could evince a greater interest in the welfare of his family than he did for the safety and welfare of his country. Every faculty he possessed was devoted to the salvation of the Union. I did not awake from my sleep until eleven o'clock in the forenoon, soon after which Mr. Lincoln came into my room and laughingly said : " When you are ready, I'll pilot you down to breakfast," which he did, and seating himself at the table near me, expressed his fears that trouble was brewing on the New Brunswick border ; that he had gathered further information on that point from the correspondence, which convinced him that such was the case. He was here interrupted by a servant who handed him a card, upon reading which he arose, saying: " The Secretary of War has received important tidings; I must leave you for the present ; come to my room after breakfast, and we'll talk over this New Brunswick affair."

On entering his room, I found him busily engaged in writing; at the same time repeating in a low voice the words of a poem, which I remembered reading many years before. When he stopped writing I asked him who was the author of that poem. He replied: " I do not know. I have written the verses down from memory, at the request of a lady who is much pleased with them." He passed the sheet, on which he had written the verses, to me, saying : " Have you ever read them?" I replied that I had, many years previously, and that I should be pleased to have a copy of them in his handwriting, when he had time and inclination for such work. He said: "Well, you may keep that copy, if you wish." The following is the poem, as written down by Mr. Lincoln.

A. M. Ross

MONTREAL, 1882.

Oh ! why should the spirit of mortal be proud ?—
Like a swift-fleeing meteor, a fast-flying cloud,
A flash of the lightning, a break of the wave,
He passeth from life to his rest in the grave.

The leaves of the oak and the willow shall fade,
Be scattered around and together be laid ;
And the young and the old, and the low and the high,
Shall molder to dust and together shall lie.

The infant, a mother attended and loved ;
The mother, that infant's affection who proved ;
The husband, that mother and infant who blest,—
Each, all, are away to their dwellings of rest.

The maid, on whose cheek, on whose brow, in whose eye,
Shone beauty and pleasure—her triumphs are by.
And the memory of those who loved her and praised,
Are alike from the minds of the living erased.

The hand of the king, that the scepter hath borne,
The brow of the priest, that the miter hath worn,
The eye of the sage and the heart of the brave,
Are hidden and lost in the depths of the grave.

The peasant, whose lot was to sow and to reap,
The herdsman, who climbed with his goats up the steep,
The beggar, who wandered in search of his bread,
Have faded away like the grass that we tread.

The saint, who enjoyed the communion of heaven,
The sinner, who dared to remain unforgiven,
The wise and the foolish, the guilty and just,
Have quietly mingled their bones in the dust.

So the multitude goes—like the flower or the weed,
That withers away to let others succeed ;
So the multitude comes—even those we behold,
To repeat every tale that has often been told.

For we are the same our fathers have been ;
We see the same sights our fathers have seen ;
We drink the same stream, we view the same sun,
And run the same course our fathers have run.

The thoughts we are thinking, our fathers would think ;
From the death we are shrinking, our fathers would shrink ;
To the life we are clinging, they also would cling—
But it speeds from us all, like a bird on the wing.

They loved—but the story we cannot unfold ;
They scorned—but the heart of the haughty is cold ;
They grieved—but no wail from their slumber will come ;
They joyed—but the tongue of their gladness is dumb.

They died—ay, they died—we things that are now,
That walk on the turf that lies over their brow,
And make in their dwellings a transient abode,
Meet the things that they met on their pilgrimage road.

Yea ! hope and despondency, pleasure and pain,
Are mingled together in sunshine and rain ;
And the smile and the tear, the song and the dirge,
Still follow each other, like surge upon surge.

'Tis the wink of an eye—'tis the draught of a breath,
From the blossom of health to the paleness of death ;
From the gilded saloon to the bier and the shroud :—
Oh ! why should the spirit of mortal be proud ?

I THINK Mr. Lincoln possessed much originality of character; that he was humane and pure, kindly disposed toward the South, and that, whatever may have been his errors or deficiencies, he always meant to act according to what he considered patriotic motives and the dictates of an honest conscience. Hence I have no hesitation to declare that I have never ceased to be convinced that his tragic death, at the time it occurred, was a most fatal event for the Southern States, which I sincerely believe would have been treated with much more liberality by him than they had the good fortune to be after his assassination.

Charles Gayarré

NEW ORLEANS, 1882.

NOW all men begin to see that the plain people, who at last came to love him and to lean upon his wisdom, and trust him absolutely, were altogether right, and that in deed and purpose he was earnestly devoted to the welfare of the whole country and of all its inhabitants. To him more than to any other man the cause of Union and Liberty is indebted for its final triumph. Lincoln was the very embodiment of the principles by which our country and its inhabitants were saved.

R. B. Hayes

WASHINGTON, 1880.

ABRAHAM LINCOLN had a sterling common sense, a vein of humor, a deep well of gentle, kindly feeling, a long-suffering patience, an unselfish patriotism, which, when viewed in connection with his death as a martyr for his country, are sufficient to secure for him a lasting place in the catalogue of the world's leaders.

George P. Fisher

NEW HAVEN, 1882.

ABRAHAM LINCOLN stands out on the pages of American history, unique, grand and peculiar. As honest, unselfish and patriotic as Washington, he was his superior as an orator and logician, and dealt successfully with larger and graver matters. In tact he has never had an equal in this country. Mr. Salmon P. Chase once said to me that " his cunning amounted to genius."

Like the mighty oak which towers far above its fellows, he was a growth of the forces of nature, which is to say, of God; and one cannot resist the conclusion that he was prepared, in a special sense, by God, for the work he had to do.

Willard Warner

TECUMSEH, 1882.

THE world will readily admit that Abraham Lincoln was a very remarkable man in his character and career, as in the achievement which crowned his life with honor; not, as is sometimes said, one of a thousand, but one of many thousands of much higher promise than attached to him in their early days; and yet his fame and the immortal character of his memory depends chiefly upon two acts, neither of which was, properly speaking, his own: one, the proclamation abolishing slavery, which was in a manner forced upon him and the country; and the other his assassination, which was brought upon him, in whole or in part, by that act: the penalty, as it were, of one of the noblest deeds on record among mankind.

It is common in this country, where no law of primogeniture prevails, to find men born in the middling classes, or even lower classes, so-called, who reach stations and positions of eminence. In this respect Mr. Lincoln sustained himself in every position he reached, or, we might almost say, that reached him.

One might easily imagine that a common rail-splitter and woodman might become a boatman, or even, under circumstances, a soldier; but who would ever dream of his becoming a lawyer, a politician, a legislator, a statesman, and, much less, the President of the nation and the head man of thirty or forty millions of people: one of the highest positions, few as they are in number, in the civilized world?

If any one had seen him splitting rails it would be natural enough to suppose he might some day become a river boatman ; and again, when acting as a river boatman, it might occur to an observer, seeing his energy and readiness, that he would ultimately become captain of a raft, but few persons would have thought of anything beyond that.

So, again, when he reached the bar—if there was any such thing as a bar at that time in the place where he practiced—it might possibly be thought, from his tact and efficiency as a counselor, that he might ultimately become a judge ; and yet again, who that ever knew him as a rail-splitter on his father's farm, or a boat-hand on the Mississippi river, or even as a lawyer, ever dreamed that he would reach the highest position in the nation— perform the highest act for human freedom ever discharged by man? It is not to be denied that Abraham Lincoln had tact, which is often the equivalent of talent, and was able to qualify and adjust himself to every position to which he was elected or reached by his own efforts or the favor of his friends.

Mr. Lincoln had acute sense of the absurd and ridiculous, of obstacles and objections, real or imaginary, and a quick wit, which held them to account and "brought down the house" on all occasions. He was fond of relating a good practical story, illustrative of human life, which were often original with him, always apt to the occasion, and told with a gusto which was characteristic, and may be said to be a quality and a passion of his distinct personality.

Strange to say, the life, career and death of President

I HAVE great admiration for Lincoln. I regard him as one of the greatest men of our time. His fame is growing every day.

[signature: Thos Burk]

HOUSE OF COMMONS, 1882.

MR. LINCOLN, next to Washington, is the great central figure of our history in another generation. As the lapse of time shall smooth the asperities of a civil war, and shall throw its mellowing influences over the stories of his early life, his public services as President, his character as a statesman and leader, will rise higher and shine more brightly, until it shall stand without a rival or a peer in the day to which he belonged.

[signature: Saml. F. Miller]

WASHINGTON, 1880.

BULL RUN found an administration zealous of interest, but irresolute as to method. It found a President seeking the right, but modestly relying upon others and showing little faith in self. It left a sad-eyed, quaint-featured man, who from that hour, with one hand resting on the heart of the people and feeling constantly how and why that heart was throbbing, from thereafter accepted all the responsibility of his place. He moved and spoke thereafter as the people would have moved and spoken, had that people sat incarnate in his seat. Forever thereafter, with humanity, but iron resolution, he directed the issue and bore himself the terrible burden of the strife.

ABRAHAM LINCOLN,

LAWYER AND CITIZEN.

BY THE "CRIER OF THE COURT."

TO remember the sayings and acts of those with whom we come in every-day contact is a task made easier when the memory of events are of a pleasant character, sweetened by high personal regard. My recollections of Mr. Lincoln are all pleasant to memory. The bitterness of political campaigns could not poison the ordinary antagonist of Abraham Lincoln into the slightest show of personal disrespect, while the influence of the genial grandeur of his nature, on one who esteemed him personally, as I did, would wipe away the gauzy webs of aspersion woven by political spiders during the heat and excitement of a canvass. Politically I shall utter not another line nor syllable in reference to Mr. Lincoln—only this—I was not of Mr. Lincoln's party, hence what I may say of him will be outside of prejudice politically. My introduction to Mr. Lincoln personally, whom I had known by reputation as a leading Whig politician of Illinois, since the campaign of 1848, was in the spring of 1854. I was engaged in conversation with Dr. Harrison and Rev. Peter Cartwright, explaining to them the "Atkins Self-Raking Reaper," when Mr. Lincoln came up and the doctor gave me an introduction. He told me to proceed with the explanation, which I did, and he seemed to take quite a lively interest. At the close of the explanation

Mr. Lincoln surprised me not a little by remarking in his peculiar emphatic manner, " Young man, I think you are just the one I am looking for," and without giving me an opportunity to ask for what purpose he wanted me, he said, "If you are through with the doctor and Uncle Peter, will you walk over to the state-house with me, I want to use you." I consented to go, remarking to Dr. Harrison, as I did so : " Doctor, I only know Mr. Lincoln as a Whig, but as the Whig party is dead, I suppose he will not be dangerous." He laughed and we started, but after going about twenty feet turned and said, " Ho, Doc ! I hope our reaper friend will have better luck than some in this county who thought the Whig party was dead !" This was evidently intended as a " twit " at some old Whig politician, as both the doctor and the pioneer of Methodism had a hearty laugh over it.

His use of me I soon learned ; he showed me a number of pieces taken from two reaping-machines—the Manny and McCormick—which had been taken to his room for the purpose of studying the various movements, to ascertain wherein one of the machines was an infringement of the patent granted to the other. Mr. Lincoln possessed but little practical knowledge of machinery, but his fondness for the study of mechanics very much interested him, and he could very readily, with but little explanation, comprehend the uses of different parts and their relation to other parts. It was a pleasurable task for me to explain these two machines ; to aid him in ascertaining their movements ; in noting the difference or pointing out the mechanical equivalents of the one for the other, or where I thought the same principle was

29

applied in the construction or operation of the various parts to accomplish a specific purpose, or where the mechanism of the one differed from the other, although the end reached was the same.

That little introduction knit two very opposite natures, in many respects, very closely together. Neither could, or at least did not, talk long upon a subject without a story was suggested, when it would flow out as natural as life, and frequently to the merriment of both. My business had naturally led me in contact with a great many stories, which it was the least of all my troubles to retain. I found one with an inexhaustible fund of them, and a taste for telling them unsurpassed.

This was my introduction to Mr. Lincoln, and each day I came in contact with him in our closer relation of lawyer and "Crier of the Court" only strengthened our "fellow feeling," until, without appearing egotistic, I really loved Lincoln, and I had many evidences of his personal regard for myself. As a "story-teller" Mr. Lincoln has been misunderstood, and in this short article, if I can place him before the country robbed of what some natures—who never knew the man—would make appear as a "trifling" attribute in his genial "make-up." The impression has been sought to be left on the minds of those who have read some of the criticisms on his character that "story-telling" with Lincoln was an indication of a "great waste of time," and "a contribution to the indolent and shiftless of social life." This view of Mr. Lincoln as a story-teller is a great wrong to his memory, and they who have measured him thus knew him not. Mr. Lincoln's stories were a recreation to him, and he only used them to relieve an over-taxed mind or to "make a point" by telling a story which would require hours of argument. As Linder once said to an Eastern lawyer, who expressed the opinion that Mr. Lincoln lost time in telling stories to a jury: "Ah, my friend! Don't lay the flattering unction to your soul that he is losing time. Lincoln is like Tansey's horse, he 'breaks to win.'" Mr. Lincoln could tell a story as no other man I ever heard make the attempt. He had a purpose in telling them before juries and on the stump. He could annihilate an opponent with a story, and the other would scarcely know what hurt him.

It will scarcely be presumed that he was *always* telling stories. It was the force of one of his well-told stories that gave him the reputation of a story-teller. Modesty would suggest to the "Crier of the Court" to close with this simple explanation. He would not have ventured thus much only to correct an error in regard to one whom those failing to understand the man would conclude that—

> "Every word he spoke,
> And even when he wrote,
> Out would pop a little joke,
> Or end with anecdote."

He told stories, very good ones, too, which we hope long to remember; but the mind which could grapple with questions requiring an army of a million men and great executive ability was made equal to the task by just such innocent recreation to self and amusement of his friends.

As I have said in my lecture, so I repeat here, "Mr.

Lincoln has puzzled wiser heads than those supposed to be carried through life on the shoulders of a Court Crier. Attempts to define and portray him are numerous. They are found floating on the sea of literature in every conceivable shape from contact with the waves of tribulation or success from the frequent jars and bumps on the rocks, as well as the shoals of criticism. I have not ventured on this sea with my flimsy bark to attempt a reputation at the expense of a lawyer I honored, a citizen whom I knew well and loved, but rather to give those not favored with the same relation a court officer bears to the attorney, a homely sketch of an honest man's private life, as a lawyer, his going in and coming out before a court, his daily walk and conversation, the little things of a great man's life which make up the great characteristics of which only the world at large sees and hears so little.

"One of the finest fields for the study of characters that more frequently rise in splendid proportions than any other in this nation, is the court-room. Certainly no field or profession has proved so prolific in the production and development of *ruling spirits*, as that of the law.

"As a lawyer Mr. Lincoln was not classed with the first of the profession in all the branches of the science. Others who still delight in having had a professional association with him—an intimate acquaintance with him—while he lived and practiced law at the same bar, could justly lay claim to and would in equity be allowed credit for a greater amount of legal attainments, a more comprehensive knowledge of the premises in particular branches than he. But he possessed a general knowledge of all the branches. He had taken a draught from nearly all the various streams that flow from the one great well-spring of a 'Rule of action,' and was, in a word, a good lawyer. Mr. Lincoln could boast that in some branches of the law he had greater knowledge than some of his brothers; had more freely than many others analyzed the medicinal properties of these waters, with a view solely to ascertain their healing virtues for the ills of litigation. Mr. Lincoln was impressed with the idea, which should govern every honorable member of the profession, that a lawyer's duty was to settle, not create litigation.

"Judge Davis—who loved Mr. Lincoln as a brother —said of him: 'He was a great lawyer, both at *Nisi Prius* and before an appellate tribunal.' It was generally thought among the members of the bar that his strength was most apparent when standing before a jury. How often have I heard his shrill and not unfrequently musical voice ring out the convincing notes from an intellect as vigorous, although not so quick to perceive, yet so comprehensive, exact and clear that they stamped him in the estimation of every listener as an able, impressive master of the intricacies of his case. He was an honest man and a lawyer, seldom, if ever, allowing himself to be found on the wrong side of a case. It was to this fact more than to any other that he owed his success at the bar. In canvassing his success as a lawyer and statesman it has been my privilege to hear almost every shade of opinion expressed of him by members of the Springfield bar. But, Crier only as I claim to have been, I think the great secret has been overlooked, and

I HAVE been requested to give my recollections touching the life of Abraham Lincoln, late President of the United States. I understand that it is not expected that I should prepare a life or biography of him, but simply give such incidents as would illustrate his character and minor life. So much has been said and written respecting the public history of the great commoner of America, that I feel that it would be a work of supererogation in me to attempt a review of his public career. ₁I shall confine myself in what I shall say to what I know of Abraham Lincoln as a man, and his political life, at home or in Illinois. In order to give assurance that I had the acquaintance, and to some degree the confidence, of the illustrious man, I will give a copy of a letter from him to me, now in my possession ; but I will first premise the circumstances under which it was written. In 1857 and 1858, William Bissell, a Republican, was Governor of Illinois. The Democrats at the session of the Legislature of those years obtained a majority in the Legislature, and passed two acts, an appropriation bill, and an apportionment bill, the latter of which the Governor intended to veto, and the former to approve. The bills resembled each other in external appearance and were both laid upon the Governor's table at the same time, and by mistake he approved of the bill he intended to veto, which was reported to the House as having been sanctioned by the Executive. In a short time the Governor was made aware of his mistake, and he instantly convened a meeting of such of his friends as could be summoned, to consult as to the best means to extricate himself from the dilemma. N. B. Judd, of Chicago, Mr. Lincoln, I believe, Gov. Koerner, of St. Clair, and I, were of the number. We advised Governor Bissell to instantly send his messenger to the House, and request the return of the bill. The majority, not suspecting anything, complied with the request, and the Governor *erased* his name. The Democrats employed General McClernand to apply for a writ of mandamus to compel the Secretary of State, Hatch, to report the apportionment bill as having received the Executive approval and become a law. Here is the letter :

"SPRINGFIELD, January 19, 1858.
"HON. JOSEPH GILLESPIE.
"My Dear Sir :
"This morning Colonel McClernand showed me a petition for a mandamus against the Secretary of State to compel him to certify the apportionment act of last session, and he says it will be presented to the court to-morrow morning. We shall be allowed three or four days to get up a return, and I for one want the benefit of consultation with you. Please come right up.

"Yours, as ever,
"A. LINCOLN."

I visited him as desired, and agreed with him as to the line of defense he should pursue, and after a few days received the following letter :

"SPRINGFIELD, February 7th, 1858.
" HON. J. GILLESPIE.

"My Dear Sir :

"Yesterday morning the court over-
ruled the demurrer to Hatch's return in the mandamus
case. McClernand was present, said nothing about pleading over, and so I suppose the matter is ended. The
court gave no opinion for the discussion, but Peck tells
me confidentially that they were unanimous in the
opinion that even if the Governor had signed the bill
purposely, he had the right to strike his name off so long
as the bill remained in his custody to control.

"Yours as ever,

"A. LINCOLN."

So much has been said about Mr. Lincoln that I
hardly know how I shall go about giving my views
touching or delineating his life and character without
traveling in old grooves. Mr. Lincoln seldom said anything on the subject of religion. He said once to me that
he never could reconcile the "prescience of Deity with
the uncertainty of events." I inferred from that remark
that his antecedents were of the *Baptist* persuasion. He
said at the same time that he thought it was unprofitable
to discuss the dogmas of *predestination* and *free will.*
After he became President he told me that circumstances
had happened during the war to induce him to a belief
in "special providences." I think his mind was unsettled
on religious matters until his election, and he surveyed
the vast responsibilities cast upon him. After that, it
seemed to me that he became religiously inclined. It was

difficult for him to believe without demonstration. He was *up* in Bible reading and quoted from and illustrated by Bible incidents. To give an instance, I called upon him, to get his opinion as to the probabilities of the conclusion of the war. He said it would very soon be ended by the overthrow of the rebellion. "Now," said I, "Mr. Lincoln, what is to be done with the rebels?" "Well," said he, "some people think their heads ought to come off, but there are too many of them for that, and if it was left to me, I could not draw the line between those whose heads ought to come off or stay on." He said he was favorably impressed with the policy of King David. Said I: "What was that?" "Well," said he, "you remember that during the rebellion of Absalom, while David was fleeing from Jerusalem, Shimei cursed him. After the rebellion was put down, Shimei craved a pardon. Abishai, David's nephew, the son of Zeruiah, David's sister, said: 'This man ought not to be pardoned; he cursed the Lord's anointed.' David said unto him: 'what have I to do with you, ye sons of Zeruiah, that ye should this day be adversaries unto me? Know ye that not a man shall be put to death in Israel.'" This reference not only indicated Mr. Lincoln's policy, but also his humanity, which is evidenced by an incident I will relate. One evening Mr. Joshua F. Speed, of Louisville, and I accompanied Mr. Lincoln to the Soldiers' Home, to spend the night with him. While we were at tea, it was announced that a delegation were in the anteroom. Mr. Lincoln immediately went to see them; Speed and I remained at the table. We soon heard that the delegation were from New Jersey, and that they were importuning the President to pardon some young men from that State, who had deserted, were recaptured and sentenced by a court-martial to be shot, in a few days. One of the delegation was a brother to one who was under sentence, and he appealed to Mr. Lincoln with terrible earnestness. The President combated his views with invincible arguments. He pointed out that it would be disastrous to the cause if he should pardon men who had deserted their colors, while the armies were confronting each other ; he had no right under such circumstances to expect the men who had remained in the ranks to do their duty. My heart almost sank within me when Mr. Lincoln dismissed them, saying that he would give them a definite answer at the White House at nine o'clock the next morning. Speed and I, after tea, had come into the room and listened to the discussion, after the delegation left. I was much afraid that Mr. Lincoln had made up his mind not to pardon the young men. Speed, who I know had more influence with the President than any living being, suggested that we should tackle him and beg for the boys, which we did in good earnest. We plied him with all the reasons we could muster, and still I was afraid we were not gaining ground. When it came to be time to retire, I said to Mr. Lincoln that I did not think I could sleep unless I knew that he was going to pardon the boys. He said : " Gillespie, I can't tell you." "Well," said I, "you can give me an inkling." Said he, " All I can say is that I have always found that *mercy bears richer fruits than strict justice.*" In the morning the delegation were ahead of time and they were rejoiced beyond measure to receive the pardon for their friends. Mr. Lincoln was a very humane man, but at the same time he was wonderfully just and firm. If it was possible for him to exercise clemency without doing wrong, he would do so. He told me, one evening, that since he saw me in the morning, he had received some distressing intelligence. He had been notified by *Ould*, Commissioner (I think he called him) for Exchange in the rebel army, that a large number of prisoners captured and paroled at Vicksburg had been put into the field. I said I did not perceive why that should distress him; that it only amounted to our having a few more to fight. "Ah," said he, "look at it in this light; these men are liable to be shot when captured unless I prohibit it, and the responsibility rests on me to say whether the laws of war shall be carried out, in the case of those men, or suspended. What would you do if in my place?" said he. I said: "It is too big a question for me." "Well," said he, "it is a momentous question, and must be decided at once, and I have about made up my mind that those men have been *forced* into the field, and that it would be unmerciful to have them shot." As a boon companion, Mr. Lincoln, although he never drank a drop of liquor, or used tobacco in any form, in his life, was without a rival. No one would ever think of putting in while he was talking. He could illustrate any incident, it seemed to me, with an appropriate and amusing anecdote. He did not tell stories just for the sake of telling them, but invariably by way of illustration of something that had happened or been said. There seemed to be no end to his fund. I could relate hundreds of his stories, but time and space forbid it. I will give a circumstance showing his power to amuse. In 1842 (I think), after

Mr. Van Buren's defeat, he and Mr. Paulding took an excursion through the West; they informed their friends that they would reach Springfield, Ill., by a certain evening. The Springfield people knew that the bad state of the roads would prevent them getting further than Rochester, about seven miles from Springfield, that day; and as accommodations at the place were horrible, Mr. Van Buren's friends concluded to meet him there with refreshments and make the night pass off as pleasantly as circumstances would permit. Mr. Lincoln, although a Whig, was pressed into the service, and was told to use his best endeavors to entertain the distinguished guests, in which he succeeded admirably. Ebenezer Peck, a great admirer of Mr. Van Buren, told me he had never passed a more joyous night. "*Lincoln told his queerest stories*; Van Buren's laugh was ready chorus." Mr. Van Buren said that for days after his sides were sore from laughing at Lincoln's humor. Physically, Mr. Lincoln was a Hercules. I first saw him in 1832, while he was engaged in a wrestling-match with one Dan Thompson, who was the champion, in that line, of the southern portion of Illinois, while Lincoln occupied that position as to what was then the northern portion. It was a terrible tussle, but Lincoln was too much for him. Mr. Lincoln was a very indulgent husband and father; while at Springfield, his children were constantly with him, romping and playing. The truth is, his affection was so strong that he had but little government over them, and it was painful to see him when allusion was made to the death of his son Willie. As a lawyer he was peculiar, and never gave an opinion until he had reflected upon the case. He went into court with his subject thoroughly analyzed, and would discard every doubtful point and concentrate all of his powers upon the *tap-root* of his case. Analysis and concentration were the characteristics of his mind. He had no ceremony in his temper, and treated every one with the utmost consideration and respect. Mr. Lincoln cared nothing about money-making, and had no conception of a speculation. He said he had no money sense. He had a realizing sense that he was generally set down by city snobs as a country Jake, and would accept, in a public-house, any place assigned to him, whether in the basement or the attic, and he seldom called at the table for anything, but helped himself to what was within reach. Indeed, he never knew what he did eat. He said to me once that he never felt his own utter unworthiness so much as when in the presence of a hotel clerk or waiter. Mr. Lincoln was very tender-hearted. I called at the White House and was detained a considerable time in the anteroom, which was filled with persons waiting their turn to be admitted to the President. While there, I met with an old lady who said she had been several days waiting to see Mr. Lincoln; that she wanted to get permission to see her son, who was a soldier lying at the point of death; that she was unable to obtain permission from the Secretary of War. I told her that if I gained admittance before she did, I would speak to the President about her case. She said she had been told that he was a very kind-hearted man. Just about this time, Mr. Lincoln's barber, whom I had known in Springfield, Illinois, came out of Mr. Lincoln's room and, seeing me, offered to take me in by a private door, which I accepted.

While shaking hands with the President, I mentioned the case of the old lady, and he remarked that his greatest tribulation consisted in the fact that it was impossible for him to give prompt attention to such cases, but he directed the old lady to be shown in, and without hesitation, granted her request. He saw in an instant that she was honest. I have heard Joshua F. Speed, of Louisville, relate an incident illustrative of Mr. Lincoln's character, which redounded to the advantage of the country. It was at a time when the want of money was paralyzing the Government. Stewart and Astor and other capitalists had assembled to consider whether they would advance funds to meet the pressing necessities of the case. While those men were conferring with the President on the momentous question, an old gentleman and lady made their appearance, who turned out to be very particular friends of Mr. Lincoln, who broke up the conference with the capitalists, to greet, in his most cordial manner, his old friends. The effect upon Messrs. Stewart, Astor and others was electrical. They declared that they would have no hesitation to aid a Government at the head of which was a man so true to his old friends.

J G Gillespie

EDWARDSVILLE, 1882.

H IS sense of humor was as logical as his mind was clear and his heart generous. I knew him well before he was Chief Executive, and he was the best companion; bigger by far in the noblest sense of courtesy and heartiness than any man I ever knew, except his great rival, Judge Douglas.

Sam'l Cox

NEW YORK, 1880.

————————

A MAN of a style of greatness which is the best product of free institutions, and of them alone; a man whose glory it was that his chief desire was to do the right, and to promote the right; whose watchword was Duty; and whose warmest aspiration the removal of all weights and hindrances which hold men back from their highest social, intellectual and religious development.

Thomas Chase.

1880.

CAVALRY GROUP OF STATUARY. NATIONAL LINCOLN MONUMENT.

Representing the rearing figure of a horse, from whose back his rider has just been thrown, and the wounded trumpeter, who is supported by a companion.

WHEN I began, a few weeks after his death, to write the life of Abraham Lincoln, I entertained a profound respect for his strong mind, his tender heart, and the memory of his beneficent life. When I wrote the last page of the book, I had become his affectionate admirer and enthusiastic partisan.

J. G. Holland

NEW YORK, 1880.

HIS services were of such inestimable value to the republic, and his life so identified with the struggle to maintain it, that no ordinary volume would be sufficient to more than touch upon them.

Anson G. M'Cook

WASHINGTON, 1880.

30

I HAVE always thought Mr. Lincoln was a man born for his time. He was a leader without seeming to be. He, more than any other man during his presidency, stood at the helm of State. Through his skill, which was only the best of common sense, we were taken by the only channel that led from secession to the true dictum of "an indestructible Union, composed of indestructible States." He died as he lived, a great statesman, who knew enough of the ways of politics to make his statesmanship practically useful.

M. R. Waite

WASHINGTON, 1882.

IF there was any one trait in the make-up of that illustrious man that stood out more conspicuously than any other, it was, to use a favorite word of his, his fairness —his habitual, ever-recurring sense of justice. As an illustration of this, I offer for the LINCOLN MEMORIAL ALBUM a few recollections of his bearing towards his great political rival, Stephen A. Douglas : for great he, too, truly was, as a popular and sensational debater and political manager, to say nothing of his acknowledged ability in other directions.

The passage of the Kansas-Nebraska Bill—of which he was the admitted champion—in the spring of 1854, in open violation of both letter and spirit of the Missouri Compromise Act of 1820, throwing out that immense district of country covered by these Territories—now States—to the baneful institution of human slavery, was claimed to be a manifest breach of national good faith ; and so repugnant was it to the sentiment of the Northern people, that it roused up a storm of popular indignation all over the North, unequaled in the previous history of the country. In no part of that country, Kansas alone excepted, did that excitement run higher than here in Illinois ; as an evidence of which, about that time, or soon after, scores of law-abiding men armed themselves with Sharpe's rifles, and fled from our midst to the plains of "Bleeding Kansas"—then so-called—whilst many others contributed freely of their means to accomplish a common object, *to wit,* make Kansas a free State; the battle-ground being almost wholly confined to that State.

Senator Douglas, having not only introduced and voted for that Bill, but making the leading speech in its support, was the object of special hostility and criticism here and everywhere. He labored to justify the act on the ground of what he denominated "popular sovereignty"—plausibly contending it was equally fair to both sections of the Union; and that, as the free State men were not only more numerous, but more active in their movements than the Southern people, they would take possession of and organize into free States both of these Territories; a view, the correctness of which—in the latter regard—was vindicated by subsequent history, though not till a series of outrages had been perpetrated, unparalleled in the history of popular governments. The opposition contended that, as that Territory had in the most solemn manner, and as a peace-offering for the preservation of the Union, been dedicated to freedom, when Missouri was admitted into the Union, the passage of the Bill exhibited an unmanly, servile pandering to the slave power of the South, that up to that time, and for many years preceding, had dominated all legislation on the slavery question, and in various ways been very aggressive on the rights of Northern people. The result was an intensely bitter political excitement; so bitter as to not only mar, but almost to destroy social enjoyment between ordinary politicians holding adverse opinions on this subject.

These two men were the Magnus Apollos of their respective parties; for although the Republican party had not then been fully crystallized into a political organization, it was in a process of formation, and Lincoln was everywhere in Illinois our admitted standard-bearer.

Notwithstanding the high party-excitement referred to, his love of fair play shone out most conspicuously. Judge Douglas, fully apprised of the state of public feeling, had given out that on his return from Washington he would address the people on the exciting topic of the times, and in pursuance thereof a Democratic meeting was called at Bloomington on the 19th day of September, 1854. After conferring with our Anti-Nebraska friends—as we were then commonly called—I opened a correspondence with Mr. Lincoln, resulting in his coming to Bloomington on that day, in order to take notes and reply to Mr. Douglas, if the way opened, on the same day, and if not, in the evening. This fact became pretty widely known, and a very large meeting, composed of quite as many Anti-Nebraska men as Democrats, met in the grove near town—no hall we then had being sufficient to hold the crowd. In order that the country people should have the benefit of the discussion, there was a universal desire, on the part of our friends, that Lincoln as well as Douglas should be heard in the day-time, and I had been requested to see Lincoln on his arrival and get his approval that we propose to, and *urge* upon the Judge to divide time, so as to have a joint discussion.

With what little ability I could command, I did so, emphasizing the fact that a large majority of those we most desired to reach could not be heard unless this arrangement was made ; and that in the absence of such an agreement it would be quite difficult to restrain within bounds the clamor of the people to hear him. I shall never forget his very prompt and decisive reply, which was substantially this: "Fell, this is not our meeting; it is Judge Douglas's meeting; he called it, and he and his friends have a right to control it. Notwithstanding all you say about our country people, and the great desire I have to talk to them, we must do nothing to defeat his object in calling it. He has heard of the great racket the passage of his Bill has kicked up, and he wants to set himself right with his people, a job not very easily done, you and I being the judges. Partly on this ground and partly to keep me from speaking, he will no doubt consume so much of the time that I'll have no chance till in the evening. I fully appreciate all you say about our country friends, and would like mighty well to talk to them on this subject. If Judge Douglas will give me a chance I will follow him out in the grove, but as he won't do this, I guess you may give it out, after he is done, that I will reply to him after candle lighting in the court-house."

This speech settled the matter. I will only add, in conclusion, our Anti-Nebraska friends were greatly disappointed at not getting his approval of some pretty active (perhaps I should say aggressive) demonstrations, to secure a division of time in the discussion; that, as we anticipated, the afternoon was consumed by the Judge; that so intense was the desire to hear Lincoln in the daytime, it was found quite difficult to repress a perfect avalanche of popular calls for our hero to be heard; and that, in the evening, he held forth at the old court-house to all that could get in it, or within hearing distance, in a most logical, eloquent and inspiring speech on the disturbed and perturbed condition of the country, and the consequent duties we owed to that country, and to a common humanity, in resisting, to the bitter end, this last aggression on Northern rights. In power and pathos, mingled with the playful and humorous, he seldom, if ever, acquitted himself more grandly.

It may not be amiss to say that before speaking commenced I called on Judge Douglas, who, as we had anticipated, politely declined the proffered debate; in do'ng which he made some amusing, though good-natured, remarks about the uncertain character of our party, which in truth was, at that time, far from being of a very compact or coherent order, either in name or creed.

I repeat, it was Lincoln's love of justice, his habitual, ever-active sense of right, and the practice of it, that made him so strong with the people; and such I know is the opinion of him whose name, more than any other, is linked with his; I mean Judge David Davis, with whom he spent so much of his life, here in Illinois, as a practicing attorney around our old judicial circuit.

In the fall of 1858, during the discussion between Senator Douglas and Mr. Lincoln, I had occasion to visit the Middle and Eastern States; and as the whole country was then agitated by the slavery question and that discussion cut a prominent figure in the agitation, I was frequently applied to for information in reference to Mr. Lincoln. I felt my State pride flattered by these inquiries, and still more to find the *New York Tribune*, and other papers, publishing copious extracts from these discussions, taken from the Chicago press. I did what

little I could to satisfy so laudable a curiosity, not thinking, at first, that anything further would come of this
discussion, in reference to Mr. Lincoln, than his election
to the Senate. At length, from the frequency of these
inquiries and public notices of the Illinois contest, an
impression began to form, that by judicious efforts he
could be made the Republican candidate for presidency
in 1860. Very soon after my return home, and after the
senatorial contest had closed, one evening, as I passed
on the south side of the public square of this city, I
espied the tall form of Mr. Lincoln emerging from the
court-house door, Judge Davis's court then being in
session. I stopped until he came across the street, when,
after the usual salutations, I asked him to go with me
into my brother's (K. N. Fell) law-office, then kept over
what is now the Home Bank. There we sat down, and
in the calm twilight of the evening, had substantially the
following conversation :—FELL.—" Lincoln, I have been
East, as far as Boston, and up into New Hampshire,
traveling in all the New England States, save Maine :
in New York, New Jersey, Pennsylvania, Ohio, Michigan
and Indiana ; and everywhere I hear you talked about.
Very frequently I have been asked : ' Who is this man
Lincoln, of your State, now canvassing in opposition to
'Senator Douglas ?' Being, as you know, an ardent
Republican and your friend, I usually told them we had
in Illinois *two* giants instead of one ; that Douglas was
the *little* one, as they all knew, but that you were the *big*
one, which they didn't all know.

  "But, seriously, Lincoln, Judge Douglas being so widely known, you are getting a national reputation *through*

him, as the result of the late discussion; your speeches, in whole or in part, on both sides, have been pretty extensively published in the East; you are there regarded by discriminating minds as quite a match for him in debate, and the truth is, I have a decided impression that if your popular history and efforts on the slavery question can be sufficiently brought before the people, you can be made a formidable, if not a successful, candidate for the presidency."

LINCOLN.—" Oh, Fell, what's the use of talking of me for the presidency, whilst we have such men as Seward, Chase and others, who are so much better known to the people, and whose names are so intimately associated with the principles of the Republican party. Everybody knows them; nobody, scarcely, outside of Illinois, knows me. Besides, is it not, as a matter of justice, due to such men, who have carried this movement forward to its present status, in spite of fearful opposition, personal abuse, and hard names? I really think so."

FELL.—" There is much truth in what you say. The men you allude to, occupying more prominent positions, have undoubtedly rendered a larger service in the Republican cause than you have; but the truth is, they have rendered *too much* service to be available candidates. Placing it on the grounds of personal services, or merit, if you please, I concede at once the superiority of their claims. Personal services and merit, however, when incompatible with the public good, must be laid aside Seward and Chase have both made long records on the slavery question, and have said some very radical things which, however just and true in themselves, and however much these men may challenge our admiration for their courage and devotion to unpopular truths, would seriously damage them in the contest, if nominated. We must bear in mind, Lincoln, that we are yet in a minority; we are struggling against fearful odds for supremacy. We were defeated on this same issue in 1856, and will be again in 1860, unless we get a great many new votes from what may be called the old conservative parties. These will be repelled by the radical utterances and votes of such men as Seward and Chase. What the Republican party wants, to insure success, in 1860, is a man of popular origin, of acknowledged ability, committed against slavery aggressions, who has no record to defend and no radicalism of an offensive character to repel votes from parties hitherto adverse. Your discussion with Judge Douglas has demonstrated your ability and your devotion to freedom ; you have no embarrassing record ; you have sprung from the humble walks of life, sharing in its toils and trials; and if we can only get these facts sufficiently before the people, depend upon it, there is some chance for you. And now, Mr. Lincoln, I come to the *business* part of this interview. My native State, Pennsylvania, will have a large number of votes to cast for somebody on the question we have been discussing. Pennsylvania don't like, over much, New York and her politicians. She has a candidate, Cameron, of her own ; but he will not be acceptable to a larger part of her own people, much less abroad, and will be dropped. Through an eminent jurist and essayist of my native county in Pennsylvania, favorably known throughout the State, I want to get up a well-considered, well-written newspaper

article telling the people who you are and what you
have done, that it may be circulated, not only in that
State, but elsewhere, and thus help in manufacturing
sentiment in your favor. I know your public life, and
can furnish items that your modesty would forbid, but I
don't know much about your private history : when you
were born, and where, the names and origin of your
parents, what you did in early life, what your opportunities for education, etc., and I want you to give me
these. Won't you do it ?"

LINCOLN.—"Fell, I admit the force of much that you
say, and admit that I am ambitious, and would like to be
President. I am not insensible to the compliment you
pay me, and the interest you manifest in the matter ; *but
there is no such good luck in store for me as the presidency
of these United States ;* besides, there is nothing in my
early history that would interest you or anybody else ; and,
as Judge Davis says, '*It won't pay.*' Good night."

And thus ended, for the time being, my pet scheme
of helping to make Lincoln President. I notified him,
however, as his giant form, wrapped in a dilapidated
shawl, disappeared in the darkness, that this was not the
last of it ; that the *facts* must come. The next year, 1859,
I was engaged much of the time as the corresponding
secretary of the Republican State Central Committee, in
traveling over the State and in carrying out plans for a
more thorough organization of the Republican party,
preparatory to the great contest of 1860. I visited personally a large majority of the counties in the State, and
nearly everywhere had the satisfaction of learning that,
though many doubted the possibility of nominating

Lincoln, most generally it was approved of. This fact became in time very apparent to Lincoln himself, whom I not infrequently met in my travels; and in the month of December of that year, feeling that perhaps it *would* "pay," I induced him to place in my hands this eminently characteristic paper. Such is the history of a paper that has already become historic, and which, to me at least, has a value I little dreamed of at the time.

"SPRINGFIELD, Dec. 20, 1859.
"J. W. FELL, Esq.
    "MY DEAR SIR:
        "Herewith is a little sketch, as you requested. There is not much of it, for the reason, I suppose, that there is not much of me. If anything be made out of it, I wish it to be modest, and not to go beyond the materials. If it was thought necessary to incorporate anything from any of my speeches, I suppose there would be no objections. Of course, it must not appear to have been written by myself.
        "Yours very truly,
            "A. LINCOLN."

"NORMAL, ILLINOIS, March 9, 1882.
"OSBORN H. OLDROYD, Springfield, Ill.
    "MY DEAR SIR:
        "It is with much pleasure that I have learned of your purpose to erect at Springfield, Illinois, a "Memorial Hall," in which is to be stored whatever is interesting as connected with, or illustrating the life and character of that most remarkable man and patriot,

Springfield, Dec. 20. 1859

J. W. Fell, Esq
     My dear Sir:

          Herewith is a little sketch, as you
requested— There is not much of it, for the reason,
I suppose, that there is not much of me—
If anything be made out of it, I wish it
to be modest, and not to go beyond the material.
If it were thought necessary to incorporate anything
from any of my speeches, I suppose there would
be no objection— Of course it must not appear
to have been written by myself— Yours very truly
                                        A. Lincoln

I was born Feb. 12, 1809, in Hardin County, Kentucky. My parents were both born in Virginia, of undistinguished families—second families, perhaps I should say. My mother, who died in my tenth year, was of a family of the name of Hanks, some of whom now reside in Adams, and others in Macon counties, Illinois. My paternal grandfather, Abraham Lincoln, emigrated from Rockingham County, Virginia, to Kentucky, about 1781 or 2, where, a year or two later, he was killed by indians, not in battle, but by stealth, when he was laboring to open a farm in the forest. His ancestors, who were quakers, went to Virginia from Berks County, Pennsylvania. An effort to identify them with the New England family of the same name ended in nothing more definite, than a similarity of Christian names in both families, such as Enoch, Levi, Mordecai, Solomon, Abraham, and the like.

My father, at the death of his father, was but six years of age; and he grew up, litterally without education. He removed from Kentucky to what is now Spencer county, Indiana, in my eighth year. We reached our new home about the time the State came into the Union. It was a wild region, with many bears and other wild animals, still in the woods. There I grew up. There were some schools, so called, but no qualification was ever required of a teacher, beyond "readin, writin, and cipherin" to the Rule of Three. If a straggler supposed to understand latin, happened to sojourn in the neighborhood, he was looked upon as a wizzard— There was absolutely nothing to excite ambition for education. Of course when I came of age, I did not know much— Still somehow, I could read, write, and cipher to the Rule of Three; but that was all— I have not been to school since— The little advance I now have upon this store of education, I have from time to time picked up under the pressure of necessity—

I was raised to farm work, which I continued till I was twenty-two— At twenty-one I came to Illinois, and passed the first year in Illinois— Macon county— Then I got to New Salem (at that time in Sangamon, now in Menard county, where I remained a year as a sort of clerk in a store— Then came the Black-Hawk war; and I was elected a Captain of Volunteers— a success which gave me more pleasure than any I have had since— I went the campaign, was elated, ran for the Legislature the same year (1832) and was beaten— the only time I ever have been beaten by the people— The next, and three succeeding biennial elections, I was elected to the Legislature— I was not a candidate afterwards. During this Legislative period I had studied law, and removed to Springfield to make, practice it— In 1846 I was once elected to the lower House of Congress— Was not a candidate for re-election— From 1849 to 1854, both inclusive, practiced law more assiduously than ever before— Always a whig in politics; and generally on the whig electoral tickets, making active canvasses. I was losing interest in politics, when the repeal of the Missouri Compromise aroused me again— What I have done since then is pretty well known—

If any personal description of me is thought desirable, it may be said, I am, in height, six feet, four inches, nearly; lean in flesh, weighing, on an average, one hundred and eighty pounds; dark complexion, with coarse black hair, and grey eyes— No other marks or brands recollected—

Hon. J. W. Fell.   Yours very truly
                                         A. Lincoln

Washington, D.C. March 26. 18/
We the undersigned hereby certify that the foregoing statement is in the hand writing of Abraham Lincoln.
                                David Davis
                                Lyman Trumbull
                                Charles Sumner

1861—1865.

THE cry for " Freedom " or for " Death " resounds,
From frozen lake to Mississippi's mouth
The rugged mind of *Lincoln* guides the North,
The gray-eyed eagle Davis leads the South.

On ! on ! they come ! the while the scythe of gray
Sweeps low the lines of blue, like autumn leaves ;
The eager mouths of earth quaff deep of gore ;
The granaries of Death heap high with sheaves.

Steel clashes steel ! and now the twofold cry
Bursts from the stern lips of the nation's head,
The patriot's cry for " Union," " Freedom " rings
Through all the land, and echoes mid the dead.

And patriotism swells the surging tide,
With mighty hosts unnumbered as the stars—
" *One country,*" stirs the patriot of the North,
And nerves his sinews for the " War of Wars !"

On ! on ! and now the banners of the South
Bend low to meet the kiss the dying give ;
The South yields to the hosts—her cause is lost—
Yet, though subdued, her Truth and Honor lives!

Now Lincoln's hand has caught the Union flag,
And firmly nailed it to the ship of State ;
He stands to pilot her into the port—
To sternly meet the stern decree of fate.

And now—a horror falls upon the land,
The pulses of the North beat wild and high;
The weary Southland sees her last hope fade,
And, with the dream of Lincoln, droop and die.

I HAVE been more deeply interested in the life and character of Abraham Lincoln, and have admired him more unreservedly, than any other American, living or dead. I have read all the biographies of which I have any knowledge, and not one of them, or all of them, have given me the high estimate of his character which was indicated in the unreserved confidence and generous love with which he was regarded by all his contemporaries, and especially by those who came in personal contact with him and knew him best.

C. C. Carpenter

FORT DODGE, 1882.

ENGLISH SYMPATHY FOR MR. LINCOLN.

THE hatred of aristocratic England of the American Union in the time of the rebellion almost made anti-slavery England pro-slavery. The anti-slavery society of Clarkson and Wilberforce were alarmed at the revulsion of principle, and issued an address to the people. They sent a copy of that address to President Lincoln, with the following letter:

"To His Excellency Abraham Lincoln, President of the United States of America.

"Sir:—It has seemed desirable to the Committee of the British and Foreign Anti-Slavery Society, to issue, at the present crisis, an Address to the friends of the Anti-Slavery cause, of which a copy is annexed.

"In directing your attention to it, the Committee would take advantage of the opportunity, to assure you of their personal respect and sympathy, and of their appreciation of the exceeding great difficulties of your position. Since your accession to office, they have watched, with deep interest, the progress of events, and especially the gradual development of a policy tending to promote Negro Emancipation. If certain measures in furtherance of that policy, and some apparently inconsistent with it, have not recommended themselves to the approval of the Committee, they have, nevertheless, recognized the majority of them with satisfaction, as conducive, in the main, to the interests of the enslaved portion of the African race.

The Committee earnestly desire, that the sanguinary conflict between the two sections of the Union may speedily cease, and that with the removal of the sole cause of this strife, a way may open for a reconciliation, upon the enduring basis of a community of interests, and a mutual forgiveness of injuries.

" On behalf of the Committee,

" (Signed)   THOMAS BINNS, *Chairman.*

" L. A. CHAMEROVZOW, *Secretary,*

27 New Broad Street, E.C.

London, 17th November, 1862."

MR. LINCOLN'S EMANCIPATION PROCLAMATION IN ENGLAND.

When it had been learned that Mr. Lincoln had been elected for a second term for the presidency, a large public meeting was called in Bristol, England, to congratulate him on his re-election, and the meeting was broken up by a mob. Afterwards the following address was prepared and signed by a number of prominent persons, representing the friends of the American Union. A few weeks later another public meeting was held in the same hall, and presided over officially by the Mayor of the city, to express their abhorrence of the assassination of our President and condolence to the nation for the loss of so great and good a man.

Address to his Excellency Abraham Lincoln on his Re-election to the Presidency of the United States.

We, the officers and members of the Committee of the Bristol Emancipation Society, in the name of a large number of our fellow-citizens, who, in meeting assembled, on several occasions, and invariably by a large majority of votes, have adopted resolutions in agreement with the tenor of this address, desire most cordially to express to your Excellency our congratulations on your re-election to the presidency of the United States, by the popular vote of your freedom-loving countrymen.

We rejoice in this result, regarding it as evincing the will and design of the American people to sustain you in the Anti-Slavery policy inaugurated under your administration by the Federal Government, a policy which, while rapidly making your country as free in fact as it has been heretofore by profession, will for the future identify your administration with the Liberation of the Enslaved.

We believe that in issuing your Emancipation Proclamation, freeing all persons held as slaves by citizens who were in arms against the United States Government after 1863, and your corresponding recommendation to purchase for emancipation the slaves of loyal persons in States not in rebellion ; and your signing the law excluding slavery from all the lands of the United States at present under a territorial form of government, together with the anti-slavery policy marking many of your acts, you have *commended your course to the approval of all* TRUE PHILANTHROPISTS.

Disclaiming any desire to mingle with the mere civil and political questions of the day, in which, among Americans, there exists a diversity of opinion, we feel that the policy of your administration, to which we have referred, *affects the great interests of humanity;* by it we are reminded afresh of the acts of our own Government in abolishing the slave trade, and slavery; and in venturing to send to you our congratulations, we would express it as our conviction that such deeds, while in harmony with the highest laws of morality, tend, of their own nature, to draw nearer to each other the two great Protestant nations, leading to their alliance and co-operation, and placing them in a position to influence, by their united example, the civilized world.

In the long struggle which has passed, and in the conflict which may yet be continued, we see the chastisement of a great and erring people, for the crime of slave-holding, and for the glaring departure from high principles and professions; and we believe that whenever the nation shall have purged away the crime of slavery, Peace and Prosperity will speedily be restored.

The address was beautifully engraved and illuminated on a sheet of parchment four by five feet, and formally presented through me, as United States Consul, to the President, who received it but a short time before his assassination.

Zebina Eastman

MAYWOOD, 1882.

MR. LINCOLN was a man, in my view, of unswerving integrity in all his private and public relations; his convictions upon all subjects that he discussed were honest and decided, and he followed them out; he was a man of great benevolence of character; there was no malice in his composition, but the widest charity for all; he was devoted to the best interests of the State of his adoption, but at the same time he was a devoted patriot, loving his whole country, and an earnest defender of human liberty, and the perpetuation of the American Union, which, if broken up, might destroy the existence of free institutions upon the American continent; he had no prejudices against the Southern people; he was one of the best friends they ever had. This is the place that will be awarded to him in history in after times. The war gave him deep distress; there was nothing he would not have done, no sacrifice he would not have made consistent with his high sense of duty to his country and to humanity, if that would have stopped the war, and saved the Union from dissolution. In the deep sincerity of his heart, I have often heard him express these sentiments, and all his Messages to Congress and other similar papers, when carefully analyzed, will prove the correctness of this estimate of him. These are my impressions formed of Mr. Lincoln in a pleasant and frequent association with him during the 37th and 38th Congresses, in both of which I was a member, and which extended through the period of the civil war.

Mr. Lincoln often spoke to me about the Emancipation Proclamation. He had no great faith in its efficacy. I heard him say a number of times it only affected those who were free, *i. e.*, those behind the Federal lines, and of course it would not reach the vast number of slaves who remained within the lines of the Southern army. This made him exceedingly anxious in reference to the passage of the 13th amendment to the Constitution of the United States, abolishing African Slavery in our country. This amendment had failed to pass during the session of Congress of 1863–64, but it was again introduced into the Senate by its author, the Hon. John B. Henderson, of Missouri, and having passed that body, was sent to the House of Representatives to be acted upon there. The President had several times in my presence expressed his deep anxiety in favor of the passage of this great measure. He and others had repeatedly counted votes in order to ascertain as far as they could the strength of the measure upon a second trial in the House. He was doubtful about its passage, and some ten days or two weeks before it came up for consideration in the House, I received a note from him, written in pencil on a card, while sitting at my desk in the House, stating he wished to see me, and asking that I call on him at the White House. I responded that I would be there the next morning at nine o'clock. I was prompt in calling upon him, and found him alone in his office. He received me in the most cordial manner : and said in his usual familiar way : "Rollins, I have been wanting to talk to you for some time about the 13th amendment proposed to the Constitution of the United States, which will have to be voted on now before a great while." I said : "Well, I am here, and ready to talk upon that subject." He said : "You and I were old Whigs, both of us followers of that great statesman, Henry Clay, and I tell you I never had an opinion upon the subject of slavery in my life that I did not get from him. I am very anxious that the war should be brought to a close, at the earliest possible date, and I don't believe this can be accomplished as long as those fellows down South can rely upon the Border States to help them; but if the members from the Border States would unite, at least enough of them to pass the 13th amendment to the Constitution, they would soon see they could not expect much help from that quarter, and be willing to give up their opposition, and quit their war upon the Government; this is my chief hope and main reliance, to bring the war to a speedy close, and I have sent for you, as an old Whig friend, to come and see me, that I might make an appeal to you to vote for this amendment. It is going to be very close; a few votes one way or the other will decide it." To this I responded, "Mr. President, so far as I am concerned you need not have sent for me to ascertain my views on this subject, for although I represent perhaps the strongest slave district in Missouri, and have the misfortune to be one of the largest slave-owners in the county where I reside, I had already determined to vote for the 13th amendment." When he arose from his chair, and grasping me by the hand, gave it a hearty shake, and said, "I am most delighted to hear that." He asked me how many more of the Missouri Delegates in the House would vote for it." I said I could not tell; the Republicans of course would,

General Loan, Mr. Blow, Mr. Boyd, and Col. McClurg. He said : "Won't General Price vote for it? He is a good Union man." I said I could not answer. "Well, what about Governor King?" I told him I did not know. He then asked about Judges Hall and Norton. I said they would both vote against it, I thought. "Well," he said, "are you on good terms with Price and King?" I responded in the affirmative, and that I was on easy terms with the entire delegation. He then asked me if I would not talk with those who might be persuaded to vote for the amendment, and report to him as soon as I could find out what the prospect was. I answered I would do so with pleasure, and remarked, at the same time, that when a young man, in 1848, I was the Whig competitor of King, for Governor of Missouri, and as he beat me very badly, I think now he should pay me back by voting as I desire him to on this important question : I promised the President I would talk to these gentlemen upon the subject. He said : "I would like you to talk to all the Border State men whom you can approach properly, and tell them of my anxiety to have the measure pass ; and let me know the prospect of the Border State vote," which I promised to do. He again said: "The passage of this amendment will clinch the whole subject ; it will bring the war, I have no doubt, rapidly to a close." I have never seen any one evince deeper interest and anxiety upon any subject than did Mr. Lincoln upon the passage of this amendment. The next day I saw both General Price and Governor King, and had a long private interview with each of them. When I mentioned the matter to General Price, he became at once quite excited, and

expressed himself, in strong language, against the amendment; and said: "Lincoln don't know that I am the
owner of seventy negroes, does he?" I said, "I don't
know; but suppose you owned a thousand negroes,
what would they amount to, compared with the stopping of this infernal war, and saving the American
Union?" I left General Price, and seeking Governor
King, took him into one of the cloak-rooms of the
House, and had a more *quiet* conversation with him
upon the subject. I asked him if he had decided in
his own mind how he should vote upon the 13th
amendment. He said he had been thinking upon the
subject a good deal, but said: "*You know my people are
opposed to it.*" I responded: "Governor, at least two-
thirds of the people in my district are opposed to the
passage of this amendment; but there are questions
sometimes bigger than constituencies, and I intend to
vote, and speak in favor of this amendment, and make
our country free in fact, as well as in name, and get
clear of this infamous rebellion." Before I left him he
said he thought he would vote for it, which he did.
I conversed with most of the Border State men who
could be approached, upon the question; told them of
the President's deep anxiety in regard to it, and I have
ever believed that the interviews had some influence
in strengthening the final vote for the 13th amendment.
It will be remembered that when the vote in
the House was taken, the amendment was carried
by a small *majority;* and, being approved, on
the 1st day of February, 1865, became substantially a
part of the Constitution of the United States, being

subsequently ratified by all the States. Several days after the passage of this amendment through Congress, I called upon President Lincoln, and I never saw him evince greater joy at the news of any victory won upon the field of battle, than he did over the passage of this amendment. He said: " I read your speech, one night, after I had gone to bed, and it is the best speech delivered in Congress during this session." I suppose that the good President felt he owed me this much on account of my earnest co-operation with him in endeavoring to put through this important amendment. It is the most important, as it is to me the most satisfactory vote I ever cast in a legislative assembly.

It was well understood, and especially in Missouri, that General Sterling Price, of Confederate military fame, immediately prior to and about the commencement of the rebellion, claimed to be a Union man, and, as such, was elected president of the convention which assembled in February and March, 1861, in Jefferson City and St. Louis, to take into consideration the then existing condition of things in the State of Missouri. He had been a warm supporter of Colonel Benton during his contest with the nullifiers of the State. It was thought by many that he went very reluctantly into the rebellion, and as late as 1863 it was frequently said, and by persons presumed to know, he was getting very tired of the Confederate cause, and that he would be gratified if he could get out of it honorably. I had a conversation with a gentleman bearing a very near relation to him, and this subject was mentioned ; he was of the same impression with others, that General Price would like to abandon the

rebellion. As he was a very popular officer, command
ing a large body of men, and most of them from Missouri, I thought it might be well to sound him upon the
subject, and to this end it was agreed that a reliable messenger be sent to him, that his real sentiments might be
ascertained. A pass was obtained by me for him through
the Federal lines, General Price at that time being in the
State of Texas ; but upon the arrival of the messenger
at the Confederate lines, some distance below Cairo, he
was not allowed to go through into the Confederacy ; determined, however, not to give up so valuable an enter-
prise, I wrote to a member of the Confederate Congress
then in session at Richmond, Va., from Missouri, to obtain
a pass through their lines for the person above referred
to. It was not long before I received an answer to my
letter, in which the gentleman stated he had submitted
the proposition to President Davis, and he promptly refused to grant the request, and in this my correspondent
said he entirely agreed with him. So the project failed,
simply because General Price could not be reached,
and his opinion on the subject could not be ascertained. At that time it would have been a grand
thing if General Price could have been induced
to abandon the Confederacy and return to his loyalty
to the United States, as he wielded an immense influence,
and could have reclaimed a large number of young men
who had been persuaded against their better judgment
to make war upon their country. About the time I conceived this thought, in August, 1863, I happened to be in
the office of President Lincoln, when I ventured to mention the subject to him. He was very much amused at

my proposition, regarding it as not at all feasible, and at the same time perpetrating quite a number of jokes at my expense. I insisted, however, that it be tried, as no harm could come of it, and we would at least find how General Price's pulse beat upon the subject, and all I asked of him was that he give the messenger a pass through the Federal lines, to see General Price. "Well, he said, "we will see what General Hitchcock says about it," and ringing his bell, he sent for General Hitchcock, who then had charge of the transmission of messages between the Governments at Washington and Richmond. In a few moments General Hitchcock made his appearance, when the President said to him : "General, here is Rollins from Missouri, who has had an intimation that General Price, now in Texas, might be induced to give up his opposition, and quit his war upon the United States, and return to his home in Missouri." They both laughed very heartily at the idea, but finally issued the pass, and also sent some papers which I had prepared through the lines to Richmond. After receiving the papers Mr. Lincoln said to me, pleasantly: "Now, Rollins, this is a very delicate business, and I don't want you to get me into any scrape about it ; this is your project, and not mine; if Sterling Price will come back, all I have to say, I will do the fair thing by him ; and if you can get him to come back and disband his men, it will be equal to a half-dozen victories to the Union side; but this thing must not go into the papers, or be spoken of outside of you, Hitchcock and myself." I then said to him : "Mr. President, I wish you would give me a memorandum showing your good disposition towards General Price,"

32

which he said he would do, and at once took up his pen and wrote a short note and handed it to me, the original of which, in Mr. Lincoln's handwriting, I have now in my possession, and is here copied, and this anecdote again illustrates his kindly feeling to those in arms against the Government of the United States.

"EXECUTIVE MANSION,
"WASHINGTON, August, 1863."
"HON. JAS. S. ROLLINS:

"Yours in reference to General Sterling Price is received. If he voluntarily returns and takes the oath of allegiance to the United States, before the next meeting of Congress, I will pardon him, if you shall then wish me to do so.

"ABRAHAM LINCOLN."

During the winter of 1864–65, as I now remember the time, a gentleman came to Washington, named Colonel Lane, who was one of my constituents, and resided in Montgomery Co., Missouri. I had known him in Missouri. He was a number of times at my rooms in Washington, and told me he had been operating with the United States detective force on the Mississippi river, he having an official connection therewith. I knew nothing to the prejudice of Colonel Lane. He had been recommended to the Government by such respectable and patriotic gentlemen as James O. Broadhead, Samuel S. Glover and Judge S. M. Breckenridge, as I now recall. On an occasion, when at my room, in giving me an account of his war experiences in running up and down the Mississippi river on steamboats, he told me at one time he had left the boat and gone out into the State of Mississippi, where he had remained some time; that whilst there he had heard a plan discussed by a number of young and warlike *gentlemen ?* as to how the President of the United States might be disposed of. He got in, so to speak, with these young fellows; he was anxious to find out more about it, and was one of them for a number of days. The plan agreed upon was to obtain a box about six or seven inches square, containing an explosive material, and which on being opened would explode, and most probably destroy the person who held it in his hand. He told me he had seen this box, and held it in his own hands; that the purpose and design was to send it to Washington directed to Mr. Lincoln, and place it in the Presidential Mansion, where he would most likely get and open it. To me this was a most extraordinary and infamous disclosure; it arrested my serious thought and attention. I could hardly credit it, and yet could see no motive for such a fabrication. I asked Colonel Lane if he was serious in what he said. He said he was, and had only related to me what he had witnessed with his own eyes. I said to him at once: "Colonel Lane, if the facts you relate to me are true, you should not lose a moment in communicating the facts to the President. Will you go up with me, call upon the President, and make the same statement to him?" Certainly, he said, he would go up, as he wished to tell President Lincoln precisely what he had told me. I then said to him: "Come to my room in the morning, in Twelfth street, when I will have a hack ready, when we will drive up to the White House." He was a little late putting in an appearance next morning, but I waited for him, and as soon as he arrived we mounted into the hack, and drove off to the President's office. It so happened there were great numbers of visitors who had preceded us, and were occupying the reception-room. I sent in my card, but so many others were in advance of me, I failed to obtain an audience that morning. We remained until one o'clock, when the messenger announced that the President would see no more visitors that day, and those present were dismissed. Colonel Lane and myself drove back to my room, intending to ask an audience at another time. This, I think, was on Saturday, and, as near as I can now remember, in the month of December or January in the year 1864–65. When I parted with Colonel Lane it was not his intention to leave Washington for several days; but he received a telegram that evening, as he informed me in a letter, calling him to Wheeling, West Va., and which compelled him to leave in the evening train. I did not see him again during that session of Congress, which terminated on the 4th of March, 1865, the day of the second inauguration of Mr. Lincoln as President. A few days thereafter, having business at the White House, I called upon Mr. Lincoln again, when I happened to find him alone, and seemingly in a very cheerful humor. He received me very cordially, as was his habit, and after dispatching the business which called me to see him, I ventured to tell him precisely what I had learned from Lane, and as I have stated it above. I observed he listened to what I had to say very attentively, and when I had finished my story, I said in an apologetic tone: " Mr. President, nothing but a sense of duty and the interest I feel in you and the country would have prompted me to have mentioned a matter of this kind to you. I have simply told you the tale as it was told to me." He thanked me kindly for what I had told him, and said he appreciated the good feeling and friendship which prompted it; but, treating the whole matter jocularly, he said: "I don't pay much attention to such things. I have received quite a number of threatening letters since I have been President, and nobody has killed me yet, and the truth is, I give very little consideration to such things." I told him the little I knew of Lane, and said to him: "Now, I hardly see why a man should get up a story of this sort unless there was some foundation for it. I believe he has witnessed what he relates." Upon rising to take leave I said, pleasantly: "Mr. President, I feel relieved in having unburdened myself in telling you what I have. I have acted from a sense of duty; and now, let me add, if you should come into your office one of those mornings and find sitting upon your table a wooden box about six inches square, I beg of you not to open it; let some one else attend to that; but if you attempt to open it, and the nation lose its President, I want it understood I have cleared my skirts." He again thanked me and laughed very heartily, and said, "Now, I will tell you—I promise you if I find any boxes on my table directed to me, I won't open them." Pausing a moment just as I was taking my leave of him, the smile which had just lighted up his face departed, and a certain melancholy expression, which I had often seen him wear, took its place, and he said seriously, and in language he evidently felt, *"Rollins, I don't see*

*what on God's earth any man would wish to kill me
for, for there is not a human being living to whom I
would not extend a favor, and make them happy if it
was in my power to do so."* It occurred to me, on leaving him, the conversation I had had with him had left
quite an impression on his mind. This occurred, according to my best recollection, in January, 1865.

Before the close of the session of Congress, I was several times in the office of the President, to see him on
business, and on one occasion, when I was about leaving
the room, he said to me, in a jocular manner: "Well,
Rollins, I have not received my box yet." I responded,
"I am gratified to hear it," but again warned him not to
open any box of the kind left upon his table, and I left
the room.

At the close of the Thirty-eighth Congress, I was
present at the second inauguration of President Lincoln,
and remained in Washington several days thereafter.
My second term in Congress having ended with the expiration of the Thirty-eighth Congress, before leaving for
Missouri I called at the White House, to pay my respects to the President and take my leave of him. I
found him in his office in a very genial humor, and I had
a pleasant conversation with him. He seemed to be
hopeful that the war troubles would soon be over, which
greatly rejoiced him. When I rose to bid him good-bye,
he gave me a cordial shake of the hand, and said: "Rollins, the box has not come to hand yet." I responded:
"That is well, Mr. President, I am glad to hear
it. I hope it may never come; but if it does, I charge

you not to open it." This is the last time I ever saw, and this was my last interview with, Abraham Lincoln.

About six weeks afterwards, when I was in the city of Chillicothe, Livingston county, Missouri, away up on Grand River, on the 15th day of April, 1865, I was most deeply shocked and grieved to hear that President Lincoln and several members of his Cabinet had been assassinated.

James S. Rollins

COLUMBIA, 1882.

MY sentiments of the life and services of Abraham Lincoln are, that he was a big-headed, big-hearted man—a man of destiny, sent, like Washington, to perform a great moral and political mission. Born in a tent, reared in poverty, in the Slave State of Kentucky, from infancy he imbibed early and lasting prejudices against slave-holders and slavery. Hence, his efforts in after life were directed by a scrupulous regard for what he esteemed a public duty. His administration evinced wisdom, forbearance, persistence, and was a success. His mission is performed. His advent and destiny will emblazon history so long as the science of government shall be read and propagated by men. A humane benevolence was amongst his most estimable traits.

RELIGIOUS ASPECTS.

ABRAHAM LINCOLN'S CAREER.

ONE of the noteworthy features of Lincoln's wonderful life was the manifest deepening of his sense of God's Presence and Providence during those later years when he bore the imperiled nation on his heart. He who is accustomed to discern a divine Hand in history must look upon Mr. Lincoln as a man raised up for a great purpose by him who lifted Joseph out of the pit to be ruler over Egypt, and exalted David from the Bethlehem sheep-fold to be Israel's king. How far Mr. Lincoln himself discerned God in Revelation or in the orderings of human life, previous to his exaltation to the Presidency, may not be fully known. He had early in his youth read the Bible and Pilgrim's Progress, and although the atmosphere of his legal and political life in Illinois was not helpful to faith, still he was known to several Christian ministers as a man of serious thoughtfulness, if of little knowledge, in the domain of Christian truth.

But the great anti-slavery debates and the nation's terrific struggle for existence were the rain and the solar heat that awakened and called forth the diviner nature, the heavenward side of this gracious and humane spirit. The contest against American slavery was essentially religious—a defense of fundamental Christian truth, the sacredness and worth of that humanity for which Christ died. The heroes of West India emancipation, Zachary Macaulay, Thomas Clarkson and William Wilberforce, were disciples of Him who came to break every yoke and let the oppressed go free. Green, the great English historian, finds the primal moral impulse which led England to free the negro in the great revivals under Whitefield and the Wesleys. Wendell Phillips says of the early American abolitionists that they "bound the Bible to their brows." This great orator of Boston has written severe things of the churches. He has scathed hypocrisy as no other man in our generation has done. But, having bowed my head in prayer with this old apostle of freedom, and having heard him seek the blessing of God through the merits of Christ, the great Emancipator, I have never had the least suspicion that the movement which destroyed American slavery was an infidel crusade! Looking into the coffin which held the form of William Lloyd Garrison, Wendell Phillips exclaimed: "Farewell for a little while, noblest of Christian men." In reviewing the anti-slavery contest, the younger generation should not forget, and are not likely to forget, that the most stirring lyrics ever sung to freedom came from the Christian lips of Whittier; that for years the most potent voice denouncing slavery sounded from Plymouth pulpit, and that the volume which converted the heart of the North, "Uncle Tom's Cabin," was written by a Christian woman, and is itself perhaps the most religious work of fiction since Bunyan wrote his immortal allegory. Charles Sumner was continually hurling the Sermon on the Mount at our great national sin, and

Abraham Lincoln derived his deeper anti-slavery convictions, as he confessed, from a sermon by the lionhearted Leonard Bacon, of New Haven.

All the world knows that when the newly-elected President was about to assume the government of the nation, he asked the prayers of his neighbors in Springfield. Lincoln's was a nature far from shallow. There was a moral sensitiveness about him, that made him weak, as an attorney, in defending a cause of uncertain righteousness. He was wont to seek after laws underlying special facts. It has been said of him that "he saw through his lawyer's brief the general principles of the Divine administration." His deeper nature developed and ripened as Providence brought him to bear the weight of majestic and solemn responsibilities. In the anxious uncertainties of the great war, he gradually rose to the heights where Jehovah became to him the sublimest of realities, the Ruler of nations. When he wrote his immortal Proclamation, he invoked upon it not only "the considerate judgment of mankind," but "the gracious favor of Almighty God" When darkness gathered over the brave armies fighting for the nation's life, this strong man, in the early morning, knelt and wrestled in prayer with him who holds in his hand the fate of empires. When the clouds lifted above the carnage of Gettysburg, he gave his heart to the Lord Jesus Christ. When he pronounced his matchless oration on the chief battle-field of the war, he gave expression to the resolve that "this nation, under God, should have a new birth of freedom." And when he wrote his last Inaugural

Address, he gave to it the lofty religious tone of an old Hebrew Psalm.

In 1873, I stood on the broad granite platform of that noble monument which has been built in Oak Ridge Cemetery above all that was mortal of Abraham Lincoln. A great crowd stood reverently in the May sunshine, while the Jubilee Singers, men and women whom the good President had liberated, sang, with the hot tears rolling down their dusky cheeks, as they rolled down our paler faces, the great "Battle-Hymn of the Republic," with its tuneful suggestions of that other Christian martyr who died at Harper's Ferry, attacking the wrong which at last had been trampled out in blood to the music of the old man's name :

" Mine eyes have seen the glory of the coming of the Lord,
He is trampling out the vintage where the grapes of wrath were
        stored,
He hath loosed the fateful lightning of his terrible swift sword,
        His truth is marching on.

" In the beauty of the lilies Christ was born across the sea,
With a glory in his bosom that transfigures you and me ;
As he died to make men holy, let us die to make men free,
        While God is marching on."

The whole scene was a chapter in the modern evidences of Christianity, witnessing to the world that the lightning which melted the shackles off from four millions of slaves is the same with that which gleamed among the clouds of Mount Sinai of old, and played above the summit of the Cross of Calvary.

All the great epochs of American history have been

profoundly religious.   John Winthrop felt that " the civil
state must be reared out of the churches."   Mulford, in
his great work on this nation, gathers together the words
of Franklin before the Convention which formed the
Constitution : " Except the Lord build the house, they
labor in vain that build it.   I firmly believe this ;" and
the words of Washington in his first inaugural : " No
people can be bound to adore the hand which conducts
the affairs of men, more than the people of the United
States ;" and the words of Jefferson : " I shall need, too,
the favor of that Being in whose hands we all are, who
led our fathers, as Israel of old, from their native land ;"
and he says of the last inaugural of President Lincoln
that " it was the unbroken expression of the spirit of these
Scriptures, and its whole thought was gathered up in their
words in the recognition of One who will establish
righteousness on the earth."

CHICAGO, 1882.

I KNEW Mr. Lincoln personally, being Mayor of the city of Cincinnati in February, 1861. It was my privilege to extend to him the hospitalities of the city on his way to Washington to take his seat as President of the United States. I respect him as a man of great nobleness of heart, purity of mind and intentions. I consider him a patriot, whose every endeavor it was to promote the interests of his country. While I differed with him essentially in politics, I have ever considered Lincoln a true man, actuated only by noble purposes. He was a great man, a good man, and his name will ever be venerated and honored as one of the brightest among that gallery of illustrious names which make our country so famous.

R. M. Bishop

CINCINNATI, 1880.

HISTORY has not left it for me or for any other man to magnify or detract from the glory of Abraham Lincoln. His record, inscribed in deeds and sealed with his blood, is known and read of all men.

A man of strong native mental and moral powers, he rose, by his own exertions, superior to all the deprivations of poverty and pioneer hardships, from the obscurity of a backwoods cabin, to command the admiration of all lands for all time.

At the most critical period of his country's history, when even its greatest statesmen stood perplexed and confounded in the midst of the political questions of the day, his penetrating logic picked every fallacy, cleft every knob of political casuistry, and discovered the *only* path to the preservation of the Union ; and through the fiercest, bloodiest civil war that a free people ever endured, with unswerving courage he led four millions of slaves to liberty, and re-established the Federal Government in its rightful supremacy. As true to humanity as he had always been faithful to his country, his last words were a prayer and benediction for his enemies.

. Before such a character I stand, with all men, in loving reverence.

Robert P. Porter,

CHICAGO, 1880.

WESTERN and Northern-bred men ought not to forget that Lincoln was of the South. In its more instinctive, less methodical school of parentage his idiosyncrasies were grown. The natural man, gazing out on the better development of the North, poetized and reasoned in admiration of it, yet with melancholy, for he was of the poorer and more shiftless race. Let us, therefore, learn from Lincoln that honest Southernhood taken into Northernhood produces the most memorable Americanhood; and that, though the North prevailed, Lincoln, Johnson, General Thomas, and many such refined and endeared the victory, and made it national.

Geo. Alfred Townsend

33

A S the character of Abraham Lincoln steadily developed with the developing demands and necessities of the position to which he was elevated, so his fame steadily grows with the increasing light which is thrown upon what he achieved in his great office; the emergencies that he met, the difficulties that he overcame and the results that he accomplished. He will always stand out, one of the grand figures in our history, one of the heroes and martyrs in the history of freedom, of cultivation of humanity.

PROVIDENCE, 1882.

I RECALL an incident of Mr. Lincoln's early life, which came under my own personal observation, and which illustrated his desire to be just and do right while yet a mere boy, and which showed his magnetic influence over men among whom he moved. It was in 1832 ; we were doing service in the Black Hawk War, and while lying at Rock Island the boys got up a wrestling match and pitted Mr. Lincoln, who was our captain, against a famous athlete and wrestler by the name of Thompson, from Union county, Illinois. We Sangamon county boys *believed* Mr. Lincoln could throw any one, and the Union county boys *knew* no one could throw Thompson ; so we staked all our slick and well-worn quarters and empty bottles on the wrestle. The first fall was clearly in Thompson's favor ; the second fall was rather in Thompson's favor, but Lincoln's backers claimed that it was what, in those days, was called a " dog-fall." Thompson's backers claimed the stakes, while we demurred, and it really looked, for some time, as though there would be at least a hundred fights as the result. Mr. Lincoln, after getting up and brushing the dust and dirt off of his jean pants, said : " Boys, give up your bet; if he has not thrown me fairly, he could." Every bet was at once surrendered, and peace and order were restored in a minute. During the rebellion in 1864 I had occasion to see Mr. Lincoln in his office at Washington, and, after having recalled many of our early recollections, he said : " Bill, what ever became

of our old antagonist, Thompson, that big curly-headed
fellow who threw me at Rock Island?" I replied I did
not know, and wondered why he asked. He playfully
remarked that if he knew where he was living he would
give him a post-office, by way of showing him that he
bore him no ill-will.

W G Greene

Tallula, 1882.

I BECAME acquainted with Abraham Lincoln in the year 1831, when he came from Decatur, Illinois, with a Mr. Hanks, on the hull of a flat-boat, for a man by the name of Denton Offutt. The building of this boat was commenced at Decatur, but, for want of lumber, was brought by water to Sangamon town and finished, as there was a little saw-mill which furnished sufficient material to complete it. It was the design of Mr. Offutt to load it with fifteen hundred bushels of corn and take it to New Orleans. The corn was bought at ten cents per bushel, and the boat was partially filled at Sangamon town; then brought to New Salem and finished. I was standing on the bank of the river when the boat was tied up, and I don't think I ever looked at as awkward a man as Mr. Lincoln was at that time. He was dressed in blue jean pants and coat, and a wool shirt and slouch hat. I viewed him from head to foot, and thought to myself, What a fool! but I had not been in his company long until I found out that I was the bigger fool of the two. We became very warm friends and strongly attached to each other. After Mr. Lincoln sold the corn in New Orleans, at fifty cents per bushel, he walked back and took up his residence at New Salem.

Mr. Lincoln was a candidate for the Legislature, but was defeated by Peter Cartwright; but was successful in being elected in 1834. He was boarding with me when he was appointed post-master at New Salem by Andrew Jackson; this was previous to his election. And while in the Legislature he appointed me his deputy, as the post-office was then in my house. I don't think I ever saw Lincoln idling any time away. He had but few books, but those few were always near him, and in going to and from his work, would read. He had a wonderful retentive memory, and was a great story-teller. He was liked by every person who knew him. While he boarded with me he made himself useful in every way that he could. If the water-bucket was empty he filled it; if wood was needed he chopped it; and was always cheerful and in a good humor. He started out one morning with the axe on his shoulder, and I asked him what he was going to do. His answer was: "I am going to try a project." When he returned he had two hickory poles on his shoulders, and in a very short time two of my chairs had new bottoms.

Caleb Carman

PETERSBURG, 1882.

AN EVENING WITH MR. LINCOLN.

THERE are some evenings, the events of which are
so impressed upon our memories, that scarcely a
word said, or an act done, can ever be forgotten; at one
time, perhaps, because of the beauty of our surroundings; at another, because the events were a surprise and
worthy of remembrance. The evening to which I refer
was noteworthy for both of these reasons.

It was, I think, in the year 1856. My husband, the
late Norman B. Judd, was attorney for the Rock Island
Railroad. The bridge over the Mississippi at Rock
Island had been destroyed by a river steamer running
into it and setting it on fire. The steamboat owners
along the Mississippi had brought a suit against the railroad company, and it was to be tried in the U. S. District
Court at Chicago. Mr. Lincoln had come to Chicago as
assistant counsel in the suit. Mr. Judd had invited Mr.
Lincoln to spend the evening at our pleasant home on
the shore of Lake Michigan. After tea, and until quite
late, we sat on the broad piazza, looking out upon as
lovely a scene as that which has made the Bay of Naples
so celebrated. A number of vessels were availing themselves of a fine breeze to leave the harbor, and the lake
was studded with many a white sail. I remember that a
flock of sea-gulls were flying along the beach, and dipping
their beaks and white-lined wings in the foam that capped
the short waves as they fell upon the shore.

Whilst we sat there, the great white moon appeared on the rim of the Eastern horizon, and slowly crept above the water, throwing a perfect flood of silver light upon the dancing waves. The stars shone with the soft light of a midsummer night, and the breaking of the low waves upon the shore, repeating the old rhythm of the song which they have sung for ages, added the charm of pleasant sound to the beauty of the night.

Mr. Lincoln, whose home was far inland from the great lakes, seemed greatly impressed with the wondrous beauty of the scene, and carried by its impressiveness away from all thought of the jars and turmoil of earth. In that mild, pleasant voice, attuned to harmony with his surroundings, and which was his wont when his soul was stirred by aught that was lovely or beautiful, Mr. Lincoln began to speak of the mystery which for ages enshrouded and shut out those distant worlds above us from our own, of the poetry and beauty which was seen and felt by seers of old when they contemplated Orion and Arcturus as they wheeled, seemingly around the earth, in their nightly course ; of the discoveries since the invention of the telescope, which had thrown a flood of light and knowledge on what before was incomprehensible and mysterious ; of the wonderful computations of scientists who had measured the miles of seemingly endless space which separated the planets in our solar system from our central sun, and our sun from other suns, which were now gemming the heavens above us with their resplendent beauty.

He speculated on the possibilities of knowledge which an increased power of the lens would give in the years to come ; and then the wonderful discoveries of late

centuries as proving that beings endowed with such capabilities as man must be immortal, and created for some
high and noble end by him who had spoken those numberless worlds into existence; and made man a little
lower than the angels that he might comprehend the
glories and wonders of his creation.

When the night air became too chilling to remain
longer on the piazza, we went into the parlor, and, seated
on the sofa, his long limbs stretching across the carpet, and
his arms folded behind him, Mr. Lincoln went on to speak
of other discoveries, and also of the inventions which had
been made during the long cycles of time lying between
the present and those early days when the sons of Adam
began to make use of the material things about them,
and invent instruments of various kinds in brass and gold
and silver. He gave us a short but succinct account of
all the inventions referred to in the Old Testament from
the time when Adam walked in the Garden of Eden until
the Bible record ended, 600 B. C.

I said, "Mr. Lincoln, I did not know you were such a
Bible student." He replied: "I must be honest, Mrs.
Judd, and tell you just how I came to know so much
about these early inventions." He then went on to say
that, discussing with some friend the relative age of the
discovery and use of the precious metals, he went to the
Bible to satisfy himself, and became so interested in his
researches that he made a memoranda of the different discoveries and inventions; that soon after he was invited to
lecture before some literary society, I think in Bloomington; that the interest he had felt in the study convinced
him that the subject would interest others, and he therefore

prepared and delivered his lecture on the "Age of Different Inventions:" and "of course," he added, "I could not after that forget the order or time of such discoveries and inventions."

After Mr. Lincoln left, Mr. Judd remarked: "I am constantly more and more surprised at Mr. Lincoln's attainments and the varied knowledge he has acquired during years of constant labor at the Bar, in every department of science and learning. A professor at Yale could not have been more interesting or more enthusiastic."

Another incident in connection with the railroad suit above referred to may be of interest.

Mr. Joseph Knox, one of the ablest lawyers in Illinois, was also engaged as counsel in the defense. Mr. Lincoln began his speech in the forenoon and spoke until the court adjourned at noon. Mr. Knox dined with us that day. He sat down at the dinner table in great excitement, saying: "Lincoln has lost the case for us. The admissions he made in regard to the currents in the Mississippi at Rock Island and Moline will convince the court that a bridge at that point will always be a serious and constant detriment to navigation on the river."

Mr. Judd's reply was in substance that Mr. Lincoln's admissions in regard to the currents were facts that could not be denied, but that they only proved that the bridge should have been built at a different angle to the stream, and that a bridge so built could not injure the river as a navigable stream. This reply was noteworthy as foreshadowing Mr. Lincoln's argument made in the afternoon. The case was decided in their favor, and although carried later to the Supreme Court at Washington, where it was

THE more the smoke of party strife clears away, as we recede from the times of Abraham Lincoln and the civil war, the grander does the form of the Martyr President stand forth as the representative of sagacious statesmanship and unsullied patriotism. It has not fallen to the lot of any American since Washington to be so loved and lamented by the whole nation, without distinction of race, section, or party. He was suddenly snatched away in the midst of his usefulness, but he has left a name behind which is a precious legacy to future generations of his countrymen, teaching ambitious youth that immortality may be most surely won, not by employing the tricks of the politician, but by unselfish devotion to the welfare of their country.

John Avery.

BOWDOIN COLLEGE, 1880.

THE ANALYSIS OF MR. LINCOLN'S CHARACTER.

ABRAHAM LINCOLN was born in Hardin county, Kentucky, February 12th, 1809. He moved to Indiana in 1816; came to Illinois in March, 1830; to old Sangamon county, in 1831, settling in New Salem, and from this last place to this city in April, 1837; coming as a rude, uncultivated boy, without polish or education, and having no friends. He was about six feet four inches high; and when he left this city was fifty-one years old, having good health and no gray hairs, or but few, on his head. He was thin, wiry, sinewy, raw-boned; thin through the breast to the back, and narrow across the shoulders; standing, he leaned forward—was what may be called stoop-shouldered, inclining to the consumptive by build. His usual weight was one hundred and sixty pounds. His organization—rather his structure and functions—worked slowly. His blood had to run a long distance from his heart to the extremities of his frame, and his nerve-force had to travel through dry ground a long distance before his muscles were obedient to his will. His structure was loose and leathery; his body was shrunk and shriveled, having dark skin, dark hair—looking woe-struck. The whole man, body and mind, worked slowly, creakingly, as if it needed oiling. Physically, he was a very powerful man, lifting with ease four hundred or six hundred pounds.

His mind was like his body, and worked slowly but strongly. When he walked, he moved cautiously but firmly, his long arms and hands on them, hanging like giant's hands, swung down by his side. He walked with even tread, the inner sides of his feet being parallel. He put the whole foot flat down on the ground at once, not landing on the heel; he likewise lifted his foot all at once, not rising from the toe, and hence he had no spring to his walk. He had economy of fall and lift of foot, though he had no spring or apparent ease of motion in his tread. He walked undulatory, up and down, catching and pocketing tire, weariness and pain, all up and down his person, preventing them from locating. The first opinion of a stranger, or a man who did not observe closely, was that his walk implied shrewdness, cunning—a tricky man ; but his was the walk of caution and firmness. In sitting down on a common chair he was no taller than ordinary men. His legs and arms were abnormally, unnaturally long, and in undue proportion to the balance of his body. It was only when he stood up that he loomed above other men.

Mr. Lincoln's head was long and tall from the base of the brain and from the eyebrows. His head ran backwards, his forehead rising as it ran back at a low angle, like Clay's, and, unlike Webster's, almost perpendicular. The size of his hat, measured at the hatter's block, was 7⅛, his head being, from ear to ear, 6½ inches, and from the front to the back of the brain 8 inches. Thus measured, it was not below the medium size. His forehead was narrow but high ; his hair was dark, almost black, and lay floating where his fingers or the winds left it, piled up at random. His cheek-bones were high, sharp, and prominent; his eyebrows heavy and prominent; his jaws were long, upcurved and heavy; his nose was large, long and blunt, a little awry towards the right eye; his chin was long, sharp and upcurved; his eyebrows cropped out like a huge rock on the brow of a hill; his face was long, sallow and cadaverous, shrunk, shriveled, wrinkled and dry, having here and there a hair on the surface; his cheeks were leathery; his ears were large, and ran out almost at right angles from his head, caused partly by heavy hats and partly by nature; his lower lip was thick, hanging, and under-curved, while his chin reached for the lip upcurved; his neck was neat and trim, his head being well balanced on it; there was the lone mole on the right cheek, and Adam's apple on his throat.

Thus stood, walked, acted and looked Abraham Lincoln. He was not a pretty man by any means, nor was he an ugly one; he was a homely man, careless of his looks, plain-looking and plain-acting. He had no pomp, display or dignity, so-called. He appeared simple in his carriage and bearing. He was a sad-looking man; his melancholy dripped from him as he walked. His apparent gloom impressed his friends, and created a sympathy for him—one means of his great success. He was gloomy, abstracted, and joyous—rather, humorous—by turns. I do not think he knew what real joy was for many years.

Mr. Lincoln sometimes walked our streets cheerily, —good-humoredly, perhaps joyously—and then it was, on meeting a friend, he cried: "How d'y?" clasping one of his friend's hand in both of his, giving a good hearty soul-welcome. Of a winter's morning, he might be seen stalking and stilting it towards the market house, basket on arm, his old gray shawl wrapped around his neck, his little Willie or Tad running along at his heels, asking a thousand little quick questions, which his father heard not, not even then knowing that little Willie or Tad was there, so abstracted was he. When he thus met a friend, he said that something put him in mind of a story which he heard in Indiana or elsewhere, and tell it he would, and there was no alternative but to listen.

Thus, I say, stood and walked and looked this singular man. He was odd, but when that gray eye and face and every feature were lit up by the inward soul in fires of emotion, *then* it was that all these apparently ugly features sprang into organs of beauty, or sunk themselves into a sea of inspiration that sometimes flooded his face. Sometimes it appeared to me that Lincoln's soul was just fresh from the presence of its Creator.

* * * * * * * * *

I have asked the friends and foes of Mr. Lincoln alike, what they thought of his perceptions. One gentleman of undoubted ability, and free from all partiality or prejudice, said : " Mr. Lincoln's perceptions are slow, a little perverted, if not somewhat distorted and diseased." If the meaning of this is that Mr. Lincoln saws things from a peculiar angle of his being, and from this was susceptible to Nature's impulses, and that he so expressed himself, then I have no objection to what is said. Otherwise, I dissent. Mr. Lincoln's perceptions

34

were slow, cold, precise, and exact. Everything came to him in its precise shape and color. To some men the world of matter and of man comes ornamented with beauty, life, and action, and hence more or less false and inexact. No lurking illusion or other error, false in itself, and clad for the moment in robes of splendor, ever passed undetected or unchallenged over the threshold of his mind—that point that divides vision from the realm and home of thought. Names to him were nothing, and titles naught—assumption always standing back abashed at his cold, intellectual glare. Neither his perceptions nor intellectual vision were perverted, distorted, or diseased. He saw all things through a perfect mental lens. There was no diffraction or refraction there. He was not impulsive, fanciful or imaginative, but cold, calm, precise and exact. He threw his whole mental light around the object, and in time, substance, and quality stood apart; form and color took their appropriate places, and all was clear and exact in his mind. His fault, if any, was that he saw things less than they really were; less beautiful and more frigid. In his mental view he crushed the unreal, the inexact, the hollow and the sham. He saw things in rigidity rather than in vital action. Here was his fault. He saw what no man could dispute; but he failed to see what might have been seen. To some minds the world is all life, a soul beneath the material; but to Mr. Lincoln no life was individual or universal that did not manifest itself to him. His mind was his standard. His perceptions were cool, persistent, pitiless in pursuit of the truth. No error went undetected, and no falsehood unexposed, if he once was aroused in search of truth. If his perceptions were perverted, distorted, and diseased, would to Heaven that more minds were so.

    *   *   *   *   *   *.   *   *   *

The true peculiarity of Mr. Lincoln has not been seen by his various biographers; or, if seen, they have failed wofully to give it that prominence which it deserves. It is said that Newton saw an apple fall to the ground from a tree, and beheld the law of the universe in that fall; Shakespeare saw human nature in the laugh of a man; Professor Owen saw the animal in its claw; and Spencer saw the evolution of the universe in the growth of a seed. Nature was suggestive to all these men. Mr. Lincoln no less saw philosophy in a story, and a schoolmaster in a joke. No man, no men, saw nature, fact, thing, or man from his stand-point. His was a new and original position, which was always suggesting, hinting something to him. Nature, insinuations, hints and suggestions were new, fresh, original and odd to him. The world, fact, man, principle, all had their powers of suggestion to his susceptible soul. They continually put him in mind of something. He was odd, fresh, new, original, and peculiar, for this reason, that he was a new, odd, and original creation and fact. He had keen susceptibilities to the hints and suggestions of nature, which always put him in mind of something known or unknown. Hence his power and tenacity of what is called association of ideas must have been great. His memory was tenacious and strong. His susceptibility to all suggestions and hints enabled him at will to call up readily the associated and classified fact and idea.

As an evidence of this, especially peculiar to Mr. Lincoln, let me ask one question. Were Mr. Lincoln's expression and language odd and original, standing out peculiar from those of all other men? What does this imply? Oddity and originality of *vision* as well as expression; and what is expression in words and human language, but a telling of what we see, defining the idea arising from and created by vision and view in us?* Words and language are but the counterparts of the idea —the other half of the idea; they are but the stinging, hot, heavy, leaden bullets that drop from the mold; and what are they in a rifle with powder stuffed behind them and fire applied, but an embodied force pursuing their object? So are words an embodied power feeling for comprehension in other minds. Mr. Lincoln was often perplexed to give expression to his ideas: first, because he was not master of the English language: and, secondly, because there were no words in it containing the coloring, shape, exactness, power, and gravity of his ideas. He was frequently at a loss for a word, and hence was compelled to resort to stories, maxims, and jokes to embody his idea, that it might be comprehended. So true was this peculiar mental vision of his, that though mankind has been gathering, arranging, and classifying facts for thousands of years, Lincoln's peculiar standpoint could give him no advantage of other men's labor. Hence he tore up to the deep foundations all arrangements of facts, and coined and arranged new plans to govern himself. He was compelled, from his peculiar mental organization, to do this. His labor was great, continuous, patient and all-enduring.

The truth about this whole matter is that Mr. Lincoln read *less* and thought *more* than any man in his sphere in America. No man can put his finger on any great book written in the last or present century that he read. When young he read the Bible, and when of age he read Shakespeare. This latter book was scarcely ever out of his mind. Mr. Lincoln is acknowledged to have been a great man, but the question is, what made him great? I repeat, that he read less and thought more than any man of his standing in America, if not in the world. He possessed originality and power of thought in an eminent degree. He was cautious, cool, concentrated, with continuity of reflection; was patient and enduring. These are some of the grounds of his wonderful success.

Not only was nature, man, fact and principle suggestive to Mr. Lincoln, not only had he accurate and exact perceptions, but he was causative, *i.e.*, his mind ran back behind all facts, things and principles to their origin, history and first cause, to that point where forces act at once as effect and cause. He would stop and stand in the street and analyze a machine. He would whittle things to a point, and then count the numberless inclined planes, and their pitch, making the point. Mastering and defining this, he would then cut that point back, and get a broad transverse section of his pine stick, and peel and define that. Clocks, omnibuses and language, paddle-wheels and idioms, never escaped his observation and analysis. Before he could form any idea of anything, before he would express his opinion on any subject, he must know it in origin and history, in substance and quality, in magnitude and gravity. He must know his subject inside and outside, upside and downside. He searched his own mind and nature thoroughly, as I have often heard him say. He must analyze a sensation, an idea, and words, and run them back to their origin, history, purpose and destiny. He was most emphatically a remorseless analyzer of facts, things and principles. When all these processes had been well and thoroughly gone through, he could form an opinion and express it, but no sooner. He had no faith. " Say so's " he had no respect for, coming though they might from tradition, power or authority.

All things, facts and principles had to run through his crucible and be tested by the fires of his analytic mind ; and hence, when he did speak, his utterances rang out gold-like, quick, keen and current upon the counters of the understanding. He reasoned logically, through analogy and comparison. All opponents dreaded him in his originality of idea, condensation, definition and force of expression, and woe be to the man who hugged to his bosom a secret error if Mr. Lincoln got on the chase of it. I say, woe to him! Time could hide the error in no nook or corner of space in which he would not detect and expose it.

*   *   *   *   *   *

Though Mr. Lincoln had accurate perceptions, though nature was extremely suggestive to him, though he was a profound thinker as well as an analyzer, still his judgments and opinions formed upon minor matters were often childish. I have sometimes asked prominent, talented and honest men in this and other States for their manly opinion of Mr. Lincoln's judgments. I did. this to confirm or overthrow my own opinions on this point. Their answers were that his judgments were poor. But now, what do we understand by the word "judgments"? It is not reason, it is not will, nor is it understanding ; but it is the judging faculty—that capacity or power that forms opinions and decides on the fitness, beauty, harmony and appropriateness of things under all circumstances and surroundings, quickly, wisely, accurately. Had Mr. Lincoln this quality of mind? I think not. His mind was like his body, and worked slowly.

    *   *   *   *   *   *

One portion of mankind maintained that Mr. Lincoln was weak-minded, and they look at him only from the stand-point of his judgments. Another class maintain that he was a great, deep, profound man in his judgments. Do these two classes understand themselves? Both views cannot be correct. Mr. Lincoln's mind was slow, angular, and ponderous, rather than quick and finely discriminating, and *in time* his great powers of reason on cause and effect, on creation and relation, on substance and on truth, would form a proposition, an opinion, wisely and well—*that* no human being can deny. When his mind could not grasp premises from which to argue he was weaker than a child, because he had none of the child's intuitions—the soul's quick, bright flash over scattered and unarranged facts.

Mr. Lincoln was a peculiar man, having a peculiar mind ; he was gifted with a peculiarity, namely, a new look-out on nature. Everything had to be newly created for him—facts newly gathered, newly arranged, and newly classed. He had no faith, as already expressed. In order to believe he must see and feel, and thrust his hand into the place. He must taste, smell and handle before he had faith, *i.e.,* belief. Such a mind as this must act slowly, must have its time. His forte and power lay in his love of digging out for himself and hunting up for his own mind its own food, to be assimilated unto itself; and then in time he could and would form opinions and conclusions that no human power could overthrow. They were as irresistible as iron thunder, as powerful as logic embodied in mathematics.

I have watched men closely in reference to their approaches to Mr. Lincoln. Those who approached him on his judgment side treated him tenderly—sometimes respectfully, but always as a weak-minded man. This class of men take the judgment as the standard of the mind. I have seen another class approach him on his reason side, and they always crouched low down and truckled, as much as to say, "great," "grand," "omnipotent." Both these classes were correct. One took judgment as the standard of the man, and the other took reason. Yet both classes were wrong in this—they sunk out of view one side of Mr. Lincoln. A third class knew him well, and always treated him with human respect : not that awe and reverence with which we regard the Supreme Being; not that supercilious haughtiness which greatness shows to littleness. Each will please to examine itself, and then judge of what I say. I have approached Mr. Lincoln on all sides, and treated him according to the angle approached.

＊   ＊   ＊   ＊   ＊   ＊

An additional question naturally suggests itself here, and it is this: Had Mr. Lincoln great, good common sense? Different persons, of equal capacity and honesty, hold different views on this question—one class answering in the affirmative, and the other in the negative.

These various opinions necessarily spring out of the question just discussed. If the true test is that a man shall quickly, wisely, and well judge the rapid rush and whirl of human transactions, as accurately as though indefinite time and proper conditions were at his disposal, then I am compelled to follow the logic of things, and say that Mr. Lincoln had no more than ordinary common sense. The world, men and their actions must be judged as they rush and pass along. They will not wait on us; will not stay for our logic and analysis; they must be seized as they run. We all our life act on the moment. Mr. Lincoln knew himself, and never trusted his dollar or his fame on his casual opinions; he never acted hastily on great matters.

*　　*　　*　　*　　*

Mr. Lincoln very well knew that the great leading law of human nature was *motive.* He reasoned all ideas of a disinterested action from my mind. I used to hold that an action could be pure, disinterested, and holy, free from all selfishness, but he divested me of that delusion. His idea was that all human actions were caused by *motives,* and that at the bottom of those motives was *self.* He defied me to act without a motive and unselfishly; and when I did the act and told him of it, he analyzed and sifted it, and demonstrated beyond the possibility of controversy that it was altogether selfish. Though he

was a profound analyzer of the laws of human nature, still
he had no idea of the peculiar motives of the particular
individual. He could not well discriminate in human
nature. He knew but little of the play of the features as
seen in "the human face divine." He could not distinguish between the paleness of anger and the crimson
tint of modesty. He could not determine what each play
of the features indicated.

     *   *   *   *   *

The great predominating elements of Mr. Lincoln's
peculiar character, were: First, his great capacity and
power of reason; secondly, his excellent *understanding;*
thirdly, an exalted idea of the sense of *right and equity;*
and, fourthly, his intense veneration of what was *true and
good.* His reason ruled despotically all other faculties and
qualities of his mind. His conscience and heart were
ruled by it. His conscience was ruled by one faculty—
reason. His heart was ruled by two faculties—reason
and conscience. I know it is generally believed that Mr.
Lincoln's heart, his love and kindness, his tenderness and
benevolence, were his ruling qualities; but this opinion is
erroneous in every particular. First, as to his *reason.*
He dwelt in the mind, not in the conscience, and not in
the heart. He lived and breathed and acted from his
reason—the throne of logic and the home of principle,
the realm of Deity in man. It is from this point that
Mr. Lincoln must be viewed. His views were correct
and original. He was cautious not to be deceived; he
was patient and enduring. He had concentration and
great continuity of thought; he had a profound analytic
power; his visions were clear, and he was emphatically

the master of statement. His pursuit of the truth was indefatigable, terrible. He reasoned from his well-chosen principles with such clearness, force, and compactness, that the tallest intellects in the land bowed to him with respect. He was the strongest man I ever saw, looking at him from the stand-point of his reason—the throne of his logic. He came down from that height with an irresistible and crushing force. His printed speeches will prove this; but his speeches before courts, especially before the Supreme Courts of the State and Nation, would demonstrate it: unfortunately, none of them have been preserved. Here he demanded time to think and prepare. The office of reason is to determine the truth. Truth is the power of reason—the child of reason. He loved and idolized truth for its own sake. It was reason's food.

Conscience, the second great quality and forte of Mr. Lincoln's character, is that faculty which loves the just: its office is justice; right and equity are its correlatives. It decides upon all acts of all people at all times. Mr. Lincoln had a deep, broad, living conscience. His great reason told him what was true, good and bad, right, wrong, just or unjust, and his conscience echoed back its decision; and it was from this point that he acted and spoke and wove his character and fame among us. His conscience ruled his heart; he was always just before he was gracious. This was his motto, his glory: and this is as it should be. It cannot be truthfully said of any mortal man that he was always just. Mr. Lincoln was not always just; but his great general life was. It follows that if Mr. Lincoln had great reason and great conscience, he was an honest man. His great and general life was honest, and he was justly and rightfully entitled to the appellation, "Honest Abe." Honesty was his great polar star.

Mr. Lincoln had also a good understanding; that is, the faculty that understands and comprehends the exact state of things, their near and remote relation. The understanding does not necessarily inquire for the reason of things. I must here repeat that Mr. Lincoln was an odd and original man; he lived by himself and out of himself. He could not absorb. He was a very sensitive man, unobtrusive and gentlemanly, and often hid himself in the common mass of men, in order to prevent the discovery of his individuality. He had no insulting egotism, and no pompous pride; no haughtiness, and no aristocracy. He was not indifferent, however, to approbation and public opinion. He was not an upstart, and had no insolence. He was a meek, quiet, unobtrusive gentleman. These qualities of his nature merged somewhat his identities. Read Mr. Lincoln's speeches, letters, messages and proclamations, read his whole record in his actual life, and you cannot fail to perceive that he had good understanding. He understood and fully comprehended himself, and what he did and why he did it, better than most living men.

    *   *   *   *   *   *   *

There are contradictory opinions in reference to Mr. Lincoln's *heart and humanity.* One opinion is that he was cold and obdurate, and the other opinion is that he was warm and affectionate. I have shown you that

Mr. Lincoln first lived and breathed upon the world from his head and conscience. I have attempted to show you that he lived and breathed upon the world through the tender side of his heart, subject at all times and places to the logic of his reason, and to his exalted sense of right and equity ; namely, his conscience. He always held his conscience subject to his head ; he held his heart always subject to his head and conscience. His heart was the lowest organ, the weakest of the three. Some men would reverse this order, and declare that his heart was his ruling organ : that always manifested itself with love, regardless of truth and justice, right and equity. The question still is, was Mr. Lincoln a cold, heartless man, or a warm, affectionate man ? Can a man be a warm-hearted man who is all head and conscience, or nearly so ? What, in the first place, do we mean by a warm-hearted man ? Is it one who goes out of himself and reaches for others spontaneously because of a deep love of humanity, apart from equity and truth, and does what it does for love's sake ? If so, Mr. Lincoln was a cold man. Or, do we mean that when a human being, man or child, approached him in behalf of a matter of right, and that the prayer of such an one was granted, that this is an evidence of his love? The African was enslaved, his rights were violated, and a principle was violated in them. Rights imply obligations as well as duties. Mr. Lincoln was President ; he was in a position that made it his duty, through his sense of right, his love of principle, his constitutional obligations imposed upon him by oath of office, to strike the blow against slavery. But did he do it for love ? He himself has answered the question : "I would not free the slaves if I could preserve the Union without it." I use this argument against his too enthusiastic friends. If you mean that this is love for love's sake, then Mr. Lincoln was a warm-hearted man —not otherwise. To use a general expression, his general life was cold. He had, however, a strong latent capacity to love ; but the object must first come as principle, second as right, and third as lovely. He loved abstract humanity when it was oppressed. This was an abstract love, not concrete in the individual, as said by some. He rarely used the term love, yet was he tender and gentle. He gave the key-note to his own character, when he said, "with malice toward none, and with charity for all," he did what he did. He had no intense loves, and hence no hates and no malice. He had a broad charity for imperfect man, and let us imitate his great life in this.

"But was not Mr. Lincoln a man of great humanity?" asks a friend at my elbow, a little angrily ; to which I reply, "Has not that question been answered already?" Let us suppose that it has not. We must understand each other. What do you mean by humanity? Do you mean that he had much of human nature in him? If so, I will grant that he was a man of humanity. Do you mean, if the above definition is unsatisfactory, that Mr. Lincoln was tender and kind? Then I agree with you. But if you mean to say that he so loved a man that he would sacrifice truth and right for him, for love's sake, then he was not a man of humanity. Do you mean to say that he so loved man, for love's sake, that his heart led him out of himself, and compelled him to go in search of the objects of his love, for their sake? He never, to my knowledge, manifested this side of his character. Such is the law of human nature, that it cannot be all head, all conscience, and all heart at one and the same time in one and the same person. Our Maker made it so, and where God through reason blazed the path, walk therein boldly. Mr. Lincoln's glory and power lay in the just combination of head, conscience, and heart, and it is here that his fame must rest, or not at all.

Not only were Mr. Lincoln's perceptions good; not only was nature suggestive to him; not only was he original and strong; not only had he great reason, good understanding; not only did he love the true and good— the eternal *right;* not only was he tender and kind—but in due proportion and in legitimate subordination, had he a glorious combination of them all. Through his perceptions—the suggestiveness of nature, his originality and strength; through his magnificent reason, his understanding, his conscience, his tenderness and kindness, his heart, rather than love—he approximated as nearly as most human beings in this imperfect state to an embodiment of the great moral principle, "Do unto others as ye would they should do unto you."

*　　　*　　　*　　　*　　　*

There are two opinions—radically different opinions —expressed about Mr. Lincoln's will, by men of equal and much capacity. One opinion is, that he had *no* will; and the other is, that he was *all* will—omnipotently so. These two opinions are loudly and honestly affirmed. Mr. Lincoln's mind loved the true, the right and good, all the great truths and principles in the mind of man.

He loved the true, first; the right, second; and the good, the least. His mind struggled for truths and his soul for substances. Neither in his head nor in his soul did he care for forms, methods, ways—the *non*-substantial facts or things. He could not, by his very structure and formation in mind and body, care anything about them. He did not intensely or much care for particular individual man—the dollar, property, rank, order, manners, or such like things. He had no avarice in his nature, or other like vice. He despised, somewhat, all technical rules in law and theology and other sciences —mere forms everywhere—because they were, as a general rule, founded on arbitrary thoughts and ideas, and not on reason, truth, right, and the good. These things were without substance, and he disregarded them because they cramped his original nature. What suited a little, narrow, critical mind did not suit Mr. Lincoln's any more than a child's clothes did his body. Generally, Mr. Lincoln could not take any interest in little local elections—town meetings. He attended no gatherings that pertained to local or other such interests, saving general political ones. He did not care (because he could not, in his nature) who succeeded to the presidency of this or that Christian association or railroad convention ; who made the most money ; who was going to Philadelphia, when and for what, and what were the costs of such a trip. He could not care who, among friends, got this office or that—who got to be street inspector or alley commissioner. No principle of goodness, of truth, or right was here. How could he be moved by such things as these ? He could not understand why men struggled for such things. He made this remark to me one day, I think at Washington, " If ever this free people—if this Government itself is ever utterly demoralized, it will come from this human wriggle and struggle for office—a way to live without work ; from which nature I am not free myself." It puzzled 'him a good deal, at Washington, to know and to get at the root of this dread desire—this contagious disease of national robbery in the nation's death-struggle.

Because Mr. Lincoln could not feel any interest in such little things as I have spoken of, nor feel any particular interest in the success of those who were thus struggling and wriggling, he was called indifferent—nay, ungrateful—to his friends. Especially is this the case with men who have aided Mr. Lincoln all their life. Mr. Lincoln always and everywhere wished his friends well ; he loved his friends and clung to them tenaciously, like iron to iron welded ; yet he could not be actively and energetically aroused to the true sense of his friends' particularly strong feelings of anxiety for office. From this fact Mr. Lincoln has been called ungrateful. He was not an ungrateful man by any means. He may have been a cool man—a passive man in his general life; yet he was not ungrateful. Ingratitude is too positive a word—it does not convey the truth. Mr. Lincoln may not have measured his friendly duties by the applicant's hot desire ; I admit this. He was not a selfish man— if by selfishness is meant that Mr. Lincoln would do any act, even to promote himself to the presidency, if by that act any human being was wronged. If it is said that Abraham Lincoln preferred Abraham Lincoln to

35

any one else, in the pursuit of his ambitions, and that, because of this, he was a selfish man, then I can see no objections to such an idea, for this is universal human nature.

It must be remembered that Mr. Lincoln's mind acted logically, cautiously, and slowly. Now, having stated the above facts, the question of his will and its power is easily solved. Be it remembered that Mr. Lincoln cared nothing for simple facts, manners, modes, ways, and such like things. Be it remembered that he *did* care for truth, right, for principle, for all that pertains to the good. In relation to simple facts, unrelated to substance, forms, rules, methods, ways, manners, he cared nothing; and if he could be aroused, he would do anything for anybody at any time, as well foe as friend. As a politician he would courteously grant all facts and forms—all non-essential things—to his opponent. He did so because he did not care for them; they were rubbish, husks, trash. On the question of substance, he hung and clung with all his might. On questions of truth, justice, right, the good, on principle, his will was as firm as steel and as tenacious as iron. It was as firm, solid, real, vital, and tenacious as an idea on which the world hinges or hangs. Ask Mr. Lincoln to do a wrong thing, and he would scorn the request; ask him to do an unjust thing, and he would cry: "Begone!" ask him to sacrifice his convictions of the truth, and his soul would indignantly exclaim: "The world perish first!"

Such was Mr. Lincoln's will. On manners and such like things, he was pliable. On questions of right and substance, he was as firm as a rock. One of these classes of men look at Mr. Lincoln from the stand-point of things non-essential, and the other looks at him from the stand-point of substance, rejecting forms. Hence the difference. Mr. Lincoln was a man of firm, unyielding will, when, in human transactions, it was necessary to be so, and *not* otherwise. At one moment Mr. Lincoln was as pliable and expansive as gentle air, and at the next moment he was as biting, firm, tenacious, and unyielding as gravity itself.

Thus I have traced Mr. Lincoln through his perceptions, his suggestiveness, his judgments, and his four great predominant qualities, namely—his powers of reason, his great understanding, his conscience, and his heart. I assert that Mr. Lincoln lived in the head. He loved the truth ; he loved the eternal right and the good —never yielding the fundamental conceptions of these to any man for any end.

All the follies and wrong Mr. Lincoln ever fell into, or committed, sprang or came out of his weak points, namely, his want of quick, sagacious, intuitive judgment —his want of quick, sagacious, intuitive knowledge of the play and meaning of the features of men as written on the face—his tenderness and mercy, and, lastly, his utterly unsuspecting nature. He was deeply and seriously honest himself, and assumed that others were so organized. He never suspected men. These, with other defects of his nature, caused all his follies and wrongs, if he ever had any of either.

All the wise and good things Mr. Lincoln ever did, sprang or came out of his great reason, his conscience, his understanding, and his heart ; his love of truth, right, and the good. I am speaking now of his particular and individual faculties and qualities, *not their combination,* nor the result of wise or unwise combinations. Each man and woman must form his or her own estimate of the man in the mind. Run out these facts, qualities, and faculties, and see what they must produce. For instance, a tender heart; a wise, strong reason; a good understanding, an exalted conscience, a love of the good, must, in such combination, practically applied, produce a man of great humanity.

Take another illustration in the combination of his faculties and qualities. Mr. Lincoln's eloquence lay, 1st, in the strength of his logical faculty, his supreme power of reasoning, his great understanding, and his love of principle; 2d, in his clear, exact, and very accurate vision; 3d, in his cool and masterly statement of his principles, around which the issues gather; in the statement of those issues, and the grouping of the facts that are to carry conviction, aided by his logic, to the minds of men of every grade of intelligence. He was so clear that he could not be misunderstood nor misrepresented. He stood square and bolt upright to his convictions, and formed by them his thoughts and utterances. Mr. Lincoln's mind was not a wide, deep, broad, generalizing, and comprehensive mind, nor versatile, quick, bounding here and there, as emergencies demanded it. His mind was deep, enduring, and strong, running in deep iron grooves, with flanges on its wheels. His mind was not keen, sharp, and subtile; it was deep, exact, and strong.

Whatever of life, vigor, force, and power of eloquence

the whole of the above qualities, or a wise combination, will give; whatever there is in a fair, manly, honest and impartial administration of justice, under law, to all men at all times—through these qualities and capabilities given, never deviating ; whatever there is in a strong will in the right, governed by tenderness and mercy ; whatever there is in toil and a sublime patience ; whatever there is in particular faculties, or a wise combination of them—not forgetting his weak points—working wisely, sagaciously, and honestly, openly and fairly ; I say, whatever there is in these, or a combination of them, that Mr. Lincoln is justly entitled to in all the walks of life. These limit, bound and define him as statesman, orator, as an Executive of the nation, as a man of humanity, a good man, and a gentleman. These limit, bound and define him every way, in all the ways and walks of life. He is under his law and his nature, and he never can get out of it.

This man, this long, bony, wiry, sad man, floated into our county in 1831, in a frail canoe, down the north fork of the Sangamon River, friendless, penniless, powerless and alone—begging for work in this city—ragged, struggling for the common necessaries of life. This man, this peculiar man, left us in 1861, the President of the United States, backed by friends and power, by fame, and all human force ; and it is well to inquire *how.*

To sum up, let us say, here is a sensitive, diffident, unobtrusive, natural-made gentleman. His mind was strong and deep, sincere and honest, patient and endur-

DEDICATED TO THE PILGRIMS

VISITING LINCOLN'S TOMB ON THE NINETEENTH ANNIVER-
SARY OF THE EMANCIPATION PROCLAMATION,
SPRINGFIELD, ILLINOIS, SEPTEMBER 22,
1881.

WE have come, fellow-men, of a dark-hued race,
On a pilgrimage to the last resting-place
Of him, who, in life, was a friend to the slave,
But whose mortal remains fill a martyr's grave.

We have come from the East, the North, South and West,
A disenthralled people, no longer oppressed,
But free as the air—as a bird on the wing—
To this hallowed shrine our oblations we bring.

Four millions of Freedmen to-day swell the song;
The blue vault of Heaven its echoes prolong.
From the gulf to the lakes, from the lakes to the sea,
The shackles have fallen—the Brother is free.

The crack of the slave-whip no longer is heard,
And hearts no more sicken, while hope is deferred;
The slave-pen and auction block never shall be
Erected again in this land of the FREE.

LINCOLN, the God-like, the friend of our race,
With a stroke of his pen did forever efface
That foul blot, so long our derision and shame,
And carved for himself an immortal name—

A name that shall live throughout all coming time,
Unbounded by country, by language, or clime.
Great-grandchildren's children, as years roll around,
Shall pilgrimage make to this hallowed ground;

And he whom we honored, what tho' he be dead,
What tho' the spirit forever has fled,
Our fond recollection time cannot efface
Of LINCOLN, the saviour and friend of our race.

He blushed when he thought of the deep-burning shame
That slavery brought on Columbia's fair name,
And the proudest day of his life was when
He struck off the chains from four millions of men.

From the depths of our hearts, for this priceless boon,
Let songs of thanksgiving our voices attune ;
Let gratitude from these dark temples arise
Like incense from altars, whose flame never dies.

If ever beatified spirits descend
And with those of mortals in harmony blend,
The spirit of LINCOLN is with us to-day,
To charm all our fears and our sorrows away.

So long as the Freedman inhabits this zone,
PHILANTHROPIST, STATESMAN, and SAGE, all in one
We'll hail him, the greatest, the wisest and best,
Who sleeps in yon "windowless palace of Rest."

Corydon, T. Corliss

INDIANAPOLIS, 1881.

BORN in the humblest walks of life, and unaided by education or by fortune, Abraham Lincoln, by his own endeavors and native resources, attained to the highest honor of the republic. He administered that great office so as to win the confidence and affection of the American people. His name will go down through all time imperishably associated with the freedom of a race, and as one of the noblest champions of liberty, humanity and charity for all, in war and in peace.

David Davis

WASHINGTON, 1880.

M R. LINCOLN'S place in the hearts of the nation and on the pages of history is so well fixed, that it seems like presumption in one like myself to write of his merits. I do it, however, because of my great admiration for his character and services. At the beginning of his administration I was very much prejudiced against him, but I was intensely interested in the successful termination of the war, and that interest was far above all prejudices or friendship; and so at last I came to recognize in President Lincoln a man of extreme conscientiousness and patriotism; to which was added an ability for the grave duties devolved upon him far beyond that of the most able men known for years in the councils of the nation. I have long held to the opinion that at the close of the war Mr. Lincoln was the superior of his generals in his comprehension of the effect of strategic movements and the proper method of following up victories to their legitimate conclusions. Had he lived, I have always believed that the long and bitter struggle over reconstruction would never have been initiated, and that substantial peace and prosperity would have followed the laying down of arms. It would seem as though the two sections of the country had not been sufficiently punished by the war, and that he was removed from his high place and that we lost the power which his character had won with the people, so that a new set of plagues might be turned loose over the land.

Wm. F. Smith

New York, 1882.

I BECAME acquainted with Mr. Lincoln in the year 1833. I moved from Kentucky to Illinois about that time, and Mr. Lincoln was then engaged in the grocery business in New Salem, Illinois. I had previously received the impression that the inhabitants of New Salem were perfect "ogres and hobgoblins," and that no one ever attempted to pass through the town without being either killed or robbed. I had some business with a friend living near there, and on calling at his house, I learned that he had gone to Salem. I scarcely knew whether it would be safe to venture there alone or not. I at length made up my mind to try it, anyhow. I reached the town without meeting with an accident; but as I neared the center my ear caught the sound of a loud voice. I began to tremble in my boots, for I felt sure the devouring angel was close at hand. I kept up my courage as well as I could, and proceeded in the direction of the voice, and a few steps brought me to the house from whence the voice issued. There sat the dreaded monster with a note-book open before him, practicing music. He at once recognized me, having been acquainted with two of my brothers, to whom I bore a close resemblance; he then introduced himself as Abraham Lincoln. We spent a very pleasant evening together, and some time after this meeting, I had an opportunity to become better acquainted with him. The family with whom he was then boarding went away on a visit, and he engaged board with a gentleman for whom I was making a frame for a house, and we soon became intimate friends and room-mates. After he became a lawyer I engaged his services in a law-suit, and on asking his charge, to my surprise he only asked me two dollars and fifty cents. I had no idea of paying less than ten dollars. When Mr. Lincoln first became a lawyer he was a general favorite with all the wild young men who knew him, and in one of his speeches, delivered after he was elected to the Illinois Legislature, he displeased some of these young bloods, and it reached his ears. He called a meeting and addressed them, saying that they had made him what he was, and if he had said anything that displeased them he was willing for them to take him to pieces limb by limb.

George W. Nance

PETERSBURG, 1882.

I CAME to Illinois in the fall of 1835, and in January, 1836, located in Petersburg, a little village recently laid out on the Sangamon river, two miles north of Salem, Mr. Lincoln's home. My earliest acquaintance with Mr. Lincoln commenced in February of that year, on his return home from Vandalia, where he had spent the winter as a member of the legislature from Sangamon county. Mr. Lincoln spent the most of the month of March in Petersburg, finishing up the survey and planning of the town he had commenced the year before, and I was a great deal in his company and formed a high estimate of his worth and social qualities, which was strengthened by many years of subsequent social intercourse and business transactions, finding him always strictly honest; in fact, he was universally spoken of in this region as "Honest Abe." After Menard county was formed out of a portion of Sangamon county, and the county seat established at Petersburg, Mr. Lincoln was a regular attendant at the courts, and as I was then keeping a hotel, he was one of my regular customers, where he met many of his old cronies of his early days at Salem, and they uniformly spent the most of the nights in telling stories, or spinning long yarns, of which Mr. Lincoln was very fond. In the early settlement of this community, when a stranger came to settle amongst them, it was their custom to try him on. This trying on was to ascertain what he was made of, and all sorts of sports were resorted to, such as running, jumping, wrestling and occasionally a knock-down, if necessary. In all these sports, Mr. Lincoln not only proved himself a match, but an over match for the most of them, and they at once became his fast friends. On one occasion, Mr. Lincoln, with a number of other persons, was descending the Sangamon river in a flat-boat. The boat leaked badly and took in a good deal of water, and when they reached the Salem mill-dam, the water was not high enough to take the boat over with so much weight, and the bow ran up high and dry on the dam. The question was, What was to be done? Mr. Lincoln suggested that they should bore a hole in the bottom of the boat and lighten it by letting the water out. This was a novel idea, but the hole was bored in the bow, and all hands went to that end, which raised the stern; the water flowed to the bow and passed off through the hole, and the boat went over the dam in safety.

On another occasion, when Mr. Lincoln and some of his friends were visiting a neighbor, a very large, fleshy, rough and uncouth old woman came in and seated herself on one of those old-fashioned, straight-backed, split-bottomed chairs, leaned back, balancing herself on the hind legs and rocking to and fro, and telling of everything going on in the neighborhood (for she knew everybody's business), Mr. Lincoln was sitting near, and being always fond of a joke, he couldn't withstand the temptation, and slyly put his foot under the front round of the chair and upset her. She fell in such a position that she could not extricate herself without his assistance; what followed can better be imagined than described.

Jn. M. Bennett

THAT Mr. Lincoln was an eminently good man—
that he was really great in all the moral aspects of
human character, is very widely if not universally conced-
ed. That he was equally great from the purely intellectual point of view, has been spoken of with more reserve.
It was not unnatural, therefore, that his extraordinary success in political life, obtained as it was without resort to
the crafty methods of the mere politician, and without
the usual personal solicitation by himself in his own behalf, should have been regarded by many as something
of a mystery—especially when considered in connection
with the fact that he was not supposed to be an educated
man. His success was largely due, no doubt, to his remarkable sagacity in determining the condition of the
public mind, and in reading the signs of the times. He
seemed to have a special gift in this direction. Perhaps
it was intuition, but so largely developed in his case as
to be almost equivalent to a separate mental endowment,
giving him, as it were, one faculty more than other men
have, and bestowing upon him a corresponding advantage over his contemporaries. But that he was intellec-
tually great, aside from this, is one of the most conspicuous facts of his life. And it is clearly evident from the
circumstances in which he was placed, during the most
important period of his political career—being the leader
alike of a new party and a new thought—that he could
not have succeeded nor laid a foundation for success, if
this had not been a fact in his favor. Whatever he may

have lacked in the way of education or scholarship, he certainly did not lack knowledge, or the ability to acquire knowledge to any extent needed at any time when wanted, nor the intelligence and skill necessary to use it to the best possible advantage. There are thousands of educated men who would rejoice to have this same power, but have it not. Such talent as this, in the field of duty to which he was called, was an ample substitute for the scholarship he did not have, and out of this talent came the giant forces which wrought his success. With these at his command, no difficulties embarrassed him, no emergencies found him unprepared, he made no mistakes, and met with no failures.

In the stirring Illinois campaign which brought him to the front as champion of freedom, and which resulted two years later in making him the nominee of his party for the Presidential office, he manifested capabilities equal to the highest and the best. The country was filled with able men at that time, men noted for great learning, eloquence, skill in debate, and wisdom of management, but it is not likely that any one could have been selected from among them all, who would have gone through that campaign, in his place, with a success and brilliancy equal to his. And yet the performance did not seem to be in any way difficult or extraordinary for him. It was only in keeping—except as to its greater importance, and the greater excitement attending it—with all his former efforts in the political field. Without pretending to be an orator, he swayed the multitudes by his eloquence as the tempest stirs the sea ; and vanquished his opponents in debate with the same easy grace and irresistible force of

36

logic with which lesser fields had been won, and which lesser foes had been taught to respect in the less trying situations of the past, and which all parties, friends and foes alike, were destined to admire. He wrought without malice; without personal animosity towards anybody; simply for his love of the right, and his hatred of the wrong, as matters of principle; and won the respect of all by the fairness and candor and good temper with which his work was done. With pleasant smiles, and keen wit, and unanswerable argument, he cleared the path before him, for himself and his party, and pointed the way to a higher and better life for the nation; and then, stepping quickly to the front, led the nation on to take possession of and permanently occupy that higher ground. And this was essentially his own work from beginning to end. He started it, and kept with it all the way through, as the most capable and efficient worker of all, and finally finished it at the end. A nobler exhibition of mental supremacy and magnificent success, in the political field, has not been seen on this earth. This is a strong statement, but it is no doubt a perfectly truthful one. If there are men now living who would withhold from him this large credit for intellectual greatness, let them explain how, from the condition of helpless poverty in which he was born, and in which he continued through all the years of childhood and youth, he could come to be the master-spirit of the nation, and to hold its highest position of official trust and power with such transcendent ability and faultless wisdom, through the most trying ordeal any nation or any ruler of a nation has ever experienced; and do all this without aid from any outside source except such as he created for himself and drew unto himself by his own efforts alone, as he advanced. His known integrity and goodness of heart were, of course, strong elements of popularity, but such success as this cannot be rationally accounted for without including among its causes that most indispensable one of all—great intellectual ability. If we call it wisdom, it means the same thing.

Mr. Lincoln was a profound admirer of our great men of the past. He studied their lives and made himself minutely acquainted with their characters, and became one of the noblest defenders of their work. Particularly is this true with regard to the men of the Revolution. He had imbibed their very spirit. The Declaration of Independence was the light which lighted him on his political way. He believed in it as sincerely and devoutly as he believed in his Bible. Its principles to him were as sacred as any earthly thing could be. He regarded them as of divine origin. And now, when he found that noble instrument assailed by gifted northern orators, and sneered at and ridiculed as containing nothing but "glittering generalities," and determined efforts being made to destroy its influence over the public mind, in order to make more room for slavery, he was naturally roused with indignation and inspired with eloquence in its defense. He came to its defense with a magnanimity and power no other man has shown. It would not be difficult to prove, if there were time and space, that he really possessed many of the leading characteristics of our great men of the past, more, perhaps, than has been manifested by any other single American. At the same time, he was wholly unlike them all in his intellectual methods—as

well as in his personal appearance—and was not equal to
any one of them, probably, in those educational advantages that come from the schools. But his great soul, man-
ifesting itself by great deeds, has won for him a reputation and fame superior to all other Americans, with the
single exception, perhaps, of Washington—and he stands
before the world an illustrious example of human greatness, creditable alike to the men who created the government and to the government which they created. They
made it possible for such a man to be produced; and he
is without any exception the grandest fruit of their deep
political foresight. He was wholly American, and
wholly a United States American, of the purest and best
type: a broad-minded, big-hearted, genial-tempered product of the prairies: with a love of country and of freedom and of man a thousand times more boundless than
the prairies,—as boundless as humanity. With such endowments of mind and such attributes of character, it is
not to be wondered at that he could move men as they
had never been moved before; nor is it a matter of wonder to those who believe in an overruling Providence that
fits the man for the hour and the hour for the man, in the
great concerns of earth, that at his chief advent into public life, the time had come for them to be so moved.

A country that has produced two such men as Washington and Lincoln during the first century of its exist-
ence--besides the large number of other great men necessarily implied in the production of these two--can afford to
be well satisfied with its laurels. Washington, the Father
of Liberty and the Founder of the Republic; Lincoln,
the Father of Freedom and the Preserver of the Re-

public :—these might not improperly be distinguishing titles of these distinguished men. No brighter names than theirs shine out from the pages of history, in ancient or modern times. The united voice of the country, and of all countries, has given to Washington his proper place, where he will stand, bathed in glory, forever. Lincoln's time has not yet come. It is too early for him to take his right place in the undivided opinion of the world. Another generation must pass—perhaps many generations—before he can be seen by all alike and in his true light. When the asperities of the war are all gone, and the memory of its bitterness has faded from the minds of men, and the prejudices excited by its passions are at an end—when the animosities engendered by party strife are forgotten, and when the losses caused by the war to the present generation are found to be an immense gain in the future, as they certainly will be—when all of these ameliorated conditions, in so far as they relate to him, shall have been reached—then the memory of his great deeds and pure life and noble character will take possession of men's minds to the exclusion of their former false views and errors, and thus being able to look upon him with unclouded sight, they will behold him exactly as he was, and as he will continue to be in reputation, one of the greatest of earth's great men.

The divine oversight and guidance of earthly affairs is nowhere more manifest than in that portion of our national history which relates to slavery. The nation has been punished, as it deserved to be, for tolerating the hideous wrong. The oppressed race has been benefited, as was right that it should be, by the continuance of that wrong. The emancipated slave comes from his bondage better fitted for the duties of civilization and better capable of self-support and self-improvement than any other equal number of his race. Shall he not share these advantages with the less-favored portion of his people? Shall he not be a missionary to his fellows of the "dark continent," still suffering under a bondage more crushing and cruel than that from which he himself has been freed? The bondage of ignorance and superstition by which they are enslaved is a bondage from which they cannot be emancipated by proclamation, but only by slow growth in knowledge through generations of instruction. Their period of instruction will come and growth in knowledge follow as one of the fruits, in part at least, of the Emancipation Proclamation issued by Mr. Lincoln; and in so far as they shall then be liberated from the gross barbarism in which they are sunk, the credit of their improved condition must proportionally be attributed to the same cause, and will in like proportion enhance the glory of that great act.

The far-reaching beneficence of this great man's life character and services cannot now be realized. Believers in the world's ultimate redemption from evil may picture to themselves the golden glories of that millennial era and rejoice in the contemplation of its purity and peace, but this is the work of the imagination. Not till the era comes shall its real brightness be seen, and not till then shall there be men wise enough to trace the blessed influences by which it was brought about,—not till then shall the full measure of his greatness be known to the children of earth.

When the freedman shall have come to his own and can speak for himself and his race with an applauding world to listen, men will look back over the landmarks of human progress, recalling the mighty agencies by which the grand result was achieved, and nowhere shall they find, in the long, bright vista of their vision, a glory more brilliant and beautiful and pure than that which rests upon the name and hallows the fame of Abraham Lincoln.

E. C. Pomeroy

BUFFALO, 1882.

I AM glad to be recorded with the many as one who had great love for Mr. Lincoln; who reveres his name and memory, and who believes that God gave him to us for the crisis we were to pass through; to lead us successfully through that four years of terrible civil war into the bright sunlight of a blessed peace, the early dawn only of which he was permitted to see, when he was cruelly and brutally murdered during an evening of recreation. We question if there was ever a man holding public office in our country who received more blame and more praise than Abraham Lincoln while President; but when he died the nation staggered under the sad intelligence; a cry of unfeigned sorrow went up from every loyal breast; even enemies had pity in their hearts; and from almost every hamlet throughout the world came expressions of sympathy for the loss of our good President. Mr. Lincoln's kind and forgiving nature should never be called in question. It was like unto the following: "Then Peter came to him and said, Lord, how oft shall my brother sin against me and I forgive him? Till seven times? Jesus saith unto him, I say not unto thee until seven times, but until *seventy times seven.*" I believe the answer which Jesus made to have been the ruling spirit of Mr. Lincoln towards his fellow-beings—friends or enemies: for he said, *with malice towards none, with charity for all.*

He was pure-hearted and pure-minded. There were times, perhaps, in our impatience we thought him wrong, and wished him to do different; but the result showed that he was about right, and did things at the proper time for the benefit of all concerned. It is not likely that any man could have filled his place during the trying time he was President, perhaps, without erring—without displeasing many; and it is certainly beyond doubt that but few would have been as conscientiously just as he. Who would have been more faithful? He stood like the noble pine, that can bend before the storm but will not break. "*He* stood when others fell!" No matter who was discouraged, it was not for *him* to be disheartened; or, at least, to show it. How well did he try to conceal the burden he had to bear; wearing a smile, and telling a story to forget his own sorrow, and to cheer up the timid and desponding. Mr. Lincoln has spoken and written some of the finest sentences to be found in our language. His speech at Gettysburg, and portions of his inaugurals, are very superior. A few words of his last inaugural, although written in prose, are really in rhyme.

> "Fondly do we hope,
> Fervently do we pray,
> That this mighty scourge of war
> May speedily pass away, &c., &c."

Many of his speeches abound with fine, tender, poetic expression. His little off-hand good-bye address to his old friends when leaving Springfield in 1861 is full of deep pathos, and will never be forgotten.

Mr. Lincoln, with his pen—and that was law—gave freedom to 4,000,000 of colored slaves. Mr. Lincoln was not looked up to with any degree of awe or reverence as some great men have been; but he was respected and truly beloved by the masses of the people for his honesty and justness to all; for his amiable temper and disposition; for his great kindness of heart; and for his unswerving integrity to the principles of free government, and the honor of his country. He was really one of the people, was for the people, and stood by the people. Mr. Lincoln was half-brother to mercy and justice. Without the rank, which is but the "guinea's stamp," he was pure gold; and from an apparently poor and humble sphere, be bounded at one leap in history to the side of Washington. Both these great men showed their virtue and wisdom through a thundering life—or death—struggle of our country. The rising generation will outdo us in appreciation of his character. The charm that lingers about the name of the immortal Washington as the Father of our Country, will also surround that of honest Abraham Lincoln as its Saviour.

Andrew Boyd.

Syracuse, 1882.

TOLLING.

(April 15, 1865.)

TOLLING, tolling, tolling!
  All the bells of the land!
Lo, the patriot martyr
  Taketh his journey grand!
Travels into the ages,
  Bearing a hope how dear!
Into life's unknown vistas,
  Liberty's great pioneer.

Tolling, tolling, tolling!
  See, they come as a cloud,
Hearts of a mighty people,
  Bearing his pall and shroud;
Lifting up, like a banner,
  Signals of loss and woe;
Wonder of breathless nations,
  Moveth the solemn show.

Tolling, tolling, tolling!
  Was it, O man beloved,
Was it thy funeral only
  Over the land that moved?
Veiled by that hour of anguish,
  Borne with the rebel rout
Forth into utter darkness,
  Slavery's corse went out.

Lucy Larcom.

BOSTON, 1882.

Printed in the United States
153548LV00005B/24/A

9 780548 590706